Cross-Border
Commemorations

Cross-Border Commemorations

Celebrating Swedish Settlement in America

ADAM HJORTHÉN

University of Massachusetts Press
Amherst and Boston

Copyright © 2018 by University of Massachusetts Press
All rights reserved
Printed in the United States of America

ISBN 978-1-62534-385-7 (paper); 384-0 (hardcover)

Designed by Sally Nichols
Set in Adobe Garamond Pro
Printed and bound by Maple Press, Inc.

Cover design by Patricia Duque Campos
Cover photo: *Escanaba, Michigan, July 1948.* Courtesy of the Swenson Swedish
Immigration Research Center, Augustana College, Rock Island, Illinois.

Library of Congress Cataloging-in-Publication Data
A catalog record for this book is available from the Library of Congress.

British Library Cataloguing-in-Publication Data
A catalog record for this book is available from the British Library.

For Emin

CONTENTS

Preface
ix

INTRODUCTION
An Entangled History of Settler Commemorations
1

CHAPTER 1
Moments of Opportunity
On Pasts and Politics
17

CHAPTER 2
Crossing Borders
Appropriating Foundational Histories
33

CHAPTER 3
Settler Colonial Histories
Memorializing a Transatlantic Legacy
63

CHAPTER 4
Mutual Modernities
Representing History through Delegation Travels
94

CHAPTER 5
Bonds of Swedishness
Festivals and the Mending of Cultural Differences
122

CHAPTER 6
Perpetual Friendships
Business and Politics in Commemorative Dinners
152

CONCLUSION
The Resilience of History
176

Notes 195
Index 239

PREFACE

When is it acceptable, perhaps even encouraged, to celebrate difficult histories such as colonialism? There is a simple answer to this complex question: whenever everyone agrees that it is a good idea. When I began to study the memory of how people from Sweden had colonized and settled certain parts of America, I grew curious about how and for what purposes people still celebrate colonialism as a positive experience. The case that had caught my attention was the New Sweden colony (1638–55), once located on the banks of the Delaware River. In memory, the colony was and is generally considered to be unproblematic. It is so benevolently regarded that in recent years it has been jointly commemorated by representatives of both the colonizers and the dispossessed. As I eventually realized, herein lay the answer to the question of acceptability: the colony is attractive because it celebrates a history that concerns not only America but also Sweden.

Commemorations frequently cross borders, more often and in more ways than we might think. Celebrations of European settlement in America are a case in point. In this book, I study twentieth-century commemorations of the seventeenth-century New Sweden colony and the nineteenth-century settlement of Swedish pioneers in the Midwest. To describe these events as ethnic, regional, or national would be reductive. Rather, they are examples of the phenomenon of cross-border commemorations. They were forums for the promotion of social, political, and commercial relations across national borders, catering to heterogeneous communities who were joined by the notion that they somehow shared the same past.

I have always been confused by the notion that "we are what we remember" and that it is crucial to "know your history." This might certainly be true on an individual level; our experiences do shape us. However, on the communal level, the assertion is less obvious. The fundamental problem is the definition of *we*. Commemorations are social events, but much scholarship on memory and commemoration includes an underlying presumption that community is local or national. In fact, community is often both international and global. The same holds true of much of history. The past has been shaped by migration, colonization, slavery, wars, exchanges of goods and ideas, and other processes that cover large geographical spaces. These are histories that concern many people. In the staging of commemorations, the question "Who might see this history as their own?" consequently ought to have both ethical and organizational implications.[1]

My road to the study of commemorations of European settlement in America began with an obscure artifact in west-central Minnesota. In 1898, a stone slab known as the Kensington Runestone was unearthed by a Swedish farmer, Olof Ohman, near the town of Kensington. It carried a curious inscription that told a story of how Norsemen on an inland travel from the east had found ten members of their group dead. According to the stone's interpreters, the voyagers had presumably been killed by "Indians." The most remarkable detail of the stone, however, was its dating: the year 1362. In 2009, I spent a week at the Runestone Museum in Alexandria, Minnesota, trying to understand how the stone (which scholarly experts had long deemed to be a late nineteenth-century artifact) could continue to garner attention in the United States and Europe. In 2003, it had been prominently exhibited at the Swedish History Museum in Stockholm under the headline "The Riddle of the Kensington Runestone." Presenting its date as an open question, the museum offered visitors pro and con arguments for its medieval dating and encouraged the public to make their own decision as to its authenticity.

The Stockholm exhibition showed that what had been described by historians as a local Minnesota curiosity was clearly more than that. The story of the Kensington Runestone, with its troubling implications of white chauvinism, was a material artifact adopted to create transnational memories of a pre-Columbian discovery of America. An artifact that in the 1890s had been used by Scandinavian immigrants who were staking a claim in the American melting pot was, a century later, presented by an overseas state agency as a matter of potential pride.[2] It is clear that histories of colonial "discoveries" and settler colonization have been central mythologies in the United States, from Plymouth Rock to the prairie settlement of the West. But these histories were also largely made through the migration of people from Europe. They do not solely belong to the United States, they have not only been celebrated in America, and their legacies are not purely a U.S. responsibility.

The project that eventually evolved into this book took shape at institutions in both Sweden and the United States. On the eastern side of the Atlantic, my academic home has been Stockholm University, where I have divided my time between the Department of History and the interdisciplinary milieu of the Research School for Studies in Cultural History. I am grateful for the intellectual vigor, the historical expertise, and the friendship and collegiality of both of these institutions. In 2013, I had the privilege of being a visiting scholar at the Immigration History Research Center (IHRC) at the University of Minnesota and at the Department of American Studies at George Washington University. My stints in Minneapolis and Washington, D.C., were formative to my study of American culture, ethnicity, and race, and they enabled me to think constructively and to write intensely. Thank you to Donna Gabaccia for inviting me to the IHRC, to Erika Lee for hosting me, and to Daniel Necas and Sara Wakefield for helping me while there, and thank you to Melani McAlister for welcoming me to George Washington University. Through the support of the history department in Stockholm, I was able to spend the fall of 2014 among the marvelous resources of the Van Pelt Library at the University of Pennsylvania. I made the crucial final revisions of this book as a research fellow in the history of ideas at the Department of Culture and Aesthetic at Stockholm University and in the history department of the John F. Kennedy Institute for North American Studies at the Free University of Berlin.

Growing up on the island of Gotland, far off the coast of Sweden in the Baltic Sea, I never dreamed of spending months doing research in places such as Dover, Delaware, and Rock Island, Illinois. I was able to do so primarily because of significant financial support from many foundations and institutions, including the Sweden-America Foundation, the American-Scandinavian Foundation, the Department of History at Stockholm University, Sven och Dagmar Saléns Stiftelse, Helge Ax:son Johnsons Stiftelse, Gunvor och Josef Anérs Stiftelse, and Gålöstiftelsen. Thanks to the Dagmar and Nils William Olsson Visiting Scholar Award, I spent an extended time at the Swenson Swedish Immigration Research Center at Augustan College in Rock Island, Illinois. The support of these institutions and foundations is a reminder that it is impossible to write international, transnational, or global history without the proper infrastructure.

It is very difficult to conduct historical research without the invaluable assistance of talented archivists and museum staff. Thank you especially to Lisa Huntsha, Jill Seaholm, and Susanne Titus at the Swenson Swedish Immigration Research Center; Anna-Kajsa Echague at North Park University in Chicago; Douglas Gustafsson and Yimei Öfverström at the National Archives in Stockholm; Randy L. Goss and Margaret Raubacher Dunham at the Delaware Public Archives in Dover; Robert Nicholl and Inga Theissen at the American Swedish Institute in Minneapolis; Jamie Nelson at Augustana College Special Collections in Rock Island; James Amemasor at the New Jersey Historical Society in Newark; Brett M. Reigh and Linda Ries at the Pennsylvania State Archives in Harrisburg; and Tracey R. Beck and Carrie Hogan at the American Swedish Historical Museum in Philadelphia. Thanks also to Samuel W. Heed of the Kalmar Nyckel Foundation and Rebecca L. Wilson at the Old Swedes Foundation, who gave me access to the Fort Christina State Park when it was still closed to the general public.

My deepest gratitude goes to two people who have commented on, criticized, and endured countless drafts of this book. My heartfelt thanks to Dag Blanck for his passion and knowledge and for his generosity in sharing them. Dag's wholehearted interest and support have been of utmost importance since the beginning. I also thank Mats Hallenberg, who has guided me through many crucial stages of my research and whose astute readings have challenged me to always improve.

For their careful readings, comments, and assistance at various stages of my writing, I want to thank Anders Andrén, Ingrid Berg, Kim Bergqvist, Olof Bortz, Anders Cullhed, Lisa Ehlin, Elin Engström, Mari Eyice, Charlotta Forss, Håkan Forsell, Peter Gillgren, Nikolas Glover, Niklas Haga, Emma Hagström Molin, Lisa Hellman, Johannes Heuman, Per Israelsson, Loraine Jensen, Otso Kortekangas, Johan Linder, Anders Lindström, Matts Lindström, Elisabeth Niklasson, Robert Nilsson Mohammadi, Oskar Nordell, Therese Nordlund Edvinsson, Margareta Nordquist, Erik Magnusson Petzell, Emma Pihl Skoog, Ale Pålsson, Magnus Rodell (who scrutinized the full manuscript in its infant stage), Elisa Rossholm, Lind H. Rugg, David Rynell Åhlén, Inga Sanner, Pelle Snickars, Daniel Strand, Anna-Carin Stymne, Birgitta Svensson, Tove Thorslund, Martin Tunefalk, Mattias Tydén, Elizabeth Venditto, Robin Wahlsten Böckerman, Adam Wickberg Månsson, and Britta Zetterström Geschwind. I especially want to acknowledge Anna Källén, whose sharp intellect and contagious energy always makes me better—on and off the court. Thank you to Gunlög Fur, Karen V. Hansen, and all the other participants in the network "Indians and Immigrants: Entangled Histories in the Midwest" for turning my attention to the complexity of settler memories.

I have greatly benefited from presenting my work at a number of workshops during the years, but I particularly want to thank the Global REM Seminar at the IHRC, the Modern History Workshop at the Department of History at the University of Minnesota (where David A. Chang made an incisive reading of an early version of chapter 4), as well as the AmStudies workshop at George Washington University. I am also indebted to everyone who contributed to my thinking at multiple conferences in North America and Europe.

This book has improved greatly thanks to the brilliant people at the University of Massachusetts Press. I am indebted to Seth C. Bruggeman for shepherding this project to the press at an early stage.

Thank you to my editor Matt Becker, who has shown a sincere interest in this project from the start, to Marla R. Miller, for her meticulously detailed and incisive comments, to Rachael Hoy and Dawn Potter for the careful editing, and to the two anonymous readers for their valuable feedback.

I am fortunate to have wonderful family and friends who remind me that there is so much more to life than work. Thank you especially to my dear parents, Monika and Michel, and my brother, Gustav, for your unreserved support and never-ending encouragement. Had it not been for this project, I would not have met my brilliant, caring, and patient wife, Nevra. She has provided invaluable comments on numerous drafts and accompanied me on tours of monuments, archives, and heritage sites (while braving all of my thoughts and ideas along the way). Thanks to Nevra, the biggest achievement during these years is not mine but ours. This book is for you, Emin, with all my love. I look forward to seeing time pass with you.

Cross-Border
Commemorations

Introduction
An Entangled History of Settler Commemorations

"Surely such a comedy cannot be allowed to take place," wrote the Swedish-American historian Amandus Johnson to Wollmar Boström, the Swedish envoy to the United States. Johnson's letter brimmed with distress, which had been triggered by Swedish-American plans for the upcoming 1938 commemoration of the colony of New Sweden (1638–55). Those plans included a suggested landing ceremony for a Swedish national delegation at The Rocks in Wilmington, Delaware, site of the 1638 arrival of the founders of the colony. According to the planning commission, the delegation would sail in on a mock replica of the colonial ship *Kalmar Nyckel*, constructed out of a ferryboat, and would be greeted at The Rocks by "five Indian chiefs." Through this series of events, they would, "in a manner, reenact the first landing of the Swedes." Johnson believed this was not only a bad plan but also "so ridiculous that we certainly cannot entertain the idea."[1]

Seventy-five years later, commemorators had no need for a mock replica. The long-standing project to build a tall ship modeled on the seventeenth-century version of *Kalmar Nyckel* had been completed, and the ship was now ready for its grandest journey to date. On a beautiful day in May 2013, Sweden's King Carl XVI Gustaf and Queen Silvia, Finland's speaker of parliament, and the two countries' ambassadors to the United States boarded the replica in downtown Wilmington to travel to the ceremonies at The Rocks. As the royals and government representatives stepped ashore, they were greeted by Mark "Quiet Hawk" Gould of the Nanticoke Lenni-Lenape Tribal Nation and Dennis Coker of the Lenape Indian Tribe of Delaware. The plan discarded in the 1930s had been realized.

Unlike the 1938 ceremony, the 2013 commemoration included Native American participants. Yet the Lenape, dressed in traditional gowns and headdresses, were not mentioned by name in any of the official statements or in most of the media coverage. Meanwhile, the king walked down the gangway, sporting a dark suit and a blue necktie, apparently embodied the notion of a modern statesman. The organizers of the commemoration, mostly representatives of local Swedish-American associations, did not seem to reflect on the fact that the Native American experience had been pushed into the background of a scene that was replaying Indian dispossession.[2] The Lenape may have been at the center of the actual historical event but were not at the forefront of a commemoration that was emphasizing the rewards of international relations.

The handshake at The Rocks is an iconic incident in American national mythology: the moment when European settlement of America began.[3] Histories of settlement are central to understanding the origins of the United States. The frequently told stories of, for example, the Jamestown colony, the Plymouth colony, and the pioneer settlements of the West have long been framed as American histories. In the axiomatic center of the United States, the Capitol in Washington, D.C., the rotunda is encircled by a frieze illustrating moments in American history. Nearly half of its nineteen scenes depict colonial landings and Native American encounters, including those of William Brewster, John Smith, and William Penn. These stories are firmly anchored in the imaginings of U.S. origins and are often connected to specific American geographies such as Plymouth Rock or Penn's Treaty Elm. Yet while Brewster, Smith, and Penn all had colonial interests in America, they all also departed from Europe on their transatlantic journeys. This is an often forgotten dimension of settling: they are histories of not only the settlers' point of arrival but also their point of departure.⁴ In this book I challenge the dominant description of the functions and meanings of settlement in America and argue that they are much more than solely American histories. Rather, they have been important for many groups in different parts of the world and have been used in the promotion of social, political, and commercial relations across national borders.

A look at recent celebrations reveals that cross-border commemorations of settler histories are a vogue of the times. Examples include the quadricentennial of the Jamestown colony in 2007; the quadricentennial of the founding of Santa Fe, New Mexico, in 2010; the 2012 celebration of Jean Ribault's 1562 landing at Fort Caroline, Florida (under the tagline "France Was Here!"); and the 450th anniversary of the Spanish settlement in St. Augustine, Florida, in 2015. French businesses and nonprofit organizations participated in the Ribault commemoration, Britain's Queen Elizabeth II attended the Virginia celebrations, and Spain's King Felipe VI and Queen Letizia made high-profile visits to the Santa Fe and St. Augustine celebrations.⁵ There are currently plans underway in England to grandly commemorate the sailing of the *Mayflower* in 2020. According to organizers, the celebration will feature "a series of major transatlantic and global events," including "United States Presidential and British Royal visits commemorating the enduring relationship between the United Kingdom, the United States, and Holland."⁶

This book explores the phenomenon of cross-border commemorations through a study of celebrations of Swedish settlement in America. People from Sweden began to settle in North America in 1638, when they established the New Sweden colony, a short-lived venture in the Delaware Valley that lasted until 1655, when it was lost to neighboring Dutch colonies. Two hundred years later, Swedish pioneers began to homestead in the Midwest, paving the way for a subsequent mass migration between 1840 and 1930, when 1.3 million Swedes immigrated to the United States.⁷ These colonists, pioneers, and immigrants have repeatedly been celebrated through cross-border commemorations in the twentieth and twenty-first centuries. The first two took place in the 1930s and 1940s: the 1938 New Sweden Tercentenary and the 1948 Swedish Pioneer Centennial, commemorating the founding of New Sweden and the nineteenth-century arrival of Swedish pioneers to the Midwest.[8] These celebrations were planned and organized by people from both sides of the Atlantic. They involved two U.S. presidents, foreign ministers from three nations (Sweden, Finland, and the United States), the Swedish royal family, Swedish Americans and Finnish Americans, homeland Swedes, business leaders, and state and federal politicians. Yet even though these groups simultaneously commemorated the same pasts, they did so for different reasons.

The 1938 and 1948 commemorations may have been only a decade apart, but they took place in different eras. Each was set in a different geopolitical reality and was influenced by different international political contexts. One was staged on the brink of World War II, the other at the dawn of the Cold War; one took place before, the other after, the rapid technological development spurred by the war years of the 1940s. They had different institutionalized conditions for public diplomacy, and they spoke to different sociocultural needs of grassroots people. But despite their differences, they also display many significant similarities. Both were organized after the end of the Swedish mass migration to the United States in the 1920s, and both were affected by an intense transatlantic exchange of ideas about the structuring of the modern state. Most importantly, the commemorations both celebrated histories of settling across national borders.

Commemorating across Borders

Commemoration is an umbrella term for an array of activities staged in the name of a celebration of the past. These activities are fundamentally social events, shaping both history and the social group performing the commemoration.[9] Because of their social character, commemorations are regularly studied to understand processes of identity construction, which scholars sometimes substitute for various forms of memory—collective, social, or cultural.[10] Such scholarship is commonly placed within a national paradigm, resting on the seldom-problematized premise that commemorations represent a specific history to a specific target group to which this history seemingly belongs. As John Gillis writes, "the core meaning of any individual or group identity . . . is sustained by remembering; and what is remembered is defined by the assumed identity."[11] Brian Conway has pointed out that the scholarship on public history and collective memory largely consists of "a significant body of literature that quarantines national collective identity formation within the boundaries of the nation."[12] The title of a recent anthology on commemorations of "the American past"—*We Are What We Remember*—illustrates this notion, which was prevalent as the research field was being shaped in the 1980s and 1990s and which remains dominant.[13]

But what if this view of identity and memory cannot explain the phenomenon of cross-border commemorations, where the same history is *not* represented to a purportedly homogenous group of people? Scholars such as Aleida Assmann, Astrid Erll, and Michael Rothberg are exploring how history and memory are formed across national borders. According to Erll, the "container-culture approach is . . . epistemologically flawed, because there are too many mnemonic phenomena that do not come into our field of vision with the 'default' combination of territorial, ethnic and national collectivity as the main framework of cultural memory."[14] As these scholars have demonstrated, memories are not limited to certain groups but are products of interactions across cultures and geopolitical borders and are subject to ongoing negotiations and cross-referencing.[15] Rothberg has made a fruitful distinction between transnational and transcultural memory that is applicable to the study of cross-border commemorations. In his definition, transcultural memory "refers to the *layering* of historical legacies that occurs in the traversal of *cultural* borders, while transnational memory refers to the *scales* of remembrance that intersect in the crossing of *geo-political* borders."[16] These two dimensions—the crossings, exchanges, and overlaps of both cultural history and geopolitical borders—are central to my analysis.

One way to approach the study of commemorations is to acknowledge the ways in which people, culture, and ideas have repeatedly made these celebrations into cross-border events. To find a better alternative to the nation as an interpretative framework, I have written this book as an entangled history. This approach incorporates

6 INTRODUCTION

FIGURE 1. The Swedish and Finnish delegations landed at the Fort Christina State Park in Wilmington, Delaware, on June 27, 1938. President Franklin D. Roosevelt, Delaware's Governor Richard C. McMullen, and other dignitaries awaited the delegations at the speakers' platform (on the left), ready to jointly inaugurate the tercentenary and officially unveil the monument created by Carl Milles (on the right). Photo courtesy of the Delaware Public Archives.

transcultural and transnational processes and acknowledges the multiple interactions that take place within and beyond the nation space; it pays close attention to interactions among various people and groups as well as to the reasons for and consequences of those interactions.[17] It has guided my project from start to finish, affecting the choices of which commemorations to include, the methodology of how to study these events, and the ways in which I theoretically and contextually interpret the sources.

The landing ceremony at The Rocks in 1938 exemplifies the implications of this approach. The New Sweden Tercentenary began on a rainy day on June 27, 1938, when the Swedish delegation disembarked in Delaware. It was led by Crown Prince Gustaf Adolf, but because he had suffered renal colic on the journey to America, his twenty-six-year-old son Prince Bertil shouldered the responsibility as temporary leader of the group. On arrival in Wilmington, the delegation walked down a gangway to set foot on The Rocks. They took a few steps on the stone and then proceeded up a second ramp to the concrete platform that surround The Rocks at Fort Christina State Park. The state of Delaware had finished construction of the park just in time for the celebrations, and the state's tercentenary commission had built a temporary stage, where President Franklin D. Roosevelt and Delaware governor Richard C. McMullen awaited the visiting dignitaries. The stage looked out over a crowd of Delaware residents and Swedish Americans from all corners of America, and it stood in front of the monument that was about to be dedicated. This monument, whose inscription declared that the New Sweden colony had "founded civilization in the Delaware Valley," had been designed by Carl Milles, a Swedish sculptor who was living and working in the United States, and financed by donations from more than 200,000 Swedes. It was a gift from Sweden, donated to the United States, to be held in the custody of the state of Delaware.

We cannot adequately understand this scene at The Rocks within a national framework. Although international cooperation stood at the center of the commemoration, it was much more than an international event. As the landing ceremony illustrates, domestic U.S. relations and regional contexts were, for example, just as pertinent as inter- or transnational dimensions in defining the relevance and meaning of the celebration.[18] Multiple interactions among different groups stand at the center of this book. The entangled history approach highlights the cooperation behind the creation of the park and the monument, the negotiations about where to place the monument and locate the opening ceremonies, and the converging and diverging historical representations that circulated in and through the monument and the ceremonies at The Rocks.[19] By studying these processes, I seek to transnationalize commemorations that previous research has nationalized.[20]

It is difficult to ascertain the number of cross-border commemorations that have been organized in the United States and Sweden, let alone in other parts of the world. This is due to the limited amount of research on the topic, a fact that can be explained by the national paradigm that has defined most previous studies of commemorations. This paradigm has also influenced the study of commemorations that display cross-border characteristics. Even when the presence of, for example, international actors in (allegedly) national celebrations are acknowledged, the reasons behind or effects of their participations are rarely analyzed.[21]

Despite the scholarly silence, there have been numerous cross-border commemorations—for example, the 1982 Dutch-American Friendship Commemoration, celebrated in memory of the 1782 signing of a treaty of amity and commerce between the Netherlands and the United States. In a proclamation, President Ronald Reagan described this two-hundred-year-old legacy as "the longest unbroken, peaceful relationship with any foreign country" (thus overwriting statements of a three-hundred-year-old friendship claimed by Swedish and American commemorators in 1938).[22] A year later, in 1983, Reagan commemorated the three hundredth anniversary of German Mennonite families' arrival in Pennsylvania, launching the German-American Tricentennial and establishing the German-American Friendship Garden in Washington, D.C. Located steps away from the Washington Monument, the garden was dedicated by Reagan and Germany's Chancellor Helmut Kohl in 1988.[23] Foreign delegations were also present when the quincentenary of Christopher Columbus's landing was commemorated in 1992—an event that was celebrated not only by the United States but also by Italy, Spain, Mexico, and several Latin American countries.[24] All of these commemorations need to be studied beyond national frameworks of interpretation. To acknowledge them as cross-border demands a fundamental change in the way we see them. It requires a shift away from methodological nationalism toward a methodology that empirically and analytically enables the writing of history in which national contexts are not the natural end point of the analysis.[25]

The New Sweden Tercentenary and the Swedish Pioneer Centennial are examples of commemorations that were organized through interactions among groups on both sides of the Atlantic. In this book,

I incorporate sources from most of these groups, which I found in fourteen different archives located in Sweden and the United States. I include material from all of the major commissions involved, representing Sweden, the United States, Delaware, Pennsylvania, New Jersey, and Swedish America in 1938 as well as Sweden and Swedish America in 1948.[26] In addition, I incorporate on-site studies of monuments and heritage sites that have been instrumental in commemorations of Swedish settlement on the American East Coast and in the Midwest.

Although Finland and Finnish America formed commissions for the New Sweden Tercentenary, I only analyze such participation when it pertains to discussions and activities in which the other commissions were also involved. There are two reasons for this choice. First, without adequate Finnish language skills, I am unable to consider all of these sources equally alongside sources in Swedish and English. This is an example of a moment in which the entangled history approach confronts the practical limitations of doing cross-border research. Second, my research at the archives of the other commissions shows that there was comparatively little communication between the Finnish and Finnish-American groups and the rest of the commemorators studied here. This silence attests to the more peripheral role of the Finnish participants in the 1938 celebration.

An important consequence of commemorations that cross borders is the geographical dispersion of their material legacies. Their traces are found in different archives, in different countries. By examining one or a selected few of these archives, one would gain only a simplistic understanding of the commemorations. My research of the vast majority of collections from the 1938 and 1948 commemorations has revealed a plethora of source materials and also identified overlaps in the archival holdings. Many of the documents—letters, protocols, telegrams, and printed matter—are located, as copies and originals, in several different archives. This is evidence that these commemorations, as both a practice and a materiality, have crossed borders and that they need to be analytically treated as such.

The organizers of the 1938 and 1948 celebrations produced commemorative stamps, coins, and pins. They issued books and printed pamphlets, staged parades and pageants, erected historical markers and monuments, created delegations that traveled around the United States and Sweden, visited historical sites as well as modern businesses and industries, organized banquets and luncheons, and held speeches at public events and via radio. As a consequence, the archives contain records in different media: texts, images, films, sound recordings, and material artifacts. The texts include protocols, letters, memos, telegrams, printed pamphlets, books, blueprints, lists, and schedules, in handwriting, typewriting, and carbon copies. There are also commemorative pins, stickers, stamps, plaques, and monuments, dispersed both inside and outside the archives.

These miscellaneous materials and seemingly inconsequential tokens play an important role in the communication of history. W. J. T. Mitchell has famously argued that "all media are mixed media." All media consist of different sensory and semiotic dimensions, but this does not imply that all media are identical. On the contrary, one needs to consider "the specific mixtures of specific media"—in other words, how different media have different sensory and symbolic characteristics.[27] Mitchell's argument is relevant for studies in public history because it encourages the acknowledgment of both the specificities and similarities of various source materials. A monument functions differently from a book, a stamp, or a film. In short, the sensory characteristics—the ways in which we perceive them through hearing, seeing, and touching—differ among the media. What they have in common is semiotics, stemming from the fact that all were produced as commemorative objects. To take this into consideration is to recognize that all of these objects have been involved in the construction of the imaginaries of Swedish settlement in America.

Settler Commemorations

Even though the past does not constitute the raison d'être of a commemoration and might not be at the forefront of the projects launched during its execution, commemorative activities must somehow relate to the past that they celebrate, even if the reference is very fleeting. Otherwise, such activities do not fit within the framework of the commemoration. Although social, political, and commercial interests shaped the 1938 and 1948 celebrations, they pivoted around claims that these were events of importance because they commemorated foundational histories.

The tercentenary and the centennial celebrated histories at the heart of the American myth of origin, commemorating the arrival of people who interchangeably were called colonists, pioneers, and immigrants. These myths are not unique to the United States. They are shared by other settler countries who also have experiences of European discovery, exploration, settling, and so-called civilizing. Settler commemorations have often adopted a set of discursive strategies in explaining and legitimizing history, either by completely erasing any notions of an indigenous past or by promoting an idealized past in which indigenous peoples and settlers coexisted harmoniously.[28] The moment of settling is the point of departure for how most Americans think about the foundational histories of any given area of the country, and commemorations—both ethnic community celebrations and those with a national scope—have in different ways contributed to shaping and calcifying these memories.

From the American Revolution to the late nineteenth century, settler commemorations were geographically focused on the East Coast, including grand celebrations of the Plymouth colony in 1820, 1870, and 1920–21.[29] As settlers and immigrants began moving into newly incorporated areas west of the Mississippi River, commemorations became a means of forging local communities and of staking claims to the settled land and to the nation. Beginning in the late nineteenth century, Swedish Americans, German Americans, Norwegian Americans, and other European immigrant groups repeatedly staged celebrations of the achievements and hardships of pioneer ancestors.[30] Old-settler societies were an aspect of these local heritage projects, and they remain an enduring legacy in the West and the Midwest. Throughout the United States, older generations of pioneers founded these societies as a means of "forging a sense of place and a sense of belonging." Some are still active in local communities, where they continue to inform memories of origin.[31] Attesting to the contemporary ramifications of these histories, the concept of settler colonialism has in recent years gained ground in studies of public history.[32]

The colonists and pioneers who founded new societies and the immigrants who moved into communities founded by the settlers were linked by their European heritage. Yet the dominating memories of their lives have been attached to the American landscape. As Davia Stasiulis and Nira Yuval-Davis have pointed out, "the settlers' ideologies involved in nation-building have a historical starting point, which occurs at the moment of colonial conquest and the beginning of settlement."[33] It is evident that the national mythological character of settler histories in the United States has overshadowed their significance in a larger transatlantic context.

Both the New Sweden Tercentenary and the Swedish Pioneer Centennial were cross-border events grounded in their celebration of settlement. While commemorators in 1938 claimed to celebrate "the first permanent settlement" in the Delaware Valley, the 1948 organizers commemorated the "actual settling" of the Mississippi Valley.[34] The significance of these histories can be exemplified by four memorial stamps that in a very condensed form emphasized the historical meanings of the celebrations.

The postal services of Sweden and the United States issued a number of commemorative stamps in time for the New Sweden Tercentenary and the Swedish Pioneer Centennial. In 1938 both countries produced stamps that represented the colonists' encounters with

FIGURES 2 AND 3. Sweden issued a set of commemorative stamps for the 1938 New Sweden Tercentenary and the 1948 Swedish Pioneer Centennial, designed on both occasions by the Swedish artist Olle Hjortzberg. © PostNord Frimärken.

American Indians. The U.S. stamp depicted the colonists arriving with open arms from the *Kalmar Nyckel,* greeted by a native chief. These signs of friendliness were echoed in a Swedish stamp, which showed a Native American man presenting a peace pipe to the colonists as two men plant the Swedish coat of arms in the newly acquired soil. These stamps were representations of acquisitions, showing the moment when replacement began.

Ten years later, the stamps depicted a very different process of settlement. The Swedish stamp showed a single man pushing a plow. Behind him, to his left, is a log cabin with a straw-thatched roof. Adjacent to the cabin and depicted as an abstract, one-sided figure and thus seemingly detached from the rest of the picture, there is a geometrically shaped skyscraper extending its body over the stamp's frame. The connection between man and land also stands at the center in the stamp issued by the U.S. Postal Service: it depicts a man leading an ox-drawn covered wagon across a prairie landscape. On either side of the picture, twelve stars represent the midwestern states where Swedes originally settled in the mid-nineteenth century.

These stamps are historical representations of Swedish colonization and pioneering in North America, from the Swedish-Native encounters in the Delaware Valley, to the covered wagon on the midwestern prairie, to the plowing man in front of the skyscraper. A crucial component of a settler colonial representation is the dual relation to indigenous populations. The violent displacement of indigenous people forms a premise of the settler project, even as the representations of this project are based on a disavowal of any foundational violence. The portrayal of the indigenous population as "vanishing" and the settled land as "virgin" or "vacant" constitutes a crucial part of the settler narrative, denying both foundational violence and Native presence.[35] These narrative strategies and structures have been imperative in the commemorations of Swedish settlement in America. They center on two mutually constituent dimensions—namely, the implicit or explicit relation to Native Americans and the claim that a modern and civilized society founded by the Swedish settlers had replaced those populations.

With the exception of interactions in the Delaware Valley, only recently have relations between Swedish settlers and Native Americans received scholarly attention. Previously, Swedish settlement was primarily discussed within a context of immigration.[36] This has been the case, as Gunlög Fur writes, "in spite of the fact that Swedish immigrants settled land just recently and more or less forcefully vacated by Indians" in the nineteenth century.[37] Swedish settlers in the Midwest benefited from American dispossession of Native lands through legislation such as the 1862 Homestead Act and the 1887 Dawes Act, which gave immigrants opportunities for land allotments.[38] Karen Hansen has studied how Scandinavian immigrants between 1890 and 1930 settled on the Spirit Lake Dakota Indian Reservation in North Dakota. "Here," she explains, "they were settler colonialists."[39] The process Hansen describes was part of the U.S. settler empire in which geographic and demographic expansion, as well as ideological and institutional structures, ensured that Native Americans continued to encounter settlers from the United States and Europe who sought to claim their land, even into the 1900s.[40]

The commemorations in 1938 and 1948 celebrated Swedish land claims in the Delaware and Mississippi valleys, lauding their replacement of Native Americans, their civilized cultivation of the soil, and their establishment of what commemorators saw as the first societal institutions worthy of notice. Although narratives of Swedish settlement begin at the point of Native contacts in the Mid-Atlantic region or in encounters with the recently vacated land of the Midwest, their impact largely derives from claims about the civilization that the settlers imposed. These claims were common in the United States, resting on the notion that Native society and culture were unmodern, uncivilized, and archaic.[41] Commemorators likewise asserted that the settlers had built new and lasting societies and that those legacies still were visible in the present-day United States. As I will show, these claims became a malleable tool in the promotion of cross-border relations.

Although settlement and its memories have been criticized in the United States, both continue to be commemorated vigorously in and beyond America. Since the 1960s, Plymouth Rock and other sites of settling have become less important as American myths of origin, yet, as this book demonstrates, they continue to be celebrated in cross-border commemorations.[42] The book consists of six chapters, each devoted to an aspect common to such commemorations, with analyses of both its planning and performance. Together, they show that the commemorations have supported contemporary cross-border relations while promoting a settler colonial history.

Chapter 1 investigates the conditions of the 1938 and 1948 commemorations, centering on the historical disposition and the political capacity needed to create fruitful circumstances for commemorative organizing. Although cross-border commemorations can be staged by regions, states, diasporas, nonprofit organizations, and businesses, they often include some representative from a foreign country. They are made possible by events of the past, by how the past has been represented historiographically, and by international political circumstances. Chapter 2 focuses on the specific contemporary motivations behind the 1938 and 1948 commemorations, showing how commemorators seized on the moments of opportunity to forward their own agendas. Although regional and national contexts were important incentives, the commemorations were eventually organized because they provided forums for the promotion of inter- and transnational relations. Chapter 3 examines which histories commemorators claimed to celebrate. The histories of Swedish settlement in America were—through monuments, speeches, texts, and even the choice of commission names—memorialized as transatlantic legacies. In their efforts to stage joint celebrations, and through their sometimes intense negotiations, commemorators entangled histories of settlement.

While chapters 2 and 3 revolve around the planning of the commemorations, the three subsequent chapters analyze its cooperative performance. Chapter 4 focuses on the travels of foreign delegations, which were the primary structuring principle of cross-border commemorations. By traveling across the Atlantic and into the American interior, these delegations represented history through reenactment. They served the dual function of, on the one hand, creating a bridge to the past by emphasizing historical links and continued legacies and, on the other, establishing a break with and a distance to the past by way of modernization. Chapter 5 centers on the public indoor and outdoor festivals and parades that attracted massive audiences to the celebrations. The festivals enabled Swedish Americans to physically interact with the representatives of their old homeland and to mutually express and negotiate different ideas about Swedishness. Chapter 6 investigates the practice of commemorative banquets and luncheons and analyzes how notions of friendship informed contemporary relations and histories of settlement. Serving as both celebrations of history and sites for international networking, they were attended by government representatives, politicians, businessmen, and celebrities, and were—through decorations, programming, and speeches—designed to stimulate cross-border relations. Finally, the book's conclusion explores the sustained practices and resilient histories in subsequent twentieth- and twenty-first-century commemorations of Swedish settlement in America.

The Atlantic world is intrinsically connected through the historical and contemporary movements of people, goods, and ideas. Along with difficult histories such as slavery and international wars, the processes of colonization, pioneering, and migration have, in essence, been about crossing borders, linking spaces, and connecting people. As researchers have repeatedly shown, commemorations of settlement speak to issues of national, regional, and ethnic identity. My book does not set out to prove this scholarship wrong but to demonstrate that studying commemorations as cross-border events provides a more complex and multifaceted understanding of this influential public historical phenomenon.[43]

CHAPTER 1

Moments of Opportunity

On Pasts and Politics

After his return to Sweden at the end of the 1938 New Sweden Tercentenary, Sten Dehlgren, the editor-in-chief of the Swedish daily newspaper *Dagens Nyheter*, reflected on his impression of the celebrations. "The Americans," he began, "had indeed not been sparing with the festival funds." Looking back at a trip to the United States during World War I, he recalled that many Americans had held rather negative attitudes about Sweden, a fact explained by the country's close cultural and political ties to Germany. Some twenty years later, however, there had been "an undeniable turn in the American manner of thinking." This turn could not, according to Dehlgren, be explained by the historical merits of the New Sweden colony—"this Swedish failure at colonization," as he called it—but by a growing general American interest in history and heritage as well as by "a determined and successful campaign of enlightenment on the part of the Swedes." It was also clear to him that the interest was stirred by politics—in particular, the attention the celebration had received from the Roosevelt administration and from other representatives of the Democratic Party. There were, Dehlgren concluded, "many contributing causes [that] gave rise to this extensive American manifestation."[1]

The timing for the New Sweden Tercentenary had clearly been right; and as Dehlgren had noted, its success was linked to both political capacity and historical dispositions. Commemorations are made possible by what has happened in the past, by how the past has been represented historiographically, and by contemporary social and political circumstances. These dimensions are central to understanding the reasons, motivations, and consequences of commemorations. In order to understand how and for what purposes they are staged, we need to explore the moments when pasts and politics merge.

The modern practice of commemoration developed in the late eighteenth century during the French and American revolutions. It had, in the words of John Gillis, grown out of "an ideologically driven desire to break with the past" and thus to distance the New Regime from the Old.[2] In the ensuing age of nationalism, history became a means of forging a sense of belonging to the imagined community of the nation. A primary means of instilling the sense of a shared past and a common future involved "the invention of tradition" in which formalized and ritualized commemorations played a key role.[3] This feature of commemorations has also made it a source of conflict; in the scholarship on public remembrance, this is reflected in the common description of memory as a "contested terrain."[4]

According to historian John Bodnar, public memory in America is forged in "the intersection of official and vernacular cultural expressions." The fashioning of memory is a consequence of the active work of cultural leaders seeking to advance the interest of a particular social entity—a local community, an ethnic group, or a branch of government—and of the patriotic and nationalistic culture of the majority population.[5] Although most commemorations have been orchestrated by dominating social groups, the friction between a majority and a minority population is embedded in studies of ethnic commemorations as well as in the ways that indigenous peoples have been able to use commemorations to engage with present marginalization and the memory of past atrocities.[6] These negotiations naturally affect how some histories are represented, and how others are not. Shaped by both memory and amnesia, commemorations are always political in the way that they offer a specific, singular, and situated perspective on history, while displaying a "tendency to obscure decisions made about who gets remembered and why." As the historian Seth Bruggeman succinctly writes: "Commemoration is an argument about the past presented as if there were no argument."[7]

The moments of opportunity for organizing a commemoration are a vortex of circumstances in which contemporary interests merge with temporal possibilities of the historical calendar.[8] It was this process that Sten Dehlgren observed in 1938. For the New Sweden Tercentenary and the 1948 Swedish Pioneer Centennial, the most important circumstances concerned the histories of transatlantic connections and international political relations of the mid-twentieth century. Together, these contexts shaped both the making and the message of the celebrations and formed the foundation for the development of the commemorations into transatlantic events.

Transatlantic Connections

European descendants inhabited the United States through colonial settlement, pioneer settlement, and mass migration. Although some Swedes settled in America during the seventeenth and eighteenth centuries, their mass migration did not begin in earnest until the 1840s. Because both commemorators and writers of popular history have conflated the history of colonialism and immigration (as I will discuss in chapter 3), it is important to point out that these events were not linked but were the products of two distinct historical processes: one connected to European mercantilism and imperialism, the other to developments of industrialization and capitalism.[9]

The Lenape called the area of the Delaware Valley that would become the location of the New Sweden colony Lenapehoking—"land of the original people." With the Susquehannocks, they inhabited the land around Lenapewihittuck, known today as the Delaware River. Contrary to popular understanding of the history of New Sweden, the Lenape had control over the majority of the Delaware Valley until the 1680s. Following Henry Hudson's 1609 sighting of Delaware Bay, Dutch explorers entered the area in 1615 and laid the foundation for the settlement of New Netherlands, situated between New France in the north and the colony of Virginia in the south. In subsequent decades, as a changing set of European countries laid claims to the Delaware Valley, the Lenape continued to uphold trade with the colonists. Despite a steadily decreasing population due to epidemics such as smallpox, they lived in close proximity with the Europeans, mingling, intermarrying, and working to maintain peaceful and beneficial relations.[10]

In early November 1637, two ships left the harbor of Gothenburg in western Sweden.[11] The larger vessel, *Kalmar Nyckel* (the Key of Kalmar), and the smaller one, *Fågel Grip* (the Griffin), had been equipped by the New Sweden Company to establish a colony along the Delaware River. The New Sweden Company was a joint Swedish and Dutch venture that was strongly backed by the Swedish crown. The vessels operated under a Swedish royal charter and carried colonists from Sweden, but a considerable proportion of the crew and the financing were Dutch. The ships' commander was the former governor of New Amsterdam, Peter Minuit. After a period of expansion during the reign of Gustavus Adolphus, the kingdom of Sweden consisted of present-day Finland, the Baltic countries, and parts of northern Germany. (As we shall see in chapter 2, this has complicated twentieth century commemorations of the colony.) Because the Swedish expansionist wars had strained the country's finances, the prospect of an overseas colony from which it could expropriate resources became an attractive solution for the shortage of capital.

The two vessels sailed into Delaware Bay in March 1638, arriving at an area that currently was not under the direct influence of any European power. A few days after their arrival, Peter Minuit met with five Lenape sachems—Mattahorn, Mitatsimint, Elupacken, Mahomen, and Chiton—who signed a deed ceding control of the land between Minquas Kill (the present-day Christina River) and Sankikas Kill (at Trenton, New Jersey). The Swedes established a garrison post called Fort Christina on the banks of the Minquas Kill. The colony soon expanded, settling primarily along the west bank of the Delaware River.

The first years of New Sweden were a great disappointment to the financial backers of the enterprise. The irregular shipments of tobacco and hides that reached Sweden from America created financial losses.

As a result, the Dutch financiers withdrew from the company after a few years. In 1642, as an effort to gain greater control of the colony, the Swedish crown dispatched Lieutenant Colonel Johan Printz to take over as governor of New Sweden. Printz was instructed to implement Swedish law in the colony and to spread the Christian faith. The colony was under pressure due to a lack of contact with Sweden: only twelve ships in total arrived there, with merely three reaching shore during Printz's ten-year stewardship (1643–53). Nonetheless, he was able to expand its control by building new garrisons. The small community included colonists from varying backgrounds, including a growing number of Finns. By the end of the colony's lifespan, Finnish settlers might have accounted for half of the population. However, the lack of support from Sweden and the problem of attracting a substantial number of colonists created distress. The population of New Sweden never exceeded a few hundred individuals. In 1654, its total population was 368. In addition, the colony's relations with the British and Dutch were strained. New Netherlands, led by Governor Peter Stuyvesant after 1647, did not appreciate the involvement of another European country so close to their colonial interests. In the summer of 1655, Stuyvesant led a fleet of vessels down the Delaware River and besieged Fort Christina and Fort Casimir (close to today's New Castle, Delaware). Without the capacity for meaningful resistance, the Swedish colonists surrendered, and New Sweden fell to the Dutch.

Unlike its neighboring British and Dutch colonies, New Sweden was never involved in an Indian war. In both historical scholarship and popular history, this fact has been explained as a result of Swedish agency, based on the notion of a special affinity between the New Sweden colonists and the Lenape.[12] As I will discuss in chapter 3, the idea of Swedish-Native friendship has been a common trope in commemorations of the colony. In reality, the lack of warfare was to a great degree due to the actions of the Lenape. Trade was the central aspect of the relations; and long before the arrival of the Swedes, the Lenape had sought advantageous trade relations with European colonists. Gunlög Fur has shown that "those with power to broker peace and create kin" in the Delaware Valley were Lenape women, who functioned as "mediators of peace" in the colonial encounters.[13]

After the fall of the colony in 1655, most settlers of New Sweden stayed in and around the Delaware Valley. Many maintained connections with Sweden through letter writing and by preserving material objects, language, and religious practices from the old country. For seventy-five years, beginning in 1696, the Lutheran state church in Sweden sent clergy to the Delaware Valley in support of the Swedish Lutheran congregations that remained in the area. The Old Swedes churches in Wilmington (Gloria Dei Church) and Philadelphia (Holy Trinity Church) both date from this period.[14] Throughout the seventeenth and eighteenth centuries, however, the influx of Swedes was sparse.

In the 1840s the first large groups of Swedish emigrants began to leave for America, part of the mass migration of more than 30 million people from Europe to the United States. Their move across the Atlantic was part of major social and economic transformations, of industrialization, urbanization, and population growth. In his seminal book *The Transplanted,* John Bodnar emphasized that the immigrants were "the children of capitalism." The immigration and its great regional and temporal fluctuations were a consequence of expanded transportation networks, the spread of cheaper manufactured goods, the rise of commercial agriculture in Europe, and the growth of American industrial capitalism.[15]

The emigration had an enormous impact on twentieth-century Swedish-American relations. Some 1.3 million Swedes immigrated to the United States between the 1840s and 1920s, the third-largest European per-capita immigration to America after the Irish and the Norwegian.[16] During this period, between one-fifth and one-fourth of the Swedish population relocated to the United States. In 1845 only sixty-five people emigrated from Sweden to the United States, but by 1854 about 14,500 had made the journey. The immigration culminated in 1879–93, with 46,500 people leaving for the United States in 1887 alone—the peak year of Swedish immigration. Unlike the early immigrants, most of whom were families who settled on farmland in the rural Midwest, the later immigration was dominated by men and women seeking work in urban areas, primarily in the northern Midwest but also in New England and the Pacific Northwest. Improved economic and social conditions in Sweden were the main reasons for the dramatic decrease in Swedish immigration in the 1920s, but changes in U.S. legislation also played a role. The United Sates adopted immigration restrictions in 1917, 1921, and 1924 that drastically reduced the number of immigrants who were allowed into the country. The most significant legislation was the 1924 Johnson-Reed Act, which was primarily aimed at restricting immigration from southern and eastern Europe. The act introduced a quota system limiting the number of immigrants to no more than 2 percent of each national group's U.S. population based on the 1890 census—a basis that was consciously chosen to have lesser effect on older immigrant groups, such as the Swedish.[17] Successive U.S. quotas restricted Swedish immigration to only 3,300 individuals per year after 1929, though by that time emigration had declined to the extent that the quota was never filled.[18]

The mass migration created deep and enduring transatlantic connections. Among those who nurtured these relations were the emigrants who returned to Sweden. Although exact numbers are hard to determine, it is estimated that the return rate for all European emigrants in the early twentieth century was about 35 percent.[19] The level, however, varied greatly among groups: while more than 50 percent of Italian emigrants returned between the 1880s and 1920s, the post-1900 remigration of Jews was only about 5 percent. The difference stems from the motivation of emigration: the Italian search for labor versus Jewish racial persecution. Of the Swedes who emigrated to America, approximately one-fifth returned to Sweden. The number of returnees before the 1880s was negligible; but as the labor emigration increased toward the end of the century, so did the share of return migrants. It was common for people to make the transatlantic journey several times.[20] Through these returnees and their presence in Sweden, the majority of the Swedish population developed a familiarity with America.[21]

In certain parts of the United States, immigration gave rise to large communities of Swedish Americans. The number peaked in 1910 with 665,000 Swedish-born persons, dropping to 560,000 in 1930 and to 445,000 by 1940. Along with second-generation Swedish Americans (those with one or two Swedish-born parents), the group numbered more than 1.5 million in 1930. While the number of Swedish-born declined steadily, the number of second-generation Swedish Americans increased, reaching 986,000 in 1930. Although that figure dropped to 856,000 in 1940, the second generation was still twice as numerous as those born in Sweden. The majority of these first- and second-generation Swedish Americans lived in the Midwest. Although a significant presence also had been established in California and Washington State, the largest populations were in Chicago and Minneapolis (110,000 and 61,000 respectively, or about 3 and 13 percent of the total population of these cities).[22]

To avoid being seen as foreigners in their land of choice, many European immigrants during the nineteenth and twentieth centuries sought to affirm their place in the United States. They claimed that their Old World identities also were American identities by asserting and celebrating different homemaking myths: foundational stories, sacrifices to American freedom such as participation in the Civil War, and ideological connections between the United States and the homeland. Through these strategies, immigrants claimed that America was their rightful home.[23] While some ethnic commemorations have grown to transcend ethnic boundaries, such as the Irish-American Saint Patrick's Day, other celebrations have been more closely connected to a particular ethnic group: celebrations of Columbus Day among Italian Americans, commemorations of the immigrant sloop *Restaurationen* among Norwegian Americans, or memorializations of Thaddeus Kosciuszko and Casimir Pulaski among Polish Americans.[24] Celebrations of ethnic heritages are American history. But as we will see in chapter 5, commemorations such as these have, by their references to histories and cultures of the old homelands, also been performed through transatlantic cooperation.[25]

The process of becoming American has, throughout U.S. history, been fraught with issues of race. The path to admission, citizenship, and equal acceptance in American society was decidedly more difficult for most other immigrants than it was for the Swedes. Their comparatively easy integration had several explanations, including the fact that Swedes were overwhelmingly Protestant and had a very high literacy rate. It can also be explained by their favorable position in the American ethno-racial hierarchy.[26] Since the nineteenth century, there has been a widespread cultural conception that Swedes virtually epitomize whiteness. But like race and ethnicity in general, notions of Swedish whiteness have changed over the course of history. A conspicuous illustration of this development comes from Benjamin Franklin. In 1755, he published his *Observations Concerning the Increase of Mankind* in which he discussed the rapid population growth in the American colonies. Franklin was deeply troubled by how immigration was transforming the colonies and argued that the only people to really be considered "white," and thus fit to populate the colonies, were the British. According to him, "the number of purely white people in the world is proportionally very small. All *Africa* is black or tawny. *Asia* chiefly tawny. *America* (exclusive of the new comers) wholly so. And in *Europe*, the *Spaniards, Italians, French, Russians* and *Swedes* are generally of what we call a swarthy complexion; as are the *Germans* also, the *Saxons* only excepted, who with the *English* make the principal body of white people on the face of the earth."[27] Franklin's account of the Swedes' "swarthy complexion" stands in stark contrast to how their image changed during the nineteenth century. In his 1916 *The Passing of the Great Race*, Madison Grant, who has been called the leader of the eugenicist movement in America, argued that "the Nordic race" was the core group responsible for the development of western civilization. The Nordic race, he claimed, was the "white man par excellence." With the large-scale immigration of "Alpines" and "Mediterraneans" to America, he feared that the heritage of the Nordic race in America would disappear, thus "sweeping the nation toward a racial abyss."[28]

Grant's writings are an example of what Matthew Frye Jacobson has described as the "fracturing of whiteness," a process underway throughout the era of mass immigration, from the 1840s to 1924. The highpoint of this development was the legislation in the 1920s that effectively ended mass immigration. Legally, the United States thus underlined that Swedes and other Scandinavians had secured an advantageous position in American society.[29] Swedish immigrants were, like Italians in Thomas Guglielmo's study, considered "white on arrival" in the United States. However, unlike Italian Americans, they had a clear social advantage in being culturally, religiously, and racially associated with the white Anglo-Saxon Protestant heritage in America. In the words of the sociologist Charles H. Anderson, the Swedes "occupied an enviable position" in the American ethnic landscape.[30] In their social as well as their public historical life in America, Swedish immigrants benefited from the scientific and political evolvement of the discourse of race.

By the time of the New Sweden Tercentenary and Swedish Pioneer Centennial, the mass migration had created strong links between Sweden and the United States. While the Swedish-American community remained substantial in cities such as Minneapolis (in 1930 Swedes were the largest foreign-born group in most sections of the city), the group was changing demographically.[31] As we will see in subsequent chapters, many of the organizers of the 1938 and 1948 commemorations were not immigrants themselves but the children of immigrant parents with a favorable social standing in American society. This development meant that Swedish America went from being a community of immigrants to becoming a community increasingly detached from the immediate migratory experience.[32] This detachment was also temporal; it effectively contributed to turning the mass migration into history, thus making it increasingly appealing to commemorate.

International Relations

Yet concerns about history were not the primary reason for why state and national governments decided to participate in the commemorations. For these commemorators, the central motives were bound up in international politics. Because cross-border commemorations draw on histories that link different geographical areas, it is not surprising that they become enmeshed in the politics of international relations. Although they can be organized by ethnic groups, regional governments, or businesses, cross-border commemorations often include some degree of national participation.

In the 1938 and 1948 commemorations, the national involvement was principal. Not only did it give the commemorations added legitimacy and international news coverage but it also (as I will discuss in chapter 2) intensified the interest of ethnic and regional commemorators. The political backdrop to the commemorations was shaped by inter- and postwar discussions about the formation of the modern state. These discussions were, in turn, influenced by an increase in transatlantic traveling. As the development of steamships and the rapid expansion of rail construction made traveling easier, faster, and cheaper, people were able to make transatlantic crossings for both work and leisure. From the 1870s to the 1930s, the number of American tourists to Europe increased from fewer than 35,000 to almost 370,000 a year. While the mass migration already had ingrained Europe into the U.S. popular imagination, the surge in overseas journeys contributed to shaping the political outlook of affluent upper- and middle-class Americans.[33] As Daniel Rodgers has shown, discussions about politics in the United States and Europe were, from the 1870s until World War II, connected through "an intense, transnational traffic in reform ideas, policies, and legislative devices."[34] The New Dealers in the United States lived, in Rodgers' words, "within a world of social policy debate and social policy invention that for two generations had extended far beyond the nation's borders."[35] As a result of these connections, Sweden—rather unexpectedly—emerged during the 1930s as a model of the modern state.[36] This positive image provided a vital impetus for the 1938 commemoration and affected many of the celebrations.

After a period of economic growth in the late 1920s, Sweden was hit by the international Depression, which led to mounting unemployment. Largely as a result of the conservative government's failure to deal with the Depression, the Social Democratic Party won the 1932 election. The new government, led by Per Albin Hansson, built its policies on a platform of Keynesian theories of economic expansion. The election began a long period of Social Democratic governance in Sweden. Except for an interim three-month period in 1936 and during World War II, when Hansson led a coalition government, the party governed Sweden without interruption until 1976. Already in 1928, Hansson had used the notion of "the people's home" (*Folkhemmet*) to describe the Swedish nation. It was a metaphor of national integration that turned into a formative idea for the role of the Swedish state. The

Social Democratic governments of the 1930s also established what has become known as "the Swedish model" based on the modern welfare state; institutionalized compromises among the state, industry, business, and trade unions; and a consensus culture across the political spectrum.[37]

Observers in the United States noted these political developments in Sweden. During the 1930s some believed the country's approach might be a way of dealing with the Depression's economic and social crisis. More than any other person, the American journalist Marquis Childs contributed to spreading this idea. In 1936 he published the influential and highly successful book *Sweden: The Middle Way* in which he argued that the nation offered an appealing alternative to communism and fascism. It combined capitalism with democracy and public and private ownership with state regulations and social reforms.[38] *The Middle Way* was instrumental in focusing the attention of New Deal politicians on the developments in Sweden. At a White House press conference in June 1936, President Roosevelt described them as "tremendously interesting" and admired how the "cooperative movements exist[ed] happily and successfully alongside of private industry." His source was *The Middle Way*, which he called "a very interesting book."[39] It was also his impetus for launching a fact-finding commission that focused on the cooperative movement in Sweden and Great Britain.[40] The impact of Childs's book was significant. The first edition alone went through nine printings; the third edition, which first appeared in 1947, was still in print by 1985.[41]

According to the political scientist Kazimierz Musiał, images of "Scandinavian progressiveness"—which included both Sweden and Denmark—had emerged during the 1930s "as a result of a constant interaction between foreign images of Scandinavia . . . and the images conceived among the inhabitants of the region."[42] The American notion of Swedish modernity was internalized in Swedish political discourse through the work of Social Democratic governments. An example was the reform of Swedish education in the late 1940s, which the American school system had inspired. The New Deal in fact became a point of reference for both proponents and opponents of the Swedish model in Sweden. While opponents of economic state intervention critiqued the Swedish and American programs, supporters of such measures pointed to the United States—the epitome of modernity—as a way of legitimizing the Social Democratic policies.[43]

The positive image of Sweden in the United States changed noticeably as a result of World War II. While the United States entered the war in December 1941 after the attack on Pearl Harbor, Sweden maintained a neutral and nonaligned position throughout the war. Its neutrality continues to be a topic of debate, especially as it relates to the morality of the country's wartime actions. The Swedish government repeatedly made concessions to Nazi Germany that violated its declared neutrality.[44] The greatest challenge to the country's neutrality came after the Nazi occupation of Denmark and Norway in April 1940. From the summer of 1940 to the summer of 1943, Sweden maintained a policy of appeasement toward Germany. After the occupation of Norway, Germany demanded that the Swedish government allow military transports across Sweden's borders. Uncertain about whether the Nazis would continue their occupation of Scandinavia, the government allowed Germany to transport unarmed personnel on Swedish trains. In total, more than 2 million German troops were transported through Sweden during the war. The concessions also included permission to use Swedish territorial waters for transports on the North and Baltic seas as well as the use of Swedish airspace. In addition, Sweden maintained a trade relationship with Germany for most of the war, including the export of iron ore to the Nazi steel industry.[45]

The wartime concessions contributed to saving Sweden from the devastation that much of Europe experienced. But its actions during the war were problematic in terms of public relations. "From being hailed as the most civilized country in the world [during the 1930s] Sweden was suddenly scorned as a traitor to democracy," claimed Naboth Hedin, the director of the press agency the American-Swedish News Exchange, after the war.[46] In February 1943, the Swedish government appointed a committee known as the America Inquiry to analyze the country's situation in a postwar world. The explicit goal of the inquiry was to "restore and develop" cultural relations and trade relations with "the trans-oceanic countries." Although the committee's work concerned both North and South America, it predominantly focused on relations with the United States. The special position of the United States was considered so self-evident that the committee had "not felt it necessary" to even discuss this focus. In its final report, the committee found that Sweden's position was precarious. Its policy of neutrality and nonalignment during the war had damaged the country's image abroad—in particular, among its political allies. These "misunderstandings" could, according to the committee, be corrected by an expanded "enlightenment" campaign.[47]

Sweden's public diplomacy in the decades after World War II was predominantly targeted against persons in the United States. As a consequence of the America Inquiry, the Swedish Institute for Cultural Exchange with Foreign Countries (later renamed the Swedish Institute) was formed in 1945 as a quasi-official agency that would promote cultural, political, and economic relations between Sweden and foreign countries. The ideal institutional mission was not to deal in "propaganda" but to communicate through objective and fact-based "enlightenment" projects. When the institute set out to change Sweden's image during its first years of activity, the focus was on a progressive Swedish state that had been created through social reform. The institute sought foreign recognition and affirmation to validate the image of Swedish modernity. In this process, American recognition was of special importance.[48]

Sweden during the postwar period has been described as America's "neutral ally."[49] Still, the countries' postwar relations remained complicated. Sweden retained its position of neutrality after the war, and until 1947 the United States had no serious concern with the position. During this time, the U.S. State Department showed limited interest in Sweden's foreign policy and was satisfied with knowing that the country had a "natural orientation toward the West," as a department report stated in 1946. However, American dissatisfaction with Swedish neutrality grew in the summer of 1947 after the beginning of discussions about the European Recovery Program, also known as the Marshall Plan. Now the United States was no longer satisfied with Sweden's leanings toward the West; it wanted its explicit loyalty and a stronger commitment to the anticommunist fight. The disagreement was most pronounced between the Swedish Foreign Minister, Östen Undén, and the U.S. ambassador to Sweden, Freeman H. Matthews. While Undén persistently protected Sweden's autonomous neutrality, Matthews was unwilling to compromise in his demand for Sweden's official support and argued that its isolationism should be met by isolation.[50]

American disapproval of Sweden's neutrality increased in the spring and summer of 1948 as Sweden initiated discussions of a joint military alliance with Denmark and Norway, called the Scandinavian Defense Union. What primarily concerned the United States was Sweden's demand that the alliance be formed on a principle of neutrality, which potentially could threaten American plans for a North Atlantic alliance.[51] In an effort to break Sweden's neutralist policy, the United States used both military and economic incentives to coax its government toward America, using Sweden's need for U.S. military technology and know-how as leverage in attempts to affect its foreign policy.[52] The turning point came with the continued negotiations of the Marshall Plan, which Sweden joined in July 1948—during the centennial celebrations. To the United States, this demonstrated Sweden's association with and loyalty to the western bloc.[53]

Although seldom mentioned explicitly during the actual planning of the 1948 centennial, the Cold War loomed in the background of the celebration. Politics was a key explanation for why the Swedish government and President Harry S. Truman took an interest in the project. The geopolitical consideration of neutrality or military alignment was, of course, not in the minds of most individual commemorators. To Swedish Americans in the Midwest, the promotion of a transatlantic sense of Swedishness was decidedly more important. Within the framework of the same commemoration, however, notions of Swedishness were combined with ideas about international relations, and both were mediated through the representation of a shared past.

༄

Since the 1938 tercentenary, the New Sweden colony has provided a suitable starting point for cross-border commemorations. But had it not been for the nineteenth- and early-twentieth-century mass migration from Sweden to the United States, the New Sweden colony would not have been elevated to its later position. By the early twentieth century, there was a significant group of Swedish Americans in the United States, mainly situated in the Midwest. Importantly, the group had a social, cultural, economic, and racial status that enabled them to connect to their old homeland on a high political level and to make such an endeavor appealing to regional and federal actors in America. Gradually looking beyond colonial history as their early past in America, Swedish Americans increasingly embraced foundational stories about Swedish pioneers, drawing on a mythology germane to the Midwest.

By the 1930s, there were new and unprecedented political connections between Sweden and the United States, with common ground created by discussions about the ways of structuring modern social and economic policies. The 1938 commemoration provided an interesting opportunity as the Swedish government sought to benefit from the heightened interest in its social democratic model and as the United States looked for inspiration for its New Deal policies. When the world was shaken by the warfare and atrocities of World War II, the commemorative landscape changed. By 1945, the United States was firmly established as a superpower, while Sweden was left on the political outskirts of Europe, its position compromised by its wartime neutrality.

The mental distance between Sweden and the United States might never have been as narrow as it was in the late 1930s. Just a few years later, this distance had grown to quite a gulf. It was within this shifting nature of transatlantic relations, within the nexus of the ethnic, the regional, the national, and the international, that the New Sweden Tercentenary and the Swedish Pioneer Centennial took place.

CHAPTER 2

Crossing Borders

Appropriating Foundational Histories

On September 14, 1888, Hans Mattson, who was a Swedish immigrant, a Civil War colonel, and Minnesota's secretary of state, welcomed his audience to the first-ever celebration of the New Sweden colony. Its setting, far from the site of the colony in the Delaware Valley, was the Industrial Exposition Building in Minneapolis. Just two years old and centrally located next to Saint Anthony Falls, the building was packed with 15,000 Swedish Americans. The three-hour celebration of "the grand achievements" of Swedes in North American history had drawn participants from all echelons of the Swedish-American community. Although heavy rain had forced the cancellation of a parade with "bands of music and banners," the crowd ought to have been impressed by the building's great hall, whose pillars and platforms were decorated in the yellow and blue of Sweden and the stars and stripes of the United States.[1]

The 1888 event marked the first time that the New Sweden colony had been commemorated. What Mattson and his Swedish-American audience did was to appropriate history, publicly naming New Sweden as their heritage. The process of appropriating the past by commemorating it in the present is a way of making history signify a particular collective entity. By calling history Swedish, American, Pennsylvanian, and so on, one not only creates contemporary access to commemorational forums but also defines the history that is commemorated.

Understanding the processes of appropriation may be the most crucial step in understanding how commemorations come to cross borders. Thus, it is imperative to examine contemporary reasons for why different groups, at particular points in time, have labeled a certain history "their own." Doing so necessitates the acknowledgment of local contexts and how they entwine with those stretching beyond local and national spheres. The commissions in the 1930s and 1940s that organized cross-border commemorations of Swedish settlement regularly acted as separate entities claiming to represent supposedly separate groups of people, yet they were also mutually dependent on other groups and other people to organize the celebrations.

In 1888, the idea of commemorating the New Sweden colony originated among a group of prominent Swedish Americans in Minneapolis, who included the ministers of Lutheran, Baptist, Mission Covenant, and Methodist churches as well as several editors of Swedish-American newspapers. In July of that year, the group published an announcement calling for "all Swedes" to participate, including "Swedish congregations and societies in Minneapolis and the state of Minnesota and Swedes in other parts of the United States."[2] The fact that this idea emerged in Minneapolis was in itself not surprising. Minnesota had at that point received more Swedish immigrants than had any other state in America. By the 1880s, Swedish Americans constituted the largest immigrant group in Minneapolis. Although cities such as Chicago had a higher number of Swedish immigrants, Swedish Americans made a greater cultural and political imprint in the smaller Twin Cities, where their considerable institutional presence included churches, clubs, mutual aid societies, and newspapers. During that decade, they also began to make a greater impact on Minnesota politics; in 1886, John Lind became the first Swedish immigrant to be elected to the U.S. House of Representatives.[3]

The 1888 commemoration was a moment made by and for the Swedish-American community. It was a celebration in which patriotism and ethno-nationalist feelings trumped religious or political discord. It was not, however, a moment that their old homeland seized upon; no people or organizations from Sweden participated in organizing the celebration. Although the Swedish-Norwegian consul in Saint Paul, Hagbarth Sahlgaard, was presented in the printed report as a representative of the Swedish government, no delegation from Sweden was present, and none seems to have been invited. A telegram to King Oscar II received a one-sentence reply from the king's chamberlain.[4] It is probable that the Swedish government's lack of interest originated in a reluctance to support a Swedish-American event at a time when the mass emigration to America was considered to be a national problem. By the 1880s, New Sweden remained a settler history whose political potential was primarily acknowledged within the ethnic community.

The memorial landscape of the colony changed dramatically in the decades leading up to the tercentenary celebrations. In the 1880s, there had been no heritage organization devoted specifically to the history of the colony, but several influential institutions had been established by the 1930s. This development also amounted to a geographical change. The secular and religious organizations that had convened the 1888 commemoration had been centered in the Midwest, but the institutional epicenter for the New Sweden Tercentenary was located on the south side of Philadelphia.

This development was intimately connected to the work of one man, the Swedish-American historian Amandus Johnson. In 1880, at the age of three, he had immigrated to Minnesota with his family. After receiving a master's degree from the University of Colorado at Boulder, he moved east and earned a 1908 doctoral degree at the University of Pennsylvania. His dissertation on the New Sweden colony was published three years later as his massive two-volume study *The Swedish Settlement on the Delaware*. In the ensuing decades, Johnson established himself as the torchbearer of the project to memorialize the greatness of the Swedish colonial heritage. Along with leading businessmen and industrialists in Philadelphia and Wilmington, he established the exclusive Swedish Colonial Society, founded in 1909 with a core membership of people who claimed ancestry from the New Sweden colony.

In the mid-1920s, Johnson led an ambitious plan to build a Philadelphia museum devoted to the colony. The project was supported by the 1924 formation of the American Sons and Daughters of Sweden, a society that Johnson had initiated with the primary purpose of raising capital for the museum. The fundraising was remarkably successful, and the construction of a white stone building modeled after a seventeenth-century Swedish palace began during the 1926 Sesquicentennial International Exposition, on land located on the exposition fairgrounds in present-day Franklin Delano Roosevelt Park. In what would be remembered as a prelude to the tercentenary, Sweden's Crown Prince Gustaf Adolf, who had made a stop in Philadelphia on a visit to the United States, laid the cornerstone. Three years later, the American Swedish Historical Museum was opened to the public, with Johnson serving as museum director and chief curator. From the start he had envisioned the museum as the nave of the upcoming tercentenary in 1938.[5] Although the commemoration eventually reached far beyond Philadelphia and the Delaware Valley, his imprint on the memory of the New Sweden colony is hard to overstate. His efforts—which were ceaseless until his death in 1974, at the age of ninety-six—laid the institutional and historiographical foundations for subsequent commemorations of the New Sweden colony.

Swedish Americans had by the 1930s secured an advanced public historical position. Along with several other established immigrant groups, they had founded historical societies that sought to ground their presence in America and prove that they belonged to their chosen homeland. The American Jewish Historical Society had, for example, been founded in 1892, and the German American Historical Society had been established in 1901.[6] Norwegian immigrants were among the earliest to found a society, opening the Vesterheim Norwegian-American Museum in 1877 in Decorah, Iowa. When Norwegian Americans celebrated the 1925 Norse-American Centennial in Minnesota, President Calvin Coolidge attended and delivered remarks.[7] In other words, Swedish Americans were by no means the first ethnic group to create heritage institutions or to celebrate history in the presence of U.S. presidents. Yet when the American Swedish Historical Museum opened, it granted them a place in the public historical landscape that in some ways surpassed the Norwegians'. It was one of the grandest ethnic museums in the country, and from the outset it supported and legitimized the organization of the tercentenary celebrations.

From Ethnicity to Regionalism

Plans to organize a 1938 tercentenary of the New Sweden colony were first launched in the 1910s by the Delaware Memorial Commission, renamed the New Sweden Memorial Commission in 1924. This group was formed out of the Augustana Synod, a Lutheran denomination founded in 1860. The synod grew rapidly during the late nineteenth century and by 1936 had close to 330,000 members, with congregations spreading to the East and West coasts. In addition to its churches, the synod managed a number of educational institutions (most importantly, the Augustana College in Rock Island, Illinois), benevolent institutions (such as hospitals and orphanages), a newspaper, and a publishing house. It was the arguably most influential Swedish-American organization in the early twentieth century.[8] Although the New Sweden Memorial Commission had substantial commemorative plans, its work, for unknown reasons, came to a halt in the mid-1920s.[9]

A decade passed before anyone took concrete and concerted steps to organize the tercentenary celebration. In February 1935, however, representatives of sixteen Swedish-American associations from around the country gathered in the boardroom of the Historical Society of Pennsylvania in downtown Philadelphia. The presidents of the Swedish Colonial Society and the American Sons and Daughters of Sweden had convened the meeting on a request from the Swedish envoy to the United States, Wollmar Boström. Unlike the Augustana Synod, these two organizations had their foundations in the Delaware Valley. After a discussion that lasted for less than two hours, participants decided to organize the Swedish American Tercentenary Association. Amandus Johnson became the commission's corresponding secretary while Oscar Solbert, a fifty-three-year-old colonel and former military attaché to Norway, Denmark, and Great Britain, was named chair of the executive committee. Solbert had emigrated from Sweden at the age of eight and was at the time of the meeting a respected executive at the Eastman Kodak Company.[10]

The Swedish American Tercentenary Association set up offices in New York, Philadelphia, and Chicago and executed its plans largely through the work of local committees around the country. Its aim was to stage celebrations in all communities that had a "considerable number" of Swedish Americans, although the minutes do not state which specific cities and areas were targeted. Local committees represented broad segments of Swedish America, including churches, civic organizations, cultural societies, and social clubs. Though much work centered on advancing the history of New Sweden, the association also had other motivations. One local committee task was to raise an endowment fund for the economically struggling museum in Philadelphia. There was thus a direct financial incentive for extensive local involvement. Another objective was to send delegates from around the country to the celebrations in Wilmington, Philadelphia, and Washington, D.C. The committees' principal task, however, was to "properly emphasize locally what Americans of Swedish origin have contributed nationally and locally to American life, and to create and maintain interest in the Tercentenary."[11] The manifestation of the contemporary cultural, economic, and civic presence of Swedish Americans was a prominent theme during the commemoration.

Meanwhile, commemorative plans were also made in Pennsylvania. In January 1935, the Pennsylvania Federation of Historical Societies passed a resolution that projected plans for a tercentenary of New Sweden in cooperation with other organizations and the states of Delaware and New Jersey.[12] The preliminary organizing committee was formally appointed by the General Assembly in 1936, which passed a legislative act calling for a commemoration of "the Earliest Settlement, the First Courts of Law, and the First Capital within what is now Pennsylvania."[13] The act created the Pennsylvania 300th Anniversary Commission. A 1937 amendment to the act emphasized that the achievements of New Sweden, not least its peaceful Indian relations, were "the foundations upon which our Pennsylvania civilization is based." According to the act, the commemoration would "arouse, stimulate, and encourage" interest and education in the founding of Pennsylvania. A more instrumental motivation, however, was based on the anticipation that the celebration would bring visitors "from the nation and the entire world," who not only would learn about Pennsylvania's greatness but also increase the state's tax revenues.[14] This idea had precedents in the Depression-era United States. Other regional commemorations in the 1930s, such as the 1936 Texas Centennial, had been celebrated with a "combination of local pride and economic desperation." The notion that the commemoration could be an economic stimulus was further reflected in the fact that the Pennsylvania commission obtained federal Works Progress Administration funds available for tercentenary heritage projects.[15]

The Pennsylvania commission chairman was a fifty-three-year-old Philadelphia lawyer named Frank W. Melvin, who by the 1930s had established himself as a prominent figure in the state's public historical life. He was the chair of the Pennsylvania Federation of Historical Societies, which had initiated the state's celebration, and the president of the Swedish Colonial Society, which made him one of the founders of the Swedish-American commission. Melvin spent considerable energy on activities outside of his law practice, especially those that nurtured his historical and genealogical interests. He claimed descent from not only the New Sweden colony but also the *Mayflower* Pilgrims of 1620. He was the vice-president of the New England Society of Pennsylvania, the deputy governor of the Pennsylvania Society of Mayflower Descendants, and a member of many other societies engaged in the promotion of colonial history.[16] For Melvin, his New Sweden ancestry was not only a Swedish cultural heritage but also a more general American colonial legacy.

Genealogical interest in the United States had surged since the Civil War. Spurred by far-reaching urbanization, industrialization, and immigration, many Americans turned to a combination of ancestor worship, nationalism, and racism to assert their own respectable social and racial status. Ideas about "pure" Anglo-Saxon bloodlines and long historical roots in America were nurtured within the growing cadre of hereditary societies. Two of the best-known were the National Society of the Sons of the American Revolution and the Daughters of the American Revolution. For many members of these associations, it was not the genealogical research that was important but the bloodlines and thus the social prestige that genealogy could establish. Beginning in the late 1880s, older immigrant groups such as the Germans, the Scots, and the Huguenots began to use genealogy to assert their own share in the founding of the United States.[17] Although this kind of immigrant genealogy was intended to counterbalance Anglo-Saxon claims about the nation's founding, the biography of Frank Melvin shows that such cultural work was not a zero-sum game; merging the dominant Anglo-Saxon narrative with immigrant genealogy could open new paths into colonial history.

Melvin's position in the Swedish Colonial Society and the state historical society was a contributing factor behind Pennsylvania's commemorative plans. Given his role at the center of both the Pennsylvanian and the Swedish-American commemorative initiatives, it is no coincidence that they occurred at roughly the same time. A similar intersection took place in Delaware's plans, where the historian George H. Ryden, like Melvin, was involved with the formation of the Swedish-American commission. After learning about the resolution passed by the Pennsylvania Federation of Historical Societies, Ryden contacted the governor of Delaware. The forthcoming commemoration, he explained, would put Delaware "more in the nation's limelight . . . than she has been for many a year."[18] In March 1935, the General Assembly of Delaware adopted a joint resolution appointing a preparatory commission to arrange plans for a state, interstate, national, and international commemoration of "the founding of the first permanent settlement and the establishment of the first permanent government upon the soil of Delaware." The resolution, which had been drafted by Ryden, described The Rocks in Wilmington as the site of "the first permanent establishment of European civilization" in the area.[19] The preparatory commission was reinstated through a new resolution in 1937 forming the Delaware Tercentenary Commission. Ryden became the commission's corresponding secretary, and the secretary of the state's historical society, Christopher Ward, shouldered the chairmanship.[20]

Ryden's father had emigrated from Sweden to the United States in 1868, with his mother following him three years later. The couple settled on farmland in Kansas that was part of the newly ceded Osage Indian Territory, where they raised a family of six children.

George, the oldest son, was born in Kansas City in 1884. He attended Augustana College before moving to Yale University, where, following a stint in Russia, where he did civilian relief work for the Red Cross between 1918 and 1920, he eventually earned a doctorate in history. He was named head of the Department of History at the University of Delaware in 1928 and two years later was appointed as the state archivist of Delaware. In this role, Ryden came to serve on several state heritage commissions. Although he made a career in the state of Delaware, he also retained personal connections to Swedish America. His younger brother Ernest was a reverend of Augustana Synod and an editor of the *Lutheran Companion,* Augustana's main journal. In the 1910s and 1920s, Ryden had also been a member of the Augustana-based New Sweden Memorial Commission.[21]

Both Ryden and Melvin exemplify the integration of Swedish Americans into nonethnically coded American institutions. Since the end of the Swedish mass emigration in the 1920s, personal associations with the old homeland had increasingly passed away together with the aging immigrants.[22] Swedish immigration had taken place over a long period, and by the time of the 1938 commemoration several generations of Swedish Americans were present simultaneously in the United States. There were indeed many newcomers, but most were second- or third-generation Swedish Americans who were generally (though not exclusively) integrated into mainstream middle-class America.[23]

There is a long-standing discussion within immigration history whether generational shifts can explain ethnic interest. The historian Marcus Lee Hansen proposed an answer to this problem through a renowned maxim: "What the son wishes to forget the grandson wishes to remember." Immigration scholars such as John Higham, Thomas Archdeacon, and H. Arnold Barton have argued that factors including social status, societal tolerance, and personal attitudes have a greater impact than the internal dynamic of individual generations in explaining the level of ethnic interest. Indeed, the second generation has often been instrumental in shaping an ethnic and historical consciousness. It is noteworthy that commemorators such as Ryden and Melvin were not immigrants themselves but persons born in the

United States who had made successful professional careers in American society.[24] Swedish Americans benefited from white privilege in the American ethno-racial hierarchy, enjoying freedoms and possibilities that were not available to everyone in the United States.[25] Although Ryden, Melvin, and others could draw on their heritage when it was wanted, they did not work from the sole perspective of the ethnic community. Their vantage point was that of white middle-class men with considerable academic and professional status.[26] This position made it possible for the previously ethnically coded histories to be reconceptualized within other frameworks.

The Delaware commission chairman's way into the commemoration was decidedly different from his Pennsylvania counterpart's. Christopher Ward was born in Wilmington in 1868 and raised in the small town of Towanda, Pennsylvania. He did not have any known Swedish or Scandinavian ancestors. After studies at Harvard Law School, he eventually moved back to Wilmington and co-founded a successful business-counseling firm. Beginning in the late 1910s, he began to cultivate a long-time literary interest and eventually established himself as an acclaimed writer, publishing his first novel in 1923. In the late 1920s, Ward increasingly began to focus on historical fiction and nonfiction; the University of Pennsylvania Press published his study *The Dutch and Swedes on the Delaware* in 1930. His interest in history seems to have originated in his youth, when he was influenced by the historical work of his grandfather, Lewis Potter Bush, who was one of the founders of the Historical Society of Delaware.[27] When Ward assumed the role of chair for the Delaware commission, he was, unlike Melvin and Ryden, not involved per se in the colony's Swedishness. For him, the history of New Sweden was the history of the state of Delaware.

The bulk of the Delaware commission's efforts focused on acquiring the tract of land surrounding The Rocks in Wilmington and transforming it into a park. Members also made significant efforts to attract foreign delegations to the forthcoming celebrations. The commissioners believed that the commemoration would draw considerable attention to the state; and even though their minutes never state explicitly what they hoped this attention would yield, it is clear that the anticipated gains were partly financial. *The Delaware Tercentenary Visitors' Guide,* which sold for twenty-five cents during the celebrations, exemplified this hope. While it included a brief history of New Sweden, the majority of the guide consisted of articles about the state's public schools, highways, vacation resorts, industries, and the University of Delaware. An article about the Chamber of Commerce stated that "Delaware business was born three hundred years ago this Spring," thus historicizing the guide's wealth of commercial advertisement.[28]

Although New Jersey was included from the start in the Pennsylvania and Delaware plans, it did not form its own commemorative commission until two years later. The state adopted its first joint resolution in the spring of 1937 and arranged its first commission meeting for the following June.[29] The resolution described New Sweden as "the beginning of a permanent government for the earliest inhabitants of this [the southwest] section of New Jersey."[30] Unfortunately, there are few records preserved of the New Jersey commission's work: there is no comprehensive archival collection, and noticeably little correspondence with New Jersey representatives is preserved in other commission archives—the natural result of a comparatively limited state organization and of less extensive celebration plans.

The initial organizing phase of the New Sweden Tercentenary was shaped by interactions and exchanges between American ethnic communities and U.S. states. Wollmar Boström, the Swedish envoy to the United States, was a link between these groups. Boström, who would turn sixty years old during the celebrations, had made a career within the Swedish Ministry for Foreign Affairs, serving as a diplomat in Madrid and Lisbon before transferring to Washington, D.C., in 1925. By the mid-1930s, he had established a considerable network of contacts in America.[31] Throughout the planning of the celebration, he functioned as an intermediary, communicating with ethnic, state, and federal commissions in the United States and continuously relaying information to Sweden.

Although the regional U.S. commissions did much of their planning separately, there were several joint meetings held by the states of Delaware, New Jersey, and Pennsylvania and the Swedish-American commission. Representatives of the commissions also traveled numerous times across the Atlantic to attend commission meetings in person.[32] In addition, there were actual overlaps among the organizations. According to Melvin, about half of the Pennsylvania commission members were also members of the Swedish Colonial Society, which in turn was one of the founding organizations of the Swedish-American commission.[33] A noticeable example of organizational overlap was George Ryden, who was a member of the Swedish Colonial Society and a former secretary of the New Sweden Memorial Commission in the 1920s; he was involved in the Swedish American Tercentenary Association, where he served as a member of the program committee; he was a member of the committee planning for the Augustana Synod's participation in the tercentenary; and he was a leading figure in the Delaware commission.

This conflation of interests was made possible by crucial changes in the ways in which the New Sweden colony was being remembered. The foundations of this change had been laid by the activities of organizations such as the New Sweden Memorial Commission and the Swedish Colonial Society. Rather than geographically centering their commemorational projects in communities with a large Swedish-American presence, these groups focused on The Rocks in Delaware, the site of the colony itself.

Both Pennsylvania and Delaware believed that the commemoration concerned the founding of their states; they did not see it as simply a seventeenth-century Swedish venture. Indeed, the commemoration in Pennsylvania did not even include the colony's name. In a radio speech, Melvin emphasized that it "is a mistake . . . to assume that this Pennsylvania 300th Anniversary Celebration is a Swedish celebration." Nor was it, he said, a Finnish, Dutch, or English celebration, although these people, too, settled along the Delaware River.[34] This was a Pennsylvania celebration, underlined by the name "Pennsylvania 300th Anniversary." Furthermore, the Delaware resolution and the Pennsylvania act explicitly declared that the scope of the celebration should be wide, incorporating state, interstate, national, and international participants. When the celebrations began in June 1938, some twenty-five other states and Canada had appointed commemorative commissions whose members were sent to the celebrations in the Delaware Valley.[35]

The three commissions from the Delaware Valley linked the celebration to other commemorations of American colonial history. The commemorative context included events such as the 1931 Yorktown Victory Sesquicentennial, the 1936 Long Island Settlement Tercentenary, and the 1938 Northwest Territory Sesquicentennial.[36] Melvin, for example, communicated with the chair of the 1935 Connecticut Tercentenary for the explicit purpose of obtaining information that could be used in the planning of this one. The commission also gathered information from the 1930 Boston Tercentenary and the 1936 Rhode Island Tercentenary.[37] Although it is unclear what these contacts resulted in, they indicate that there was a regional American context of colonial commemorations that was important as the New Sweden Tercentenary was being planned.

The transformation of an ethnic commemoration into one pushed by U.S. states should be understood in relation to American regionalism. Animosity grew in the 1920s toward the dominant representations of the nation's founding moments, a mythological role often assigned to New England and the 1620 landing of the Pilgrims in today's Plymouth, Massachusetts. The federally supported 1920–21 Pilgrim Tercentenary received massive criticism, most forcefully from southerners who claimed precedent for the Jamestown colony, which was thirteen years older. During the 1930s, local commemorations such as the celebrations at Yorktown and Long Island grew in popularity when they could assert regional or national significance, preferably on par with Plymouth Rock.[38] In the words of John Seelye, the symbol of Plymouth Rock is a New England story "of the struggle by that region to retain its hegemony" vis-à-vis other regions.[39] In this regional competition, commemorations could be used as leverage for contemporary causes.

Economic and political incentives also shaped Delaware's and Pennsylvania's participation. The commemoration was a platform for foreign affairs and was framed as an opportunity to focus domestic and international attention on the states. Scholars from Frederick Jackson Turner onward have argued that domestic regional diversity is important for understanding U.S. foreign policy. According to Peter Trubowitz, conflicts over foreign policy "grow out of the uneven nature of the nation's economic development and integration into the world economy." He has identified the 1930s as a period of intense conflict over foreign policy. The North—particularly the cities of Baltimore, Boston, Chicago, Cleveland, Detroit, Philadelphia, Pittsburgh, and New York—was by the 1930s the center of U.S. industry and manufacturing. This development made the region dependent on the world economy, with its representatives in Congress supporting free trade and access to open markets. The internationalism of the Roosevelt administration was backed by the urban northern centers' alliance with agricultural southerners, who, in contrast to the western regions, also were dependent on foreign markets and free trade.[40]

Where Trubowitz emphasizes regional economic factors, other scholars have maintained the importance of ideology. It might be, as Joseph Fry contends, that regional influences on foreign policy "have been most significant when one party dominated a region."[41] This was the case in the Delaware Valley at the time of the 1938 tercentenary. Both Delaware and Pennsylvania had for decades been solidly Republican. That changed in the mid-1930s when both states elected Democratic governors. In 1934 Pennsylvania elected George H. Earle, a businessman and former U.S. minister to Austria, and Delaware's new governor in 1936 was Richard C. McMullen, a prominent Wilmington businessman and manufacturer. The 1936 election also gave the Democratic Party control of the Senate and House of Representatives in Pennsylvania as well as the House of Representatives in Delaware.

Both Earle and McMullen were greatly involved in celebrating the New Sweden Tercentenary. At the time of the commemoration, they were outspoken New Deal proponents; Earle's tenure as governor has been termed the "Pennsylvania Little New Deal."[42] The connection between regional New Dealism and these states' interest in the commemoration was also highlighted by the 1937 visit of Governor Earle to Sweden (see chapter 4), where he spent time inspecting welfare relief systems and public housing programs implemented by the Swedish Social Democratic government.[43] This regional American attention to Swedish social and economic policies was influenced by the Roosevelt administration's interest in Sweden as "the middle way" between socialism and capitalism.

New Jersey's comparatively low interest in the tercentenary may be explained by political factors. The stark shift in political government in Delaware and Pennsylvania coincided with the states' push for the commemoration. In New Jersey, however, both Republican and Democratic governors occupied the office during the 1930s. A Republican governor, Harold G. Hoffman, replaced Democrat A. Harry Moore in 1935, but Moore then won the subsequent election and resumed office in 1938. Although he was a Democrat, Moore was "very uncomfortable" with the New Deal and sought to reduce state spending.[44] In other words, during the majority of the tercentenary planning, the New Jersey governor was either a Republican or a New Deal critic, something that might have affected their participation in a regional celebration so clearly colored by New Deal commemorators and overseas welfare state proponents.

The 1920s and 1930s regionalism, together with the upward mobility of Swedish Americans, helps explain why New Sweden was appropriated by U.S. states in 1938. This regionalism was multidimensional, informed by cultural history, Depression-era economics, and New Deal politics. It is difficult to ascertain which of these dimensions was most important; probably, at least to some degree, they worked in tandem. Together, these contexts were activated through interactions. The commemoration was locally connected to the Delaware Valley but had a much larger claim. The New Sweden colony was declared to be the founding moment not only for an ethnic group but also for a region. Regional pride and recognition, the production of a more localized foundational history, international economic interdependency, and regional political dynamics were contributing factors in explaining the enthusiastic involvement of Delaware and Pennsylvania.

National Interests in Foreign Relations

As Delaware's and Pennsylvania's planning made headway, preparations began in Sweden. In January 1935, the business magnate J. Sigfrid Edström—then the chair of the electric company ASEA, the vice-president of the International Olympic Committee, and the president of the Sweden-America Foundation—contacted the Swedish minister for foreign affairs, Rickard Sandler, with a proposition about commemorating New Sweden. Edström stressed that the Swedes had made a significant contribution to "the civilizing of the continent" and the founding of the United States. Participating in the commemoration would, according to him, "forcefully contribute to the raising and manifesting of Sweden's reputation in the United States, and further strengthen the existing friendly relation between this country and our own and forge stronger the links, that will bind American citizens of Swedish descent to the land of their forefathers."[45]

For Edström, the project of connecting Sweden and the United States was personal. After receiving a civil engineering degree in Sweden in 1891, he had spent two years working in Switzerland and then moved to the United States in pursuit of practical engineering experience. Between 1893 and 1897, he worked for electrical engineering companies in Pittsburgh and Cleveland before transferring to General Electric in Schenectady, New York. In 1896, on a voyage back to the United States after a short visit to Sweden, Edström met Ruth Randall, born in Wilmington, Illinois. They became a couple and married three years later.[46] Thus, the prospect of a joint Swedish and American celebration served both his private and business interests. Edström's proposal found immediate support in Sweden, and the Ministry for Foreign Affairs hosted preliminary meetings in Stockholm to discuss the country's preparations.[47]

This interest was a sharp contrast to the Swedish indifference a few decades before. What had changed in the half-century since the 1888 commemoration? The answer is that prevailing attitudes in Sweden toward the mass emigration and the Swedish-American immigrant group had been transformed in the early twentieth century. In 1900 Sweden had been a country in need of social, economic, and political reforms. There was a widespread notion that the country was lagging behind, and the catalyst for that notion was the persistent high rate of emigration. Many believed that it was draining Sweden of its young and vigorous population. In 1907, as a response to these debates, the Swedish parliament launched the Royal Commission on Emigration. Although the commission acknowledged that political, social, and religious conditions had played a role, it suggested that the main cause of emigration was economics. One of the commission's goals was to discover what Sweden could learn from the United States in order to modernize itself, especially in the fields of business and public education, and hence limit emigration. The issue was framed as a national problem that needed to be rectified. But as the mass emigration to America came to an end in the mid-1920s, the antiemigration debates faded.[48] These changes set the stage for a Swedish reconceptualization of the Swedish-American immigrant group and the history of New Sweden.

Despite initial enthusiasm in Sweden, officials decided in September 1935 that no further action should be taken without a formal invitation from the U.S. government.[49] During the fall and spring Wollmar Boström worked toward this end with assistance from the U.S. envoy to Stockholm. Because the State Department and the Roosevelt administration did not want to act before the matter had passed through Congress, Boström worked behind the scenes, primarily by approaching congressional members from Delaware and Pennsylvania. According to him, that lobbying was successful.[50] The resolution was processed by the State Department, passing in Congress during the spring of 1936, with an invitation extended to the Swedish government in the summer.[51]

The congressional resolution also established the federal U.S. commission, officially named the United States Delaware Valley Tercentenary Commission, comprised of fifteen members jointly appointed by the president and Congress. Its chair was Senator Joseph F. Guffey of Pennsylvania, a close associate of President Roosevelt.[52] The formation of the commission took place just as the federal government was beginning to take a more active role in celebrating and memorializing American history. Previous administrations had been reluctant to fund commemorations, but this began to change during the 1920s and became more institutionalized in the work of New Deal agencies in the 1930s. The increased federal attention to history was also apparent in the expansion of historic programming and historic preservation within the National Park Service, as encouraged by Roosevelt's signing of the Historic Sites Act of 1935.[53]

The U.S. commission's purpose at this transitional moment was not to initiate any celebrations but to extend an invitation to the Swedish government and to participate in the state-planned festivities. The appointment of the commission can thus be characterized as a reaction rather than an action; it was a national response to the regional initiatives of Delaware and Pennsylvania and their expressed objective of inviting Sweden to the celebrations in their states.

The Swedish plans were elaborate, and they began even before the first meeting of the Royal New Sweden Tercentenary Memorial Commission in September 1936. Thirty-three people were appointed to the commission: several members of parliament, the chancellors of major universities, the national archivist, the national librarian, the national antiquarian, a bishop, and several representatives from the business sector. J. Sigfrid Edström became the commission chairman. Though state institutions—political, cultural, religious, and academic—were well represented, the executive committee had more of a corporate character, and its members included several business leaders. In his opening remarks at the September meeting, the minister for foreign affairs stressed that there "is currently in the United States a strong interest in Sweden." The invitation from the United States provided a "favorable opportunity" for Sweden to strengthen its relations with America.[54]

With an implicit nod to the awakened American interest in Swedish politics (as spurred by Marquis Childs book), the Swedish commission made it clear that their participation "should be concentrated on a representation of Sweden of today."[55] Unlike the upcoming New York World's Fair to be held in 1939, the tercentenary was a chance for Sweden to stand alone in the American spotlight. As Edström wrote in a letter to Sweden's prime minister, Per Albin Hansson, "[in New York] we will compete with the nations of the world and invest millions to participate in the exhibition, . . . [but in Delaware] we are alone, with the eyes of the whole American nation aimed at us."[56] For Sweden, the tercentenary was first and foremost a matter of public diplomacy.

Now that the U.S. invitation to Sweden had been presented and plans among all involved commissions were proceeding swiftly, Pennsylvania decided to invite Finland to the commemoration. This turned out to be a difficult issue to handle. Finland's participation originated in conversations between the Finnish envoy to the United States, Eero Järnefelt, and representatives from Pennsylvania. Järnefelt had met the state's governor during the summer of 1936 and had asked why Finland—which, for six centuries, until its 1809 incorporation into Russia, had been considered the eastern half of Sweden—had not been included in the invitation to Sweden. Pennsylvania moved quickly on the matter; and when its legislative act was passed in July 1936, Finland was included in the proposed commemorative plans.[57] In the discussions that followed, Pennsylvania's action was used as leverage toward convincing the State Department and Congress to secure Finland's official participation.

Despite objections from Boström and Swedish-American representatives, a motion amending Finland to the original U.S. resolution passed in the Senate in April 1937. When the amendment was introduced in the House of Representatives, it triggered a lengthy discussion about Finland's good relationship with the United States. A congressman from New Jersey even claimed that the nation "should be invited to every celebration that is held in the United States." The Finns, he said, "are an incentive to the whole world, they are an example to the whole world, and they have certainly shown us that if there is one country in this world friendly to the United States, it is Finland, by having paid its obligations to us on the day they were due, and I hope this resolution passes. (Applause)."[58]

The small, recently independent nation of Finland was the only country to have, at that point, paid its national debt to the United States, something that made it popular among U.S. politicians and the public.[59] The resolution passed in the House of Representatives, and Congress asked the president to forward an official invitation to Finland.[60] Secretary of State Cordell Hull's advice to Roosevelt was to proceed with the invitation, but the hope was that Finland would decline it due to lack of time for preparations. This, however, did not happen, and Finland was on track to participate in the tercentenary.[61]

The initial Swedish response to news of Finland's invitation was "restrained," according to the historian Max Engman. Although the U.S. envoy to Stockholm expressed opposition to the invitation, there was little that Sweden could do about the situation. It did not want to openly oppose the participation and upset its national relations with Finland, so its opposition took place behind the scenes.[62]

Because Swedish and Swedish-American representatives could not challenge the U.S. admiration for Finland, they adopted historical arguments that sought to undermine the country's right to participate. They claimed that Finland had been a de facto province of Sweden in the seventeenth century, which meant that all New Sweden colonists had been Swedes. If Finland were to be invited, the argument went, then so should the Baltic States because they, too, had been part of Sweden in the seventeenth century. In the opinion of the Swedish and Swedish-American commissions, such a development would be unrealistic.[63]

The notion that Finland would be granted an equal part in a celebration that Sweden and Swedish America had planned for a long time was a source of great concern. Yet other groups in the United States also had concerns, and they were the cause of another conflict in the Delaware Valley. Parallel to the behind-the-scenes conflict between Sweden and Finland was a regional fight between Pennsylvania and Delaware that centered on the question of who should have the celebratory spotlight during the commemoration. As I will detail in chapter 3, the primary issues involved the location of a monument to be donated by Sweden and the debarkation point for the official delegations from Sweden and Finland. Essentially, the question focused on whether the center of celebration should be in Pennsylvania or in Delaware.

Pennsylvania and Delaware had completely different attitudes toward Finnish participation. Pennsylvania was, along with Finnish Americans, the driving force behind the push for a Finnish invitation. New Jersey similarly amended its legislative act to include Finland.[64] Delaware, on the other hand, never included Finland explicitly in its celebrations. Responding to the news that the Finland amendment had passed in the U.S. Congress, Christopher Ward described the situation as "complicated." In his opinion, the U.S. government was in no position to invite Finland because it would be sending an invitation to a celebration that it would not host. At this point, however, not much could be done. "Our Commission," he wrote, "is keeping quiet about the matter. If the Finns come, we will do the best we can but we are not anxious to have them."[65]

George Ryden had been critical already when Pennsylvania's act passed in 1936. The act was "inaccurate," he argued, because the event it referred to did not take place in 1638. The first Finnish colonists had settled in 1641, and the colony's capital had not been transferred from Fort Christina, in present-day Delaware, to Tinicum Island, outside today's Philadelphia, until 1643. In the words of Ryden: "Although Pennsylvania know[s] it full well, they will not acknowledge that the first permanent settlement in the Delaware River Valley was on Delaware soil, that the first capital of [the] New Sweden colony was Ft. Christina, and that their right to share in the celebration of 1938 is based only on the fact that the land claims of the colony of New Sweden extended in the year, 1638, to the Schuylkill River."[66]

Ryden's letter offers explanations for Delaware's stubborn position concerning Finland as well as for Pennsylvania's interest in securing a Finnish invitation. In it, he argued that Pennsylvania did not have the same historically valid connection to the founding of New Sweden as Delaware did. The 1638 establishment of the colony had taken place "on Delaware soil." Therefore, present-day Delaware should be the center of celebrations. To acknowledge the equal involvement of Finland would be to historically legitimize the equal involvement of Pennsylvania. Such a representation was certainly what Pennsylvania sought, which explains their interest in inviting Finland. The conflict between Sweden and Finland was thus tied up in a tug of war between Pennsylvania and Delaware. The dimensions of nationalism and regionalism were commingled and mutually constituent. Two interconnected reasons explain why the U.S. Congress and President Roosevelt decided to engage in the commemoration: it united regional American commemorations under a national umbrella while taking charge over the foreign-relations dimension of the event. As the Sweden-Finland and Delaware-Pennsylvania battles showed, the latter dimension had become an important aspect of the project.

A Reclaimed Swedish-American Initiative

The 1948 Swedish Pioneer Centennial was held just ten years after the New Sweden Tercentenary. Despite the small gap in time, the two commemorations took place in different eras. But even though they were separated by a world war and their circumstances were different, essential elements connected them. Moreover, both were initiated within the same Swedish-American milieu, and both came about through cross-border cooperation.

As with the tercentenary, the idea of celebrating a centennial originated from the Augustana Synod in the Midwest. Since 1940, the synod had been making plans for a centennial celebration of its own to be held in 1948, a way to acknowledge "the building of the first Lutheran churches on the banks of the Mississippi."[67] In the fall of 1945, the Swedish-American journalist and author Naboth Hedin made a journey to Augustana College in Rock Island, Illinois. Hedin was born in Sweden and immigrated to the United States in 1900 at the age of sixteen. After studying at Harvard University, he worked for the *Brooklyn Daily Eagle* and was stationed for a few years as a correspondent in Paris. In 1926, Hedin became the head of the New York office of the American-Swedish News Exchange (ASNE), founded in 1921 to spread information about Sweden in the United States and to facilitate Swedish commerce with America.[68] Hedin went to Augustana to find out if Sweden could join its celebration.

On his return to New York, Hedin wrote a lengthy report to the ASNE board of directors in Stockholm. After mentioning the tercentenary, he informed the board that yet another anniversary was approaching, "the one hundredth anniversary of the much more important settlement in the upper Mississippi valley." The importance was due primarily to the extent and permanency of the immigration, two factors that made this history more consequential than that of the New Sweden colony. "In the Delaware region we have five or six churches, built by descendants of the original Swedish colonists; in the Middle West there are churches by the thousands, club houses, schools, colleges, flourishing farms, large factories, even towns and parts of cities, built and owned and managed by the descendants of the second wave of immigrants. . . . Here the Swedes were among the first settlers, or 'sod-busters' as they were called; here their descendants feel they belong and here they mean to stay."⁶⁹

Hedin's inquiries and emerging interest in the idea among midwestern Swedish Americans prompted the synod to begin planning for the celebration. Its members issued an invitation to a meeting, where they intended to create a commission for commemorating the nonreligious aspects of Swedish immigration. The invitation explained that there was "a common ground for all to join in an observance which will honor the pioneers of Swedish immigration to America."⁷⁰ In December 1945, several midwestern Swedish-American organizations met in Chicago. The delegates represented civic, professional, and religious associations. Except for a local historical society from Rockford, Illinois, the organizations were not heritage-oriented; they represented a cross-section of different factions and interest groups from around Swedish America, ranging from churches to mutual aid societies to singing clubs.

The gathering resulted in the creation of a preliminary coordinating committee charged with inviting representatives from throughout the Midwest to join in planning the commemoration. Its chairman was forty-nine-year-old Conrad Bergendoff, who came to play a leading role in the centennial. Born in Nebraska of Swedish-American parents, he had been a student at Augustana College and in 1921 became an ordained minister in the Augustana Synod. In 1928, after a stint in Sweden with studies at the universities of Uppsala and Lund, he received a doctorate degree in history from the University of Chicago. Since 1935, he had served as the president of Augustana College, and he was a firm believer that the Lutheran religion and Swedish heritage were inseparable.⁷¹ To him and to others within the synod, the Pioneer Centennial was an opportunity to celebrate this historical connection. Reportedly, the synod president, P. O. Bersell, considered the fact that this was to be a Swedish-American celebration, not an event governed by Sweden, to be of utmost importance.⁷²

The backdrop to Bersell's sentiments was a conflict that had appeared ten years before, when a disagreement had surfaced during the planning of the 1938 commemoration. After prolonged negotiations with the Swedish-American commission, Augustana was eventually granted a spot on the program, with a Lutheran celebration at the Convention Hall in Philadelphia. The slot, however, clashed with an official dinner hosted by the state of Pennsylvania and might also have been inadequately publicized in itineraries and programs. As a consequence, no representative from the Swedish royal family attended the Augustana event. Bersell blamed the Swedish-American and Pennsylvanian commissions as well as Wollmar Boström, who all had displayed "great resistance" to the plans and thrown the Augustana event "into the discard."[73] According to the synod, religious organizations had not been properly represented at the tercentenary. Even though Bersell did not blame the overseas guests, the conflict shows that Sweden had considerable leverage during the commemoration, as the celebrations were largely governed by the travels of the official delegations and the presence of royalty. Lack of recognition from Sweden was the main cause of Bersell's frustration, even though the Swedes were not the targets of his criticism.

The locus of the 1938 tercentenary had been the "authentic" site of the colony in Delaware. Because Delaware and Pennsylvania had emphasized the significance of place, the celebration was centered on the East Coast. Augustana's roots, however, were in the Midwest—in particular, Illinois. A Swedish Pioneer Centennial would provide an opportunity for celebrations that, in terms of authenticity, needed to be centered in Augustana's midwestern heartland. This enabled commemorators to more closely tie Swedish heritage to Lutheran heritage and thus to argue for both components' continued importance. The life of the pioneers should, according to Bergendoff, not be "that of the Delaware colonists, who were lost to American history until our own days."[74] As Thomas Tredway succinctly writes about Bergendoff's view of the 1938 tercentenary and the upcoming 1948 commemoration, "if Lutherans and other Swedish-American Christians were to be given due place in such festivals, they better take charge of them."[75]

Although the late 1940s have been described as years when ethnic sentiments in the United States were "at a low ebb," they were also a time when Swedish Americans were boosting their ethnic pride.[76] The Swedish Pioneer Centennial offered such an opportunity. The commemoration took place when cultural leaders in the Swedish-American community had reached a secure sociopolitical position in American society and could assert their ancestral culture and history without appearing to be nationally separatist. This meant that they were able to maintain and manifest ethnic culture within a framework of American patriotism.[77] Because Sweden's reputation had been tainted by its wartime neutrality and its policies of Nazi appeasement, the Pioneer Centennial was an opportunity for Swedish Americans to enhance the image and self-perception of their ethnic heritage while underlining their American patriotism.

The Swedish Pioneer Centennial Association had its first meeting in January 1946, with Bergendoff as chairman. It gathered a heterogeneous group of midwestern representatives from Swedish-American churches, organizations, and newspapers as well as representatives from education, industry, and government. The range of invited groups resonated with the meeting's announcement that it was "not to observe a large central celebration, but rather to help the various communities to celebrate in their own way."[78] For the organization to function, it was necessary to form local committees, but initially very little happened during the spring and summer. The association had no funds, was not yet incorporated in Illinois, had not met since its formation in January, and by July had no new meetings scheduled. Explanations for this varied, ranging from the current economic crisis, to the fact that the election year was featuring several Swedish-American candidates, to the notion that some secular and religious groups disliked the influence of the Augustana Synod.[79] There were fears that the celebration would not be realized. According to the Swedish ambassador to Washington, D.C., the plans were "dead in the water."[80]

Both the Swedish Pioneer Centennial and the New Sweden Tercentenary had their origins in the United States. But while the tercentenary was linked to regional colonial commemorations, the immediate cultural context of the centennial was that of other ethnic commemorations. For example, organizers gathered information about and made a visit to the 1947 Holland Centennial in the city of Holland, Michigan, which celebrated a century of Dutch immigration to the

Midwest.[81] Unlike the Swedish American Tercentenary Association in 1938—which cooperated with, and sometimes worked from inside of, state organizations—the Swedish Pioneer Centennial Association strove for a decentralized organization. In the eyes of midwestern commemorators, it was to be a bottom-up celebration, primarily intended for Swedish Americans. Although organizers encouraged interactions among different factions of Swedish America, they effectively sought to limit the influence of other groups in the planning of the commemoration. Yet they also wanted to cooperate with Sweden, and this interaction became the commemoration's turning point.

Growing by Way of Sweden

Naboth Hedin's journey through the Midwest had created the impetus for the organization of the Swedish-American commission, but it had also stimulated activity in Sweden. In November 1945, the ASNE board of directors had met in Stockholm to discuss Hedin's report and the ideas about a centennial. The celebration, Hedin had written, was an opportunity for Sweden "to renew both personal and cultural relations." The plan identified Swedish Americans of the Midwest as "large untapped reserves of good-will."[82] His letter, sent less than two months after the end of World War II, landed squarely in the midst of a domestic discussion about Sweden's postwar situation, and it offered an enticing way of improving the nation's postwar image. But parts of Hedin's message were apparently lost in the communication with Sweden. To the ASNE board of directors, as well as to Gösta Oldenburg—the Swedish consul in Chicago and the main intermediary between Sweden and the Swedish-American commission—the impression was that the celebration should be a comprehensive religious celebration.[83] In an attempt to clarify his idea, Hedin stated that the intention was not only to include churches but "all groups, all affiliations."[84]

Oldenburg changed his attitude after the January 1946 meeting of the Swedish-American commission in Chicago. It was now "obvious," he said, "that a commemoration of this kind will bring benefits to Sweden in terms of propaganda and Hedin has naturally . . . thought about the opportunity to somewhat raise our stock in the American consciousness."[85] A year later, Oldenburg dressed the project in other words, saying that the commemoration was not primarily a Swedish propaganda campaign but that "the Swedish folk element out here [in the Midwest] should remind and enlighten their American brothers about the contributions made by the Swedish pioneers."[86] The commemoration would thus be a chance for Sweden to strengthen relations with the Swedish-American community while broadening its cultural and political relations with the United States. It thus echoed the need of improving Sweden's foreign relations that had been identified by the 1943 report of the America Inquiry. Although Sweden's interest in the commemoration differed from those of the Swedish Americans, which largely concerned issues of ethnic maintenance, both regarded it as an opportunity to mutually manifest their transatlantic relations.

The commemorative progress was slow. After encouragement from the Swedish ambassador in August 1946, however, the Swedish-American commission convened. In late November, it extended invitations to the Swedish government and the royal house.[87] The invitation was accepted, and the first meeting of what became known as the Swedish Commission for the Pioneer Jubilee was held in March 1947. The organizations invited to participate included the Swedish Institute for Cultural Exchange with Foreign Countries, the Ministry for Foreign Affairs, the Sweden-America Foundation, as well as associations and federations representing women, employers, industry, students, and sports. The minister of commerce, Axel Gjöres, was elected commission chair.[88] If the 1938 Swedish commission mainly represented the government bureaucracy, the 1948 commission was chiefly composed of various interest groups.

It gradually became obvious to the Swedish-American commission that they had entered a new stage in the organizational process. They needed to employ someone full time to manage the organization. This came as somewhat of a surprise to Bergendoff, who claimed to be stunned by Sweden's interest in the commemoration. The celebration, he declared, has now "become a bigger thing than we ourselves have the time to plan and carry through."[89] In his view, a major problem was that Sweden was "expecting and preparing for a much more elaborate observance" than the organization could handle. The celebration therefore needed to be more modest than Sweden was anticipating.[90]

This anxiety speaks to transatlantic power relations. While the initiative lay in the United States, Sweden had entered with enthusiasm. It had much at stake in the commemoration and needed a project of public diplomacy that could reestablish its relations with the United States. The interactions with Sweden generated a commemoration that stretched far outside of the Midwest. Although the celebration was a result of the Swedish-American commission's own work, its members initially did not seem prepared for the consequence of their actions.

Because of the increased workload, the Swedish Pioneer Centennial Association employed Nils William Olsson, an assistant professor of Scandinavian languages and literature at the University of Chicago, as the organization's executive secretary. The appointment changed the pace of operations, and local committees were eventually formed in Chicago, Minneapolis–Saint Paul, and twelve other cities around the Midwest.[91] In the winter of 1948, the embassy in Washington, D.C., encouraged the Swedish commission to cooperate more closely with Olsson and the Swedish-American commission. The Swedes found that it was difficult to establish good communication with commemorators in the United States.[92] To the Swedish-American commission, however, the primary job was not to serve as an intermediary link to Sweden but, in the words of Olsson, to "enlighten . . . the Swedes in the Middle West about the Centennial."[93] During the year that passed between his appointment and the beginning of the celebrations, Olsson never met in person with representatives of the Swedish commission, and no member of the Swedish commission visited the United States.

Federal involvement constituted a marked difference between the 1938 and 1948 commemorations. No U.S. commission was created for the Swedish Pioneer Centennial, and (with the exception of brief information relayed about the travels of the Swedish delegation and President Truman's invitation to the celebrations in Chicago) there was no cooperation with the State Department or the White House.

The federal government did issue a centennial stamp, but the process was lengthy and involved a presidential veto on the ground that a similar stamp had been issued less then a decade before, commemorating New Sweden.[94] After the resolution's Illinois sponsors argued that the president had been ill advised and that the sale of the stamps would yield a profit to the government, Truman withdrew his veto.[95]

The veto was an indication of the lack of federal interest in the commemoration as a forum for foreign relations as compared to significant U.S. involvement in the 1938 celebration. It is clear that in the context of intense discussions over the Marshall Plan, the North Atlantic Treaty Organization, and the political developments in the emerging eastern bloc, neither the White House nor the State Department considered Sweden to be a priority. Compared to the claimed absence of Swedishness in the Pennsylvania celebration of 1938, there was an unmistakable Swedish overtone to the 1948 commemoration. Postwar American interest in cross-border relations was predominantly governed by ethnicity and strongly encouraged by Sweden.

⁓

The 1938 tercentenary and 1948 centennial had many similarities but also key differences. They displayed varying degrees of interactions during their planning, showing that they were enmeshed in asymmetrical power relations. Although separate commissions were formed for the New Sweden Tercentenary, the boundaries among them were porous. This was not the case with the Swedish Pioneer Centennial, which had clear lines of demarcation between the commissions and committees and where communication was much less intense than it had been in 1938. Even though the commissions were constituted as separate entities, it was impossible to compartmentalize their constitutions. At the center of the process of appropriations were interactions between groups and people and across borders.

The contemporary, and sometimes local, contexts were catalysts in the appropriations of history. The contexts concerned American state politics, regionalized commercial and cultural interests, ethnic maintenance, and international affairs. They included the end of the mass migration from Sweden to the United States and the upward mobility of the Swedish-American community; the political commonalities between the New Deal and the Swedish state shaped by the advancement of the Social Democratic Party; Sweden's economic and sociopolitical modernization; projects of public diplomacy; regionalism and economic interests in the wake of the Great Depression; and foreign relations in the pre- and postwar periods of international political unrest. These dimensions, some of which were teased out in chapter 1, will be further developed in the remainder of the book. The effect of these multiple interests, merging at these specific moments in time, was the organization of two commemorations that became greater than the sum of their parts.

CHAPTER 3

Settler Colonial Histories
Memorializing a Transatlantic Legacy

The ethos of commemorations is always the histories that they celebrate. When it comes to cross-border commemorations, these histories concern movements and flows across large geographical spaces, and encompasses, for example, migration, colonization, wars, slavery, and trade. All of these histories in one way or another have come about through exchanges across borders. The histories of Swedish settlement in America are part of the global history of European colonial settlements in all continents of the world. The representations of departure, landing, encounters with indigenous populations, the signing of treaties and settling of the land bear great resemblance to accounts of other colonial ventures. These stories lie at the heart of the foundational mythology of America. Together with stories of first contact and discovery, settler histories are a predominant feature of how Americans have related to the past.

The contemporary concerns of the 1938 and 1948 commemorators were paired with a historicizing gaze that centered on three archetypal figures: the colonist, the pioneer, and the settler. (Here, I use the singular to distinguish the archetype from actual historical characters.) These three figures are associated with different meanings and values. A settler is a founder of political order, and both the colonist and the pioneer can be understood as historically specific versions of a settler. In terms of temporal and spatial connotations, the colonist in the United States is situated before independence in 1776 and is, despite French colonial presence in the Midwest and Spanish in the Southwest, most often associated with the founding of the nation on the eastern seaboard of America. The pioneer, however, is part of the nineteenth-century westward expansion. In the words of John Bodnar, the pioneer is the "most powerful historical symbol" of "ordinary people" in the United States.[1] Its geographical location is mainly in the West and the Midwest and on the Great Plains.

The migrant is different from the colonist and the pioneer because it evokes varying notions of innocence and the exercise of power. While settlers are characterized by their assertion of sovereignty, migrants lack sovereign entitlements and are characterized by having renounced a political order in their old homeland and having encountered a society that already is constituted. Settlers, whether colonists or pioneers, are part of the literal construction of new societies, breaking ground and building cities in places previously described as wilderness. Unlike colonialism, in which an external metropolitan core dominates a colonized demographic majority, this type of settler colonialism is "premised on the domination of a majority that has become indigenous" through "the permanent movement and reproduction of communities."[2] Migrants, in contrast, move into already existing societies as individuals striving for personal freedom. They are not as clearly—or at all—involved in processes of displacement, dispossession, and land taking.

The histories at the heart of the 1938 and 1948 commemorations encompassed both settling and migration. Although there is a qualitative and important difference between a settler and an immigrant, commemorators regularly conflated their usage and adopted them interchangeably. As we will see, this conflation functioned as a narrative strategy to crack open the significance of history in the present. It was at the heart of claims that the legacy of settlement and migration was thoroughly transatlantic in nature. It did not belong to one group or one constituency, but was a memory connecting places, peoples, and cultures.

Creating a Foundational Site

Amandus Johnson made his first visit to The Rocks in Wilmington, Delaware, in 1910. The site was located in a shipyard owned by the Wilson Line. Reminiscing about the event some fifteen years later, Johnson remembered being pointed to a site in "a deplorable condition," causing him to swear "a holy oath, that if I lived long enough one of the purposes of my life would be to see that that place would not be a rubbish heap."[3]

Swedish-American interest in this Wilmington "rubbish heap" proceeded from the assumption that the rock formation along the Christina River, on the eastern side of the city, was the landing site of the colonists in the spring of 1638. This was the site, they claimed, of the founding of New Sweden. In the early twentieth century, The Rocks were surrounded by industrial complexes in a socioeconomically struggling part of town. When Delaware began planning for the 1938 tercentenary, the site was still described as "a waste and a desert sparsely occupied by a few flimsy buildings of wood or corrugated iron."[4] Clearing up the area surrounding The Rocks and turning it into a park became a prioritized project of the Delaware commission, for it was seen as a nearly sacred historical place.[5]

According to the Delaware commission, The Rocks "bear to all of this region the same relation that 'Plymouth Rock' bears to New England. As the New Englanders have cared for and hallowed their Rocks, so the people of Delaware should care for and hallow 'The Rocks.'"[6] The Rocks was thus what W. J. T. Mitchell has called a "foundational site"; the fact that history always "takes place" somewhere generates processes of "keeping place" by which certain locations, seemingly out of necessity, become sacralized and monumentalized.[7] Representatives of Delaware and Swedish America both considered The Rocks to be the exact spot of the beginning of civilization in the Delaware Valley.

As the Swedish commission began its preparations in 1936, one of its projected plans was the erection of a monument. A central discussion concerned its location. The commission's initial intention was to place the monument in Philadelphia. This idea was consonant

FIGURE 4. Before the construction of Fort Christina State Park, the shipyard of the Wilson Line was described as a "rubbish heap." In 1932, the Delaware Historic Markers Commission erected a sign next to the stone wharf that constitutes The Rocks, stating that this was the "First Landing Place of the Swedes, 1638. Site of Fort Christina." Courtesy of the Delaware Public Archives.

with the plan to stage the landing of the Swedish delegation, and thus the inauguration of the commemoration, in that city.[8] However, the commissions of Delaware and Swedish America did not automatically agree with the plan.

In an attempt to persuade Sweden to put larger commemorative emphasis on The Rocks, Delaware representatives showed the site to a visiting Swedish commission member and to the Swedish envoy to Washington, D.C., Wollmar Boström.[9] A few days later, Boström sent a telegram to Stockholm giving his view on the monument location: "The commemoration refers to the landing in Delaware sixteen hundred and thirty eight nothing substantial happened then in Philadelphia stop the committee therefore believes the monument that are gratefully accepted should stand [at the] landing site not

[in] Philadelphia who already have [a] monument in the [Swedish-American] museum stop. . . . I too believe that the monument should stand at the landing site."[10]

Two weeks later, the Swedish commission proclaimed its intention to place the monument at The Rocks in Delaware.[11] The Pennsylvania commission was not pleased to hear that Sweden had suddenly changed its preferred location for the monument, and perhaps also for the landing of the Swedish delegation. The chair of the Pennsylvania commission, Frank Melvin, explained to Pennsylvania's governor, George H. Earle, that it would be "a psychological, and political, blunder" to let Wilmington "grab the show."[12] Melvin argued in a letter to Boström that if the landing were set in Philadelphia, it would be "more impressive, will interest far more people, and will more effectively grip the imagination of our two countries." But, he added, "due to historical analogy, it may be proposed that preliminary landings be made at 'The Rocks.'"[13]

In February 1937, the governor of Delaware, Richard McMullen, was informed that the Pennsylvania commission was looking for a site to place the monument.[14] The chair of the Delaware commission, Christopher Ward, was noticeably distressed about the situation. A bill supported by the Delaware commission was introduced in the state legislature in March, directing and authorizing the state's highway commission to acquire The Rocks from the Wilson Line. According to Ward, if this bill did not pass and the park was not ready for the delegation's arrival, the commission, the state, or both would be "very shamefaced."[15] The "whole celebration will go to pieces," he wrote to McMullen, "the monument will be erected in Philadelphia, there will be no such ceremonies here and, in that case, our whole celebration might as well be abandoned."[16] Ward's fears were immediately assuaged, and at the end of April the bill to acquire the land from the Wilson Line was passed and signed into law.[17] The acquisition laid the foundations for the 1938 construction of Fort Christina State Park.

The struggle between Delaware and Pennsylvania was connected to the dispute over Finland's participation (see chapter 2). Finland, like Sweden, intended to erect a monument commemorating the colony. On being advised by the Pennsylvania commission that it would

FIGURE 5. The newly opened Fort Christina State Park in Wilmington, Delaware, with The Rocks (lower lefthand corner) and the New Sweden monument by Carl Milles. Although the parkland had been cleared, it was still surrounded by shipyards and industrial complexes. Courtesy of the Delaware Public Archives.

be "a blunder" to place the Finnish monument in competition with the Swedish donation at The Rocks, it was instead placed in Crozer Park in Chester, Pennsylvania. Its location in Chester is in the vicinity of several other sites related to New Sweden—in particular, the settlements of Finland and Upland in present-day Pennsylvania, which were a part of the colony, as well as Finns Point in New Jersey.[18]

It is also close to Tinicum Island. A few miles southwest of Philadelphia, the township of Tinicum in Essington, Pennsylvania, had been the site of Printzhof, the settlement established by Governor Johan Printz in 1643. This was the tract of land on which Pennsylvania in 1938 created Governor Printz Park. According to the Pennsylvania commission, it was the site of "the first capitol and the first government building in Pennsylvania."[19] The land had been donated to Pennsylvania by the Swedish Colonial Society, which had been harboring an idea of creating Governor Printz Park on the site since at least the late 1920s.²⁰ The park became a prestigious project of the Pennsylvania commission, likely through the efforts of Frank Melvin. The commission also secured $57,000 from the Works Progress Administration to archeologically excavate the site and improve its landscaping.²¹ When it became clear that the park would not receive the Swedish monument, Pennsylvania tried to secure another gift from Sweden to place in the park. "Governor Printz Park is my baby," Melvin wrote to the Swedish commission chair, emphasizing that he was "keenly disappointed that nothing has worked out so that we may have a real Swedish memorial in our park." During the spring of 1938, Pennsylvania hoped to be able to buy the seventeenth-century manor house, Gunillaberg, which had belonged to Johan Printz. The manor, located near the small town of Bottnaryd in southern Sweden, was his home after he stepped down as governor and in 1654 returned from the colony. Melvin's idea was to dismantle Gunillaberg, transport it to the United States, and reassemble it in Pennsylvania. Even though the project was planned and found support in Sweden, it was never completed.²²

An even more remarkable project was the plan to bring the remains of Johan Printz from the Bottnaryd parish church to Pennsylvania and to build "a fitting mausoleum" over him in Governor Printz Park. The Commonwealth of Pennsylvania, the Pennsylvania Historical Commission, and the U.S. Delaware Tercentenary Commission drafted a resolution asking President Roosevelt to issue a request to Sweden that "the body of Governor Johan Printz . . . be returned to the Commonwealth of Pennsylvania."²³ There is no indication that this resolution ever reached Roosevelt or that a request of this nature was ever submitted to Sweden.

Pennsylvania's focus on Tinicum Island, its interest in Johan Printz's remains, as well as the invitation of Finland were signs of a retreat from The Rocks. There was an inherent pedagogical problem in the idea that a place outside Pennsylvania's borders should constitute the foundational site for the state's civilization. Consequently, the Pennsylvania commission sought to establish or identify other sites, even ones overseas. During Governor Earle's 1937 visit to Sweden, the state's delegation made a stop in Bottnaryd to visit Printz's tomb.

The governor, who reportedly was "visibly affected" by the moment, placed a wreath at the base of the tomb and gave a speech declaring, "Here is the beginning of Pennsylvania." The purpose of this somewhat odd statement, as well as of Pennsylvania's other memorial measures, was to show that several non-Delaware places could be seen as foundational sites of the New Sweden colony.[24]

Pennsylvania's actions were arguments for the state's equal inclusion in the commemoration. Before 1938 the location of New Sweden's foundational site was clearly malleable. The Rocks served this function for Delaware, Sweden, Swedish America, and the United States. For Pennsylvania, Finland, and Finnish America, that site was being created on and close to Tinicum Island. Although Pennsylvania's attempts to locate New Sweden's beginnings on its own territory were unsuccessful, they forced Delaware and Swedish America to clearly articulate their counter-arguments. Those discussions show the power of regionalism at play in the commemoration and demonstrate how the history of New Sweden became entangled, with everyone claiming a superior right to its legacy.

"Every foundation is built upon destruction, the ruins of something prior, the ground beneath the foundation," writes W. J. T. Mitchell about foundational sites. "Every act of founding is also an act of losing."[25] Narratives of founding are often conditioned on narratives of replacement; they rely on both memory and amnesia. Perhaps best illustrated by Plymouth, Massachusetts, the quintessential "birthplace of a nation," stories of settler origins in America have relied on the erasure of previous pasts in the service of a history of beginnings.[26] The building of Fort Christina State Park also demonstrates how the interrelation between remembering and forgetting can overwrite a deeper precolonial history as well as a more recent one. By creating the park, commemorators subsumed a plot of land previously associated with the industrial landscape of Wilmington into a story of first contact.

The Settler and the Indian

Sites of settling are contact zones between European colonists and indigenous populations. They are the locus of stories about encounters, figuring—although in decidedly different ways—in the imaginaries of settler nations and in the mythologies of indigenous peoples.[27] As a consequence, settler sites in the United States have always been charged with meaning in relation to Native American history. The stories of Swedish settlement are no exception. Regardless of disputes in 1938 over which specific history to commemorate, the relation to Native Americans proved to be a resource to which both Swedish and American commemorators could subscribe.

The public memory of Native dispossession in America was long framed as a story of disappearance. It is a narrative epitomized by James Fenimore Cooper's 1826 novel *The Last of the Mohicans*. An example contemporary with the Swedish settler celebrations was the 1938 centennial of the Trail of Tears in Chattanooga, Tennessee. This "removal commemoration," as Andrew Denson has called it, told the dramatic story of the injustices that had taken place in and around Chattanooga. Because few Cherokees lived in the present-day city, however, this amounted to a safe atonement for white southern commemorators. The expressions of regret for the removal were, in the minds of the organizers, not a cause for political action but a way to strengthen their ties to the possessed land. Although later commemorations and public history sites, from the 1960s onward, have offered a more accurate description of the Cherokee removal, the general narrative has persisted. As Denson points out, the narrative "remains a story about vanishing Indians."[28] In recent years, public historians such as Laura Peers and Amy Lonetree have critically engaged with Native American public history and noted a change in how it is represented, staged, and performed in museums and at heritage sites. Although this history was once overwhelmingly curated and directed by non-Natives, indigenous groups are now asserting more influence and taking increasing control over its production.[29]

At the time of the tercentenary, however, such agency was firmly in the hands of white commemorators. At the core of both the tercentenary and the centennial were claims that Swedish settlement had been an essential moment in the history of the continent, that in some sense the histories of the Delaware and the Mississippi valleys had begun with the arrival of the Swedes. The foundation for the 1938 commemoration was the claim that the colony had constituted the first permanent, civilized settlement in the Delaware Valley. For instance, the Delaware resolution stated that the colony had formed "the first permanent establishment of European civilization" in the area, and the Pennsylvania act described it as "the [state's] earliest settlement, the first courts of law, and the first capital," thus constituting "the foundations upon which our Pennsylvania civilization is based."[30] New Jersey held the colony to be "the beginning of a permanent government for the earliest inhabitants" of its southwestern region, thereby writing the Native American population completely out of existence.[31]

Unlike English, Dutch, and Spanish settlements in North America, the New Sweden colony was both short lived and relatively small. Nevertheless, it was part of a concurrent European colonization of the eastern seaboard. Both north and south of New Sweden, other colonies were affected by violent conflicts between European settlers and Native Americans. Although Gunlög Fur notes that it would "be erroneous to perceive the area as free of intercultural tension," the New Sweden colony did not face large-scale violent conflicts with the Lenape that were on par with the experiences of other colonizing countries.[32] The absence of warfare and a lack of manifest hostilities between the Lenape and the New Sweden colonists—which, as we have seen, was largely due to the actions of the Lenape—has been beneficial for latter-day commemorators, enabling representations of first contact without foundational violence. In a speech at Rodney Square in Wilmington on the day of the delegation's landing, Crown Prince Gustaf Adolf elaborated on the colonists' relations with the Natives: "The Swedish settlers were from the beginning dedicated to peace, to friendly relations with their neighbors and to law and order amongst themselves. I think we are entitled to say that the Swedish settlement was built on the best traditions of the mother-country. . . . The relations of the Swedish Colonists to the Indians were always friendly. By treating the native tribes in a humane manner they won their friendship, and I think this policy explains why the Delaware Valley did not have the sanguinary Indian wars experienced by other colonies."[33]

During the same event, Secretary of State Cordell Hull addressed the colony's history at length: "Though the first colonists were soldiers," he said; "no violence marked their arrival." In this history, there were no threats, no wars or massacres to stain the colony of New Sweden.[34] At a commemorative banquet in Philadelphia a few days later, several speakers talked about the legacy and inspiration of New Sweden. The colony, according to Governor Earle, was the story of how "the dawning of our culture" was realized by the Swedes who "conquered the wilderness" and built schools, churches, and law courts. In the mind of Governor McMullen, the settlement was a place of "peace and happiness."[35]

The romantic image of Indian and Swedish contacts has its roots in the seventeenth century.[36] This image is not unique to New Sweden. Other groups have made similar claims of a special affinity with Native Americans. It has, for example, been a fixture of Jewish imagination, based on notions that both share experiences of acculturation and the negotiation of tribal identity. In Germany, this idea was popularized in Karl May's late-nineteenth-century novels about the Apache hero Winnetou.[37] Even though Swedish colonial ventures today are treated as marginal episodes in national historiography, this was not always the case. Historical scholarship and popular history in Sweden during the nineteenth and early twentieth centuries included accounts of Swedish colonialism and expansionism. Until World War II, and as demonstrated by the crown prince's speech at Rodney Square, colonialism was represented as a source of national pride. The pride in New Sweden rested on two assertions: that the colonists had treated the Lenape with respect and that the colony's foundational notions of civilization and piety remained a legacy in the United States. These notions were present in Gustaf Adolf's and Hull's addresses, which portrayed Sweden as a righteous colonizer characterized by democratic and humanitarian principles.[38] These were useful representations that enabled a denial of foundational violence and a manifestation of Native American replacement.

Conflating Colonial Settlement and Migration

The moments of settlement had taken place many decades, even centuries, before the commemorations. They were thus detached from the present and had no obvious connections to contemporary circumstances. However, commemorations rely on making history relevant in the present, and they do so through different strategies. One is to make analogies, drawing on similarities between past and present circumstances as a way of highlighting the lessons of history for contemporary society. Another is to emphasize continuities. This latter approach was a common argument in both commemorations, but was most conspicuous in the 1938 tercentenary. By conflating histories of colonization in the seventeenth century with a longer and more recent history of immigration, commemorators could temporally extend the significance of history. The histories of settlement proceeded from founding moments but received a more profound meaning in temporalities leading up to the present.

The idea of constructing a monument for the tercentenary initially came from the Swedish commission. From the start, opinions on the matter were also solicited from the United States. During the first Swedish commission meeting, it was proposed that Swedish sculptor Carl Milles should design the monument. Milles had significant standing in the United States. He had lived in Michigan since 1931, where he held a professorship at the Cranbrook Academy of Art, near Detroit. He had received an honorary doctorate from Yale University in 1936 and had been commissioned to create major works in cities such as St. Louis and Saint Paul.[39] After having discussed several design alternatives—including a statue of seventeenth-century king Gustavus Adolphus—the commission settled on a proposal submitted by Milles himself: a representation of the colonial ship *Kalmar Nyckel* riding on a stylized wave and resting on a grand, relief-covered block of black granite.[40] Such a monument, he wrote, would be both popular and "historically correct."[41] After a meeting in the United States with members of the Swedish-American commission, a Swedish commission member had "a very strong impression, that people over here in America almost consider it a necessity that the monument is made by Milles."[42]

The Swedish commission accepted Milles's proposal. Because of technical difficulties in obtaining a massive granite block, the sculptor decided to place the ship and the wave on a tall granite column. He himself chose two of the monument's reliefs: those depicting

FIGURE 6. The New Sweden monument (1938) designed by Carl Milles, at Fort Christina State Park in Wilmington. Photo by the author.

"Governor Printz buying land from Indians" and "Runaway horse returned by Indians to Swedes."[43] The notion of a peaceful relationship between Swedes and Natives had inspired him to include these reliefs. The "friendship between Indians and Swedes," Milles explained, "was remarkable, since the Dutch and the English were enemies with them."[44] He consulted with Amandus Johnson and Wollmar Boström about the other relief motifs—in particular, those with historical figures. Johnson recalled "work[ing] for three days with the sculptor helping him to select the scenes for the reliefs, and to find wordings for the inscriptions."[45] The Swedish commission drafted the main inscription that was inserted onto the column and had the monument carved in Stockholm before shipment to Wilmington, thus making the production symbolize its cross-border quality.[46]

The Swedish commission's decisions regarding the monument design and the appointment of Milles were largely dictated by real or imagined notions of opinions "in America."[47] It is difficult to tell which group or people they specifically referred to, although they probably included a combination of people from Swedish America, Delaware, and Pennsylvania. The monument was one in a series of Milles's projects that during the 1930s and 1940s centered on themes from American history, such as the *Monument of Peace* in Saint Paul (1932–36) and the *Pony Express* built for the 1939 New York World's Fair. Each in various ways dealt with the relation between settlers and Native Americans.[48]

Carl Milles's 1938 New Sweden monument still stands in Fort Christina State Park. The park's name commemorates the fort once located close to the site and does not directly link to the Swedish seventeenth-century queen.[49] The name received renewed significance in 1937 when the General Assembly of Delaware passed an act changing the name of the river that runs past The Rocks from Christiana River to its present-day name, Christina River.[50] The monument is an eight-sided black granite column with concave surfaces. On top of the column rests the ship, slightly tilted in the wind. The column is covered with several panel reliefs, four large and five smaller, with inscriptions in Swedish and English. The main inscription declares the monument to be a gift from "the people of Sweden" to commemorate

FIGURES 7 AND 8. The reliefs on the New Sweden monument narrate the history and significance of the colony. Here, one of the reliefs shows the *Kalmar Nyckel* crossing the ocean, traveling from Gothenburg (upper righthand corner) to Delaware (lower lefthand corner), on a journey from culture to nature. The other depicts "Swedes Buying Land from the Indians." Photos by the author.

"the first Swedish settlement on American soil." To a viewer, the panel reliefs appear to have been placed randomly on the column, indicating no chronology or narrative coherence. However, because of the high placement of the reliefs (six to ten feet from the ground) and the narrow shape of the monument, the viewer is encouraged to circulate it and hence piece together a narrative of departure, landing, and settlement. Even though the reliefs are not linearly placed, the monument is in fact pedagogical and particular in form, leaving little room for individual interpretations.

The four larger reliefs represent the broad outlines of the colony's history. The ship *Kalmar Nyckel* crosses an ocean inhabited by various monsters. It travels from Gothenburg, lined with long rows of houses, toward Delaware, with its natural landscape inhabited by a beaver, a bear, a horse, an eagle, and fish. On arrival, three males dressed in nonspecific Native clothing meet two males dressed in European seventeenth-century-style clothes, holding a sign with the Swedish coat of arms: the three crowns. Above the heads of the Indians a beaver, a bear, and an eagle hover. Another relief features three men, one bare-chested with nonspecific Native attire, surrounding a horse that, according to the inscription, had run away and been returned by the Natives. Lastly, a large relief depicts "New Sweden" with a woman holding a child, surrounded by figures doing agricultural and cultural work: plowing land, fishing, sowing crops, cutting wood, and building houses. Three of the five smaller reliefs provide more historical specificity by depicting people associated with the New Sweden colony: Governor Johan Printz, King Gustavus Adolphus, and Queen Christina. One relief shows Fort Elfsborg, the "First permanent settlement in the Delaware Valley." Seemingly ending the narrative is a relief with a man stepping ashore on a gangway, a sequence identified as "William Penn welcomed by the Swedes."

The monument can be read as a linear narrative, introduced by the adventurous journey of the wave-riding ship that crowns the monument. This journey is broken down in the larger reliefs. The voyage from Sweden to the Americas is one from culture to nature; the Swedes' land treaty with the Natives is one of benevolence and respect; the settling and cultivation of colonial soil is connected to virtues such as hard work, family, and religion; and the relations with the Natives are characterized as friendly through the somewhat peculiar story of the runaway horse. A short, solitary inscription signals the end of the venture and the impact of the narrative: "And thus the Swedish colonists established civilization in the Delaware Valley." The welcoming of William Penn functions as a bridge from the past to the present. It emphasizes that the colonial civilization is an actual but long neglected source of present-day Delaware Valley society, a memory that reverberates into the future.

The New Sweden monument is anchored in the particularities of the colony. It emphasizes peaceful settlement without military presence and the building and raising of a sustainable, civilized society. The ways in which the monument associate the Lenape with nature and wildlife and the Swedish colonists with culture and farming fit into a notion of progress in which Natives are defined as belonging to an archaic past contrasting with the modern world of the settlers.[51] With two exceptions—Queen Christina and the image of the mother—all of the figures on the monument are men. They reiterate the masculine projects of an adventurous ocean crossing, making treaties, and settling land as well as the femininely coded task of nurturing new generations of settlers. These two dimensions—land taking and regeneration—are equally important in a settler colonial project that relies on the indigenization of the settler and the making of a society that supersedes itself.

A crucial aspect of the monument was its representation as a national gift, a symbolism secured through a national subscription. The symbolic impact was further emphasized when a list of the nearly 170,000 Swedes who had donated money was bound into forty volumes and displayed at the American Swedish Historical Museum in Philadelphia. A subscription invitation was released in December 1936, supported by, among others, Sweden's crown prince, prime minister, and minister for foreign affairs. The following January, the petition was printed in the majority of Sweden's newspapers. By proceeding from the transatlantic bonds created by the migration, the petition declared that the subscription was a chance to commemorate Sweden's role in "the establishment and development" of the United States and to celebrate "the first Swedish emigration to North America

FIGURE 9. President Franklin D. Roosevelt, his aide, and Prince Bertil standing on the stage in Fort Christina State Park for the inauguration of the New Sweden Tercentenary on June 27, 1938. Courtesy of the Delaware Public Archives.

in 1638."[52] The subscription would ensure that the monument was "a gift from the Swedes of this country to the ones who emigrated to America and their descendants."[53] The petition was an effort to memorialize settler history as a transatlantic legacy, and it did so by framing colonialism as an early migration.

The inauguration of the monument at The Rocks coincided with the landing ceremony of the delegation. At the presentation of the monument, Prince Bertil, who gave the unveiling and inaugural address in lieu of his sick father, emphasized that the national subscription was a sign of the importance of the transatlantic genealogies created by the emigration. He continued by emphasizing the emigrants' contributions to America. "It is with pride we recall the memory of those almost legendary pioneers who braved the Atlantic in their little vessel, the 'Calmar Nyckel,' and who came to found the Colony of New Sweden. . . . We are happy to feel that in some measure they, as well as their successors during the intervening three centuries, were able to contribute to the development into greatness of your country, the country of their adoption."[54]

By describing the colonists as pioneers, Prince Bertil signaled the subsequent conflation of the history of the colonists with those of "their successors." The second speaker, President Roosevelt, struck a similar note in his welcoming and monument-acceptance speech: "Your Royal Highnesses: It is a privilege to make grateful acknowledgement of the outstanding contributions made to our national life by men and women of Swedish blood. To this spot came the pioneers. But in the succeeding centuries tens of thousands of others have come to our shores and added their strength and their fine qualities of citizenship to the American nation."[55]

Governor McMullen ended the verbal handing over from Prince Bertil (representing the people of Sweden) via President Roosevelt (representing the people of the United States) and accepted the monument to be kept in the custody of the state of Delaware.[56] In their speeches, neither Prince Bertil nor Roosevelt explicitly talked about the founding of civilization. Instead, both stressed that The Rocks was the place from which subsequent generations of Swedes had flowed into the United States. This overlap did not explicitly exist in Milles's monument, which focused on New Sweden's history as a colonial settlement. By stating that the colonists and the subsequent immigrants had made contributions to the United States, the speeches emphasized continuity from the landing in 1638 to the present day, bridged by the nineteenth-century migration.

Milles's monument effectively downplayed the Swedishness of the colonial project. It focused on the founding of civilization, building on histories that constitute the core of American national mythology (first contact, treaties with Native Americans, and settling of land). Through its funding as well as the narratives adopted during its making and unveiling, it also incorporated subsequent immigrants into its representation of the colonial legacy. This representation was not new. Swedish Americans had long conflated the histories of Swedish colonization with the subsequent mass immigration. It dominated the 1888 commemoration in Minneapolis and had been part of the ethnic group's "homemaking" in America.⁵⁷ Nor was this solely a Swedish-American strategy; Italian Americans had, for example, asserted that "Columbus was the first immigrant to America," a claim that eventually enabled U.S. politicians to embrace Columbus as a figure of an American, not an ethnic, experience.⁵⁸ The conflation of histories of colonization and immigration had their foundations in the nineteenth-century context of U.S. immigrant integration. By the 1930s, however, the narrative no longer belonged to the Swedish-American community but served to legitimize relations across the Atlantic.

Founders of the Modern Age

Compared to the clear-cut incentive for organizing the commemoration in 1938, the situation in 1948 was more complicated. One reason was the imprecise dating and the uncertain place of the history that was commemorated. The ambiguous foundation of the Swedish Pioneer Centennial made it necessary for commemorators to repeatedly explain what they actually intended to celebrate.⁵⁹

The first issue of the Swedish Pioneer Centennial Association newsletter, published in November 1946, explained that a hundred years ago "the waves of immigration began which brought eventually hundreds of thousands from Sweden to America, especially to the new settlements in the Mississippi Valley." The newsletter offered no definite answer to why 1948 was the centennial year, conceding that "almost any of a half-dozen dates might be chosen" for the celebration.⁶⁰ "One could have chosen a different year than 1848," a daily Swedish newspaper concurred. Referring to the Lutheran congregation formed in New Sweden, Iowa, the newspaper explained that 1848 was the year when a Swedish settlement was founded that could "display an ecclesiastical-Lutheran gathering."⁶¹ Listing possible events to commemorate, Conrad Bergendoff mentioned the Iowa congregation but also Gustaf Unonius's settlement in Pine Lake, Wisconsin, in 1841; Erik Jansson's settlement in Bishop Hill, Illinois, in 1846; and the foundation of Lars Paul Esbjörn's congregation in Andover, Illinois, in 1849.⁶²

According to Nils William Olsson, the commemoration sought to celebrate the "actual settling" of Swedes in the Mississippi Valley.

With reference to the lack of sources about the early settling, the year 1948 was chosen so that "all of the early settlements could be commemorated as one."[63] Religion was the common characteristic of all events listed by the Swedish-American commission. All were histories of the founding of Christian denominations or communities, and all involved people who had been ministers or preachers. This focus corresponded to the commemoration's decentralized, midwestern organization as initiated by the Augustana Synod. The targeted histories were united by Protestantism.

The centennial was similar to the tercentenary in the sense that it also referred to a story of foundational histories, a central concept of pioneering. In 1948, however, there was no concrete, uncontested, figure of a historical pioneer to which the centennial could be attached. Moreover, the past to which the centennial related was hard to locate in an exact geographical place. Describing possible activities to stage during the commemoration, Naboth Hedin touched upon the problems of erecting a monument similar to the one donated by Sweden in 1938. The place at The Rocks had been "well identified," but this time, he stated, "there is no such spot": "The settlements took place so gradually and in so many scattered places that it would be impossible to select any particular site." Therefore, he argued, there should not—and could not—be a monument to the Swedish pioneer similar to the one at The Rocks.[64] The past of the pioneers was a geographically and temporally ambiguous historical process. The absence of a specific place in which history could be properly commemorated eliminated the competition among groups and the urgent need to claim preferential rights that had permeated the tercentenary. The Swedish pioneers could be represented without connecting them to a specific foundational site, as long as that site was somewhere in the Midwest.

While it is important to note that Native Americans also were depicted in some parades and pageants in the centennial (see chapter 5), their most common representation in 1948 involved replacement and dispossession. In an effort to boost the organization of the centennial, Conrad Bergendoff in the summer of 1946 published an article in the *American Scandinavian Review* outlining the significance of the upcoming commemoration. The article, simply titled "A Centennial of Swedish Pioneers," was one of the longest coherent texts produced by a centennial commemorator to delineate the meaning of pioneering. Its core was a call to study the vast number of Swedes who had migrated to the Midwest, whose heritage could still be seen in the region, and whose records were easily available to researchers. The importance of this history was emphatically expressed in the article's first paragraph:

> How Aeneas the son of Anchyses left ancient Troy and after many difficulties landed on a new shore to begin the history of Rome, became the theme of one of the world's great poems, Virgil's Aeneid. In more modern times the story of the Pilgrim Fathers who laid the foundations of a new nation on a new continent has become a subject for poet and orator. The migration of peoples fires the imagination and touches the emotions of any generation which reflects on the birth of something new in human experience. It is not only the distress and peril of individuals who make the pilgrimage which awakens the interest of the thoughtful, but the sense of something significant taking place, something heralding the passing of one age and the coming of another.[65]

By comparing the coming of the Swedes to the Mississippi Valley with the founding of Rome and the Plymouth Colony, Bergendorff accentuated the historical neglect of the Swedish pioneers. The East Coast colonies were not adequate for describing the development of "American civilization and American culture." Rather, the history of the pioneers and the subsequent immigrants was a tale of those who "broke the prairies and built the villages which grew into cities." The migration westward and the movement of the frontier, Bergendoff claimed, brought "something new" to America: "Plymouth Rock is but one of the foundation stones of the New World." He maintained that it was the task of a modern Virgil to write this alternative foundational history.

The settling of the frontier is one of the most mythic origin stories in American history. Bergendoff's argument borrowed heavily from that of Frederick Jackson Turner, whose *The Significance of the Frontier in American History*, first delivered as a lecture in 1893, became one of the most influential historical texts in the United States.[66] Turner's central argument was that the "existence of an area of free land, its continuous recession, and the advance of American settlement westward explain American development." The wilderness of the frontier experience, he claimed, gave rise to individualism and antipathy toward domestic government control as well as to the East Coast's British legacy and relations with England. The idea was that the frontier experience had "Americanized" immigrants and had been instrumental in "the promotion of democracy."[67] Turner's emphasis on the distinctively American nature of the frontier charged the already existing concept of a frontier with new meanings.[68]

In Bergendoff's description of the passing of an old age, when the land was virgin and wild, and the rise of a new and modern age, Swedes were—to borrow a quotation from Jean O'Brien—"the first people to erect the proper institutions of social order worthy of notice."[69] In this representation, the 1948 commemoration relied on the supposed premodernity of Native Americans. All settlements considered as possible points of origin for the centennial were discussed because of the social orders the settlements were claimed to have established. In these representations, the Natives were present—although often silently—in the dichotomy of civilized/uncivilized (activated by the word *modern*). An example was the 1948 speech, titled "The Swedish Invasion," delivered at the State Coliseum in Detroit by Edwin Carl Johnson, a U.S. senator from Colorado:

> They came not armed with guns, but with plows. They came, not clothed in military armor, but with stout hearts and eager hands they set about their task of conquest. They came, not to take, but to give; not to destroy, but to build. And especially do I emphasize this point—they came not in the usual manner to ride rough-shod over helpless natives, but they came in ever-increasing numbers to create out of a magnificent wilderness comfortable homes and richer living conditions for their loved ones.[70]

Johnson argued that the pioneers did not violently conquer the Native Americans. Rather, the massive influx of immigrants had founded a settler civilization in what, despite the Native presence, he described as a wilderness. Even though he talked about an invasion, his story disavowed both foundational violence and Native interaction.

Commemorators from Sweden also adopted the theme of a rupture in the history of the continent. As the leader of the 1948 Swedish delegation, Prince Bertil gave what was his arguably most important speech of the centennial, delivered in front of President Truman at Chicago Stadium. Although he praised the contribution of Swedish immigrants to the United States, the majority of the speech was devoted to contemporary issues, such as the modernization of Swedish society and industry, American influences in Sweden, and the perils of war and economic distress. In his conclusion, he connected the last decade's fight for freedom and democracy with the struggles of the nineteenth-century pioneers: "It seems to me to be a most appropriate thing at this moment to remember the pioneers of the Middle West. Although under quite different material circumstances we live as they did on the frontier of civilization, in a new strange world, eye to eye with forces of nature that we shall only be able to control by mustering all our courage—and all our faith."[71]

Bergendoff and Prince Bertil described the arrival of the Swedes in the Midwest as the beginning of the modern era on the North American continent. While Bergendoff implied that the frontier had closed, the prince saw a new frontier in the evils of totalitarianism. By depicting their own side of the frontier as representing civilization, freedom, and democracy, they implied that the other side of the frontier signified the opposite.[72] The Swedes were, in their depictions, not the agents of Native American removal but people "armed with plows," conquerors not of the Natives but of the land itself.

The love of land was likewise the tenet of the memorial plaques in Andover, Illinois, and Saint Paul, Minnesota, that were unveiled during the centennial. The marker at the Jenny Lind Chapel in Andover explains that "among the first of the Swedish emigrants" who came to the Mississippi Valley "were the earnest and devout men and women who broke the prairie and built their homes and schools and churches in these regions." Striking a similar note, the plaque to the "fur trader, mail carrier, [and] missionary" Jacob Fahlstrom in downtown Saint Paul states that he "farmed in this region before 1838."[73] This was, according to Prince Bertil, also the story of the New Sweden colony, whose history showed "the deep Swedish love for the soil which was to be demonstrated in the Middle West some two hundred years later."[74]

Opening the prairie and cultivating the soil are recurrent tropes in the story of American pioneering and continental expansion. They form a narrative used by many early European immigrant groups to claim belonging to the landscape of the United States and have become a central theme in iconic American literature.[75] In Willa Cather's *My Antónia* (1918), the pioneer family is Bohemian and lives on the plains of Nebraska, while the Norwegian pioneers in Ole Edvart Rolvaag's *Giants in the Earth* (1927) settle in the Dakota Territory. Similar stories—of hardships on the frontier and struggles to form new homes under rough conditions—were pushed by pioneer boosters in the late nineteenth and early twentieth centuries through "Old Settler" societies established in the West and across the United States.[76] The land-taking and civilizing achievements of the Swedish pioneers were a source of pride to many, both in and beyond America.

The Transatlantic Pioneer

The histories commemorated in 1948 were intended to be not only manifestations in the present but also preserved and promoted for the future. Unlike the New Sweden Tercentenary, whose historicizing projects were grand and pedagogical, the centennial aimed for smaller participatory projects intended to establish foundations for present and future history writing. From the start, its primary purpose was "to understand what . . . contributions" the Swedish pioneers "made to American life." The Swedish-American commission encouraged local organizations to publicize histories of Swedes in America.[77] This project soon became one of three goals of the commemoration, the two others being "to observe fittingly" the Swedish pioneers and to "take cognizance" of their contributions to America. The commission's newsletter stated that the commemoration should be used to "assemble, preserve and publish books, records and documents of historical value and significance" because "American historians need this information."[78]

Professional historical research on Swedish migration to the United States was still limited in the 1940s, although, since the late nineteenth century, there had been published a number of filiopietistic books on Swedes in America, most of them authored by Swedish immigrants. Among the more influential were the works of Johan Enander, which often focused on the pre-Columbian, colonial, or Revolutionary eras and offered general tropes about Swedish contributions to the United States.[79] By the early twentieth century, scholars at U.S. universities had produced some academic immigration histories—for instance, those by Theodore C. Blegen, Arthur Schlesinger, Sr., and Marcus Lee Hansen. An important contributor to this scholarship was George M. Stephenson, a professor of history at the University of Minnesota, who in the 1920s and 1930s published several works on Swedish-American history.[80] Stephenson, however, faced strong competition from the historical genre represented by authors such as Amandus Johnson.[81] Before 1948, the market was still dominated by popular and often chauvinistic historians and editors of Swedish-American history.

In this research context, commission members envisioned the projects and purposes of the centennial as a way to encourage the writing of histories that did not yet exist. The commemorators did not set out to write these histories themselves, as was the case in 1938, when the commissions of Sweden, Delaware, and Pennsylvania all sponsored publications of New Sweden history.[82] In 1948, the writing of history was realized indirectly, through two different projects that related to the decentralized structure of the commemoration.

The first was an essay contest sponsored by the Swedish American Line in cooperation with the Swedish-American commission, with the theme "The Influence of Swedish Settlers on a Community or Region." The contestants were specifically asked to consult primary sources and use oral history and to write a biography "of a person, man or woman, of Swedish birth or descent," who had lived anywhere in the United States or Canada "during the past 200 years."[83] More than 2,000 essays were submitted to the competition, most of them stories about immigrants, their families, and their efforts at community building. Thirty selected contributions were published in Stockholm and New York as an edited volume titled *The Will to Succeed: Stories of Swedish Pioneers*. The book was intended to make people better appreciate the history of the pioneers and their descendants, and the volume's editor, Adolph Benson, a professor of Swedish descent at Yale University, saw its purpose as "a comprehensive perspective or evaluation of the Swedish influence in our American civilization."[84]

The second project was to form a lasting historical society. More filiopietistic historical societies had existed in the past, of which the most important was the Swedish Historical Society of America (1905–34), but they had not survived the transitional period after the end of Swedish mass immigration.[85] The chair of the Chicago committee warned that the centennial could soon be forgotten. Somehow, he argued, it needed to be transformed into an organization or society so that it could "be responsible for a completion of a permanent record of the accomplishments of the Swedes" in the Midwest.[86] Shortly after the celebration ended, commission members founded the Swedish Pioneer Historical Society (SPHS), renamed the Swedish-American Historical Society in 1983. The historical society was a way for the ethnic community to academically legitimize its history in America.[87] The organization of the SPHS followed the pattern of the Norwegian-American Historical Association, founded in 1925, and took inspiration from its structure and mission. Both societies sought to move away from chauvinism and to promote historical scholarship that was methodologically sound while still maintaining good relations with the ethnic communities.[88]

The essay contest and the historical society came about through cooperation between the central commission and its subcommittees. Whereas the New Sweden monument attested to the commemoration's top-down structure and had a clear international dimension, the 1948 projects were based on visions of a bottom-up remembrance mainly targeted at the ethnic community. The structure of the centennial was intended to empower the local Swedish-American communities that hosted the celebrations rather than the more powerful states and nations who had asserted considerable influence over the tercentenary celebrations. As a consequence, there were fewer openings for the Swedish commission to launch or control large-scale memorializing projects. Yet Sweden was an integral partner in the commemoration and could consequently not be detached from the history it celebrated.

An example of this was the discussion in Sweden on what to name the upcoming commemoration. In the spring of 1947, the Swedish commission's secretary, Per Sandberg, put forward suggestions for possible names in the Swedish language. They included (in literal translation) the Commission for the Swedish-American New-Builder Jubilee 1948, the Swedish Commission for the Mid-Western Emigrant Jubilee 1948, and the Commission for the Memory of the Nineteenth-Century Swedish Westward Pioneers. Sandberg explained that he had translated *pioneer* as *nybyggare* ("new-builder") because "pioneer has a somewhat different meaning in Swedish."[89]

The word *pioneer* carries specific meanings in a U.S. context that do not easily translate into Swedish. The commemoration's name—the Swedish Pioneer Centennial—had been coined in the United States, where, as Naboth Hedin explained, it "described the type of worker we intend to honor and fixes the period."[90] As a name, the Swedish commission eventually decided to adopt Swedish Commission for the Pioneer Jubilee (*Svenska kommittén för pionjärjubileet*), dropping proposed descriptions such as "Westward," "Mid-west," "Nineteenth-Century," and "1948." Such words would have functioned to pedagogically situate the commemorated history in time and place. Instead, Sweden appropriated the concept of the pioneer as defined in the United States.

In his 1992 discussion of pioneer commemorations, John Bodnar juxtaposes representations of the pioneer with representations of the patriots of the American Revolution. While pioneers are commemorated for "starting families and local communities" and for preserving traditional values mainly in the Midwest and the Great Plains, patriots are celebrated for "founding a nation" in an upheaval beginning on the East Coast.[91] The frontier myth is indeed central to the story of America. The pioneer might not have been a Founding Father, but he—the representation is often assigned a male gender—was a nation builder.

The word *pionjär* carries far less significance in Sweden than it does in the United States. A pioneer in Swedish could be described as an individual who breaks and cultivates the soil, but generally it identifies a person as a pathfinder, a groundbreaker, or a torchbearer.[92] More importantly, the Swedish definition does not emphasize settling and is not historically and geographically situated in the notion of an American nineteenth-century frontier. These essential dimensions are lost in the Swedish translation. But even though pioneering carries different meanings in a Swedish context, there is an essence of the pioneer in one of the dominant national mythologies in Swedish nineteenth- and early twentieth-century nationalism—the mythology of *odalbonden*.

Odalbonden is the title of a poem published in 1811 by the historian and author Erik Gustaf Geijer, who wrote nationally influential romantic depictions of Vikings as the heroic ancestors of Sweden.[93] It depicts the life of a freeholding member of the Swedish peasantry (the very word means "freeholding farmer"). Geijer constructed *odalbonden* as the foundation for the Swedish nation, in terms of both its economy and its constitution. The poem gave rise to claims that the nation had developed out of landowning peasant families and the associations of free farmers. The mythology represented an inseparable connection between popular or folk government and royal power, as the latter had developed out of the former. This emphasized an alliance between the king and the people.[94] It was the mythology's evocative connection between a strong state and a popular government that made it linger into the twentieth century. When the Social Democratic Party came to power in the 1920s, its members assumed these ideas in their self-representation as both a folk movement and a governing party.[95]

The nationalist mythology of *odalbonden* in Sweden shows many similarities to American mythology about the pioneers, who, in turn, share many similarities with Thomas Jefferson's ideas about the yeoman farmer. It should be noted that this is not a causal relationship but a correlation of representations. *Odalbonden* represents an ideal figure of Swedish independence, where the freedom of man was seen as the result of a historically deterministic process. It is a mythology that displays similarities to ideas about the United States as the Promised Land and the guardian of individual freedom.[96] The Swedish peasant as a land-tilling, landowning, independent man echoed key aspects of the American pioneer mythology. Much like discourses about the Swedish peasant, the American pioneer was constructed during the late nineteenth century as a promoter of American democracy.[97] The celebration of the pioneer was a celebration of independence and individualism, which resonated well in Swedish contexts.

When Per Sandberg voiced the question of what to name the Swedish commission, the issue was really about whether Sweden wanted to subscribe to the American national mythology about the frontier. The word *pioneer*, he underlined, indeed meant something different in a Swedish context. As the following chapters will show, the decision to include that word in the official name of the commission resonated in commemorative speeches of the Swedish delegates. It exemplified the way in which Sweden subscribed to the frontier myth—although from a Swedish perspective that was charged with somewhat different associations.

In different ways and through different means, the 1938 and 1948 commemorations both celebrated settler colonial histories. In the 1930s, Swedish and American commemorators eschewed a narrative that denied Native Americans a role in history, placing Swedish-Native encounters at the center of attention. Writing Native Americans into the history of New Sweden was beneficial rather than problematic for tercentenary commemorators because it indicated the supposed righteousness of the colonial venture. The situation was different in 1948. In the majority of representations of Swedish pioneering and subsequent immigration, Native Americans were no longer present. This is not surprising, considering the dominant mythology of the "Vanishing Indian," the notion of the "Virgin Land," and the idealization of the western landscape as a "wilderness."[98] What is noteworthy is how these histories were manifested by both American and non-American commemorators. In the cross-border celebrations of the 1930s and 1940s, the foundational settler histories became transcultural memories, influenced foremost by American mythologies.

The celebrations of the colonists, pioneers, and immigrants rested on the conflation of histories that spanned three centuries. By promoting these histories, commemorators maintained that they had cross-border significances. They were memorialized as transatlantic legacies, not as those whose relevance was circumscribed to America. The settler colonial claims did not simply establish certain sites in the United States as locations for the remembrance of Swedish settlement. Rather, the processes of memorialization were, from the outset, produced to undergird the promotion of cross-border relations. This dimension was grounded in the assertion that Swedish settlers, through the nonviolent replacement of Native Americans, had founded permanent civilizations in certain parts of America. It was a claimed accomplishment that could be honored on both sides of the Atlantic.

CHAPTER 4

Mutual Modernities

Representing History through Delegation Travels

"Prince Bertil Travels the Same Way as the Swedish Pioneers in the USA," reported a Swedish newspaper a couple of months before the start of the 1948 Swedish Pioneer Centennial. Sporting a picture of the prince on a motorcycle, the article continued, "The official delegation from Sweden will travel exactly the same way as the tough, adventurous immigrants one hundred years ago."[1] The prince was the head of an official delegation appointed by the Swedish government. Its arrival at LaGuardia Airport in New York City on June 1, 1948, was the start of a month of celebrations that would take its members through cities such as Chicago and Minneapolis–Saint Paul and as far west as Nebraska.

Since the 1930s, official representatives of Sweden have attended every major commemoration of Swedish settlement, and have been joined by delegates from Finland at celebrations of the New Sweden colony. These representatives were appointed by their respective governments to represent the country at celebrations in the United States. But even though foreign delegations have occupied such a prominent position at cross-border commemorations in general (recent examples include the visits of British and Spanish royalty to commemorations in Virginia, Florida, and New Mexico), the implications of their travels are seldom analyzed.

Recent scholarship on transcultural and transnational memories indicates the usefulness of studying delegations. In the 1980s, Pierre Nora introduced what during past decades has been the most influential theory on the location of memory. He argued that history is the means through which modern societies try to grapple with memory loss. To stop the process of forgetting, he claimed, we create memory sites (*lieux de mémoire*) that fixate history and "materialize the immaterial." Modern memory can therefore, according to him, exist only in specific places.[2] This idea has in recent years been scrutinized and criticized—for example, by Julia Creet, who maintains that "migration rather than location is the condition of memory." Creet thus turns Nora's assertion on its head, arguing that movement and migration are what produce memory and, in turn, our anxiety to localize it in certain places. This argument counters the idea that there is "an origin moment for memory" that can be found by searching for stability.[3] Perhaps, as Astrid Erll writes, "*all* cultural memory *must* 'travel,' be kept in motion, in order to 'stay alive,' to have an impact both on individual minds and social formations." This "travelling memory" involves individuals who participate in rituals, performances, and displays and who become carriers of memory.[4] The first step in understanding how commemorations function as cross-border events is thus to intimately explore the acts and functions of traveling delegations.

The act of leisurely or business (as opposed to migratory) travel is a performance of power. This is true as much for personal travels— necessitated by economic means and facilitated by sociocultural status—as it is for international relations. As Christopher Endy has shown, the increase in American overseas travel in the early twentieth century was widely regarded as a manifestation of the growing global power of the United States. The global presence of American citizens alongside those from European imperial powers was regularly seen as an expression of the rise of U.S. international influence. Moreover, American travel writers and commentators, including early voyagers such as Thomas Jefferson, used their experiences from Europe to formulate political positions in their homeland. During the Cold War, the connection between politics and travel became a federal policy as the U.S. government pushed overseas traveling as a part of the Marshall

Plan. The idea was that American touristic consumption would help to rebuild the western European economy. The very act of traveling, in this way, became a "soapbox" for the formation of foreign policy.[5]

The practice of reenacting past travels is common in commemorations of settlement. The same year as the New Sweden Tercentenary, in 1938, the sesquicentennial of the first white settlement in the Northwest Territory was commemorated with a reenacted pioneer trek. A pioneer caravan followed the exact historic route of the eighteenth-century settlers, from Massachusetts to Marietta, Ohio. Using an ox-drawn Conestoga wagon, and with pageants staged along the way, the participants intended to reach as many people as possible in a large geographic area.[6] Unlike such lavish historical reenactments, however, delegation tours are acts of commemoration that seem to have little to do with the actual histories commemorated. They are not apparently historicizing. Yet the practice of reenactment is not restricted to people who stage a feeling of pastness by using costumes and theatrical performance to represent history. The delegations in 1938 and 1948 did not represent history through dramatization or refer to themselves as reenactors, but they still performed reenactments in the ways in which they related themselves to the past. One aspect of this practice was their means of transportation. For while the delegations were said to travel "in the footsteps" of history, thus bridging the past and the present, they did so in the name of genealogical bloodlines and transatlantic modernization as a way to demonstrate that Sweden was part of a North American settler colonial trajectory.

Embodying the Modern State

As a rule, Swedish delegations have traveled to the United States to participate in cross-border commemorations, not the other way around. The one exception in the 1930s and 1940s was a 1937 tour of Sweden made by a delegation from Pennsylvania as part of a prologue to the New Sweden Tercentenary. Consequently, the two largest delegations of the commemorations represented Sweden.[7] The invitations from the U.S. Congress in 1938 and from the Swedish-American commission in 1948 were directed to the Swedish government. In both cases, the government responded by organizing official delegations to represent the country in the United States.

In April 1938, the Swedish government appointed a delegation of forty-one members plus twelve accompanying wives and nine journalists.[8] It was conceived as "a good and complete expression of the cultural, material, and not least, the democratic Sweden of today." The delegation incorporated people from a wide range of Swedish organizations and institutions, including members of the government and parliament, and representatives of the government bureaucracy, the state church, museums, universities, social welfare organizations, industry, the business and maritime trade, the sciences, the press, agriculture, and labor organizations. Many of the groups had specific interests in Swedish-American relations, such as the Swedish American Line and the National Society for the Preservation of Swedishness Abroad, founded in 1908 to maintain the international use of Swedish language and culture. Among the people in executive or leading positions who commonly make up the membership of official delegations were two representatives of factory workers and farmers.[9] There was strong representation from various branches of the state civil service, but there was also considerable representation from businessmen and secular and religious social movements with an interest in America.

Shortly before the delegation's departure to the United States, the Swedish chairman, Sigfrid Edström, felt compelled to write to the Pennsylvania chairman, Frank Melvin, to clear up some misconceptions. One issue was to explain why so many of the delegates did not speak English. The reason, according to Edström, was to be found in the political success of Swedish social democracy. "Coming from the working class many of them do not speak English. That is why they do not want to live in private families. That is why I bring so many secretaries. These secretaries speak English and know [the] U.S. . . . You wonder why we bring such men along who do not speak English—well, *it is the Sweden of today that shall visit you*. And as the government pays for more than half of my delegation it is government people who go and enjoy this trip."[10]

The delegation's English skills were an aspect of "the Sweden of today" that could not be negotiated. The government that Edström referred to was Social Democratic. Having formed a minority government in 1932, the party, through successful economic intervention and progressive social policies, had strengthened its popular support and gained 46 percent of the votes in the 1936 elections.[11] The problem was not that Melvin or the Pennsylvania commission had an issue with the Swedish delegation as a representation of the modern state. It was rather a question of how this representation was made. Edström's letter attests to the differences in the social and cultural perceptions about how the state was being embodied.

The discussions during the preparations for the Swedish Pioneer Centennial show many similarities to those during the New Sweden Tercentenary. In 1948, a preparatory committee stated that the official delegation "should reflect different sides of Swedish social life."[12] As the Swedish commission began planning for the appointments, its members asked a visitor from the Swedish-American commission for advice. His response included requests for representation from agriculture, sports, health care ("particularly the organization of hospitals"), churches (Methodist, the Salvation Army, and Mission Covenant), the temperance movement, adult education, the cooperative union, social politics, the army, and—what was "especially emphasized"—the industry and labor market.[13] When the delegation was appointed in May 1948, it included members from the government, the Swedish Federation of Labor, the Swedish Employers' Confederation, the Swedish Workers' Educational Association, the Swedish Farmers' Association, the Swedish Institute for Cultural Exchange with Foreign Countries, and representatives of education, free churches, and professional women's groups. It was a significantly smaller group than the one in 1938, totaling fifteen people.[14] The Swedish commission chair, Minister of Commerce Axel Gjöres, was forced at the last minute to abstain from joining the delegation due to negotiations involving import treaties and the Marshall Plan.[15] Because Prince Bertil was the chair of the Swedish Sports Confederation, the requests from the Swedish-American commission about the delegation appointments were met—or merely corresponded to the ideas in Sweden—in almost every area.

Sweden's official participations in both the interwar New Sweden Tercentenary and the postwar Swedish Pioneer Centennial were tailored to represent the country as a modern state. The delegations were appointed in ways that made them represent Sweden by standing for the nation. They did not act for the people of Sweden (by being representative in a similar way to a parliament in an indirect democracy); they were conceived to be embodiments of the nation and were appointed by the government to act as the nation abroad.[16]

There were many similarities between the 1938 and 1948 delegations. Both included representatives of government, parliament, businesses, and social movements. But there were also differences, primarily a comparatively stronger presence of state civil service and cultural institutions in the 1938 delegation. In that year, the delegation displayed a nation that incorporated social movements, workers, and farmers, but these groups were outnumbered by state institutions and thus dwarfed in relation to the delegation's size. The 1948 delegation, by contrast, contained fewer representatives of the state civil service, thus allowing the representation of social movements and the corporatist state to make a greater impact.

The reasons for why the Swedish government sought a delegation to embody Sweden as a modern state in the United States were bound up in the transatlantic exchange of political ideas. The composition of the delegations as incarnations of the Swedish nation rested on the shared Swedish and American interest in progressive socioeconomic policies. It was a discussion fueled by the success of the journalist Marquis Childs, whose book about Sweden as a political "middle way" was new and current during the height of the tercentenary planning.[17] Childs identified three crucial factors in the successful control of capitalism: the strength of consumer cooperatives, state intervention in the economy, and the impact of trade unions.[18] It is worth noting that the fields covered by his book—most prominently that of consumer cooperatives and trade unions—were represented in both Swedish delegations.

The only commemorative delegation that traveled to Sweden from the United States is a further example of the impact of these transatlantic discussions about the modern state. During the fall of 1937, Pennsylvania's governor, George H. Earle, led an official delegation to Sweden. The delegation's nineteen members came mainly from

FIGURE 10. The Swedish delegations, especially the royals, received considerable attention during their U.S. travels. In Escanaba, Michigan, the younger population prepared for the July 1948 arrival of the Swedish delegation by honoring Prince Bertil. Courtesy of the Swenson Swedish Immigration Research Center, Augustana College, Rock Island, Illinois.

the state administration, such as the chief justice of the Pennsylvania Supreme Court, the commander of the Pennsylvania National Guard, and the state's attorney general. It also included Philadelphia businessmen, accompanying wives, and a few relatives of the governor.[19] The selection of the Pennsylvania delegates mainly represented the state government. Earle received approval from President Roosevelt to make the tour but was ordered to go not as a representative of the president but of the state of Pennsylvania.[20] It appears that this delegation was the first official visit to Sweden ever made by a current elected representative from the United States.

Pennsylvania's engagement in the tercentenary was strongly informed by policies and political discussions of the New Deal.[21] An example is the Pennsylvania commission's use of funding from the Works Progress Administration. The federal government accepted six such projects for work at Governor Printz Park.[22] Connections between Pennsylvania's political program and those of contemporary Sweden became clear after Earle returned from his overseas visit, profoundly impressed by what he had seen of the country's policies. Newspapers reported that the visit had given him new ideas, especially about welfare relief and housing. Several newspapers quoted the governor saying that Sweden had "practically eliminated poverty and reduced unemployment to a minimum." This was largely due to its housing program, whose excellence had left him "perfectly amazed." The Swedish system, he thought, should be implemented everywhere in America.[23]

The appointment of the delegations, especially the selection of included groups, was influenced by cross-border ideas about social, political, and economic modernization. But the most visible members of the delegations were, of course, their leaders, and these individuals added yet another dimension to the travels. All delegations traveling from Sweden to the United States have been headed by a member of the royal family.[24] Royal visits to America have always garnered considerable public attention. Massive audiences appeared for the first British royal visit in 1860, when Albert Edward, the Prince of Wales, toured the United States and Canada. This pattern was repeated in subsequent royal visits, as when Prince Henry of Prussia visited the United States in 1902.[25] It is therefore hardly surprising that the appointment of the Swedish delegation in 1938 began by soliciting a representative from the royal house. For the tercentenary, it was decided that fifty-five-year-old Crown Prince Gustaf Adolf should represent the Swedish head of state. King Gustaf V had turned eighty in 1938, so the month-long arduous trip to North America was never an option for him. The crown prince was joined by his second wife, Crown Princess Louise (formerly Louise Mountbatten), as well as twenty-six-year-old Prince Bertil, the third son from Gustaf Adolf's previous marriage to Princess Margaret of Connaught, who, like Louise, had been a British citizen.[26] The royal party was well suited to the journey. Gustaf Adolf had a passionate interest in history and was widely known as an avid amateur archeologist, and all three were excellent English speakers.

Because his father fell sick on the journey across the Atlantic, Prince Bertil shouldered much larger responsibilities during the celebrations than had been initially intended. Although Crown Princess Louise was present at most events, she was never a speaker and was rarely an active performer at the celebrations. Instead, Prince Bertil stepped in to represent the family at ceremonies and deliver his father's speeches during the first nine days of the commemoration. He did this to great acclaim, speaking confidently in impeccable British English and receiving positive attention from American journalists for his winning charm, good looks, and unmarried status—prompting many newspapers to cover stories about the women who dined, or merely talked, with the prince.[27] Reporting on the prince's appearance at a Philadelphia Museum of Art luncheon, the Pennsylvania commission described the arrival as a "triumphal entry of a conquering monarch into the city." It was not a far-fetched analogy, the report stated, because Bertil "with his democratic grace, charm and good nature had indeed captured the hearts of all those with whom he came in contact."[28] These sentiments were widely shared in the United States.

As a result of the prince's success in 1938, the Swedish Pioneer Centennial Association requested that he return to the United States for the celebrations in 1948, representing the now ninety-year-old King Gustaf V.[29] Since the last commemoration, Bertil had further increased his international experience. After having served as the deputy naval attaché at the Swedish embassy in London during the war, he had in 1946 been dispatched to South America as the figurehead of a delegation of businessmen to promote Swedish industry.[30]

Bertil was put into the spotlight immediately upon the delegation's arrival at LaGuardia. The Swedish press reported that journalists had instantly swarmed around him. According to a Swedish newspaper, after being interviewed by both the print press and television, Bertil walked over to the cars where "the forgotten Swedish delegation" was waiting.[31] Americans had, according to the Swedish consul in Chicago, preconceptions of a prince as "a blasé person, surrounded by etiquette." Bertil, though, showed none of those traits, making an impact with his "manliness, powerful voice, and solid diplomacy."[32] As the delegation continued its travels around the United States, public admiration of the prince continued. It was clear from the start that Swedish royalty was bringing most attention to the delegation.

Using royals to represent the idea of modern Sweden might seem paradoxical, especially in the American republic. Viewed from a different perspective, however, the presence of royals in the same delegation as people from the working class symbolized the essence of Swedish modernity. President Roosevelt had stressed his great interest in the Swedish developments, with "a royal family and a socialist government and a capitalistic system, all working happily side by side."[33] This transatlantic sense of modernity, one characterized by progressive equality, in which even a prince could be described as having "democratic grace," permeated the celebrations.

The selection of delegation members was made to reflect larger communities. But regardless of whether the delegations were limited in size or more inclusive, the performance of local commemorative events was, as a rule, heavily influenced by the presence of certain figureheads: Governor Earle, Crown Prince Gustaf Adolf, and Prince Bertil. As the Swedish commission report of 1938 aptly explained, "the delegates were nothing but the extras in a show in which the Crown Prince and the Crown Princess and Prince Bertil were the stars."[34] To receive a visit by a delegation meant that it was easier to draw large audiences, attract publicity, and thus gain revenues and support for certain causes.

Following in the Footsteps of the Past

As Prince Bertil pointed out in 1938 during his opening address at The Rocks, the delegation had "landed on the very same spot, where, 300 years ago, our forefathers first set foot on western soil."[35] Ceremonial disembarkations at the original landing sites and the sailing of replicas of colonial vessels have, since the early twentieth century, been a common feature in settler celebrations. The best-known reenactments of colonial landings involve the *Mayflower* in Plymouth, but they have also taken place at Jamestown, Virginia (with John Smith), St. Augustine, Florida (with Pedro Menéndez and Juan Ponce de León), and Bradenton, Florida (with Hernando de Soto).[36] The notion of being on the same spot is powerful and influential and seems to be a common, perhaps even global, cultural-historical phenomenon. There is a widespread notion that it is possible to follow in the footsteps of the past.[37]

As the Swedish American Line flagship *Kungsholm* was about to leave Gothenburg harbor carrying the Swedish delegation, the crown prince gave a radio address describing the journey on which they were embarking: "I am about to leave Sweden on board the good ship Kungsholm," he said, "to make the same journey as these daring colonists in 1638."[38] The delegation's journey was essentially imagined as a reenactment of the past voyage of the colonists. This was clearly exemplified in the discussions about the landing of the delegation in Wilmington.

Oscar Solbert of the Swedish-American commission had far-reaching ideas about the landing procedure in Wilmington. He imagined that it would "try to repeat in a modern way the arrival in 1638." The delegation would sail up the Christina River on a Swedish warship and disembark at The Rocks.[39] The idea replaced an abandoned plan "to rig up a ferry boat or some other such contrivance to look like the *Kalmar Nyckel* and put the royal guests on it" and then have "five Indian chiefs come up to smoke the Peace Pipe and to inaugurate other pageants."[40]

The Swedish delegation left Gothenburg on June 18, 1938, and arrived in Wilmington on June 27. There they met unseasonably bad weather, with cold, hard winds and violent rain. Due to the depth and width of the Christina River, organizers decided against using a larger ship for disembarkation and instead used smaller longboats from which the delegation stepped onto the Rocks–the stones where the colonists were said to have landed in 1638. That is, rather than disembarking onto the concrete bulkhead of the newly constructed Fort Christina State Park, the guests made their entry onto U.S. soil by walking a gangway down to The Rocks, taking a few steps on the rock, then proceeding along another gangway up toward the park.[41]

The 1938 tercentenary included not only the historical landing of the colonists but also their departure. This took place during the Pennsylvania visit to Sweden. The idea of the visit seems to have originated in the Swedish commission and was realized through discussions between the Historical Society of Pennsylvania, Swedish-American representatives, the Swedish royal family, the Swedish Ministry for Foreign Affairs, the U.S. embassy in Stockholm, and the Swedish embassy in Washington, D.C.[42]

The ways in which the visit to Sweden represented history are visible in the Pennsylvania commission's final report. After arrival in Gothenburg in November 1937, "at exactly the same spot" from which the New Sweden colonists had departed, the delegation traveled eastward to Stockholm, made an excursion to Uppsala, visited museums, historical sites, and factories, attended luncheons and banquets, and then returned to the western coast. Two days later, members left Gothenburg from "the same spot" at which the *Kalmar Nyckel* had left for North America three hundred years earlier.[43]

Earle's delegation only extended its tour as far east as Stockholm. They did, not, in other words, go to Finland. There were attempts to invite Earle to Helsinki, but these were dismissed by Sweden due to lack of time.[44] There was, however, a greater significance involved in the delegation's decision not to visit Finland, something that Fred Morris Dearing, the U.S. envoy to Stockholm, explained in a confidential letter to Secretary of State Cordell Hull:

> It occurs to me therefore that this special and outstanding visit to Göteborg [Gothenburg] of Pennsylvania's Governor and his party, from the Swedish point of view, has been an effort to restore relative positions somewhat to where the Swedes feel they should be. Governor Earle comes conspicuously to Sweden. He does not go to Finland and there is no self-evident reason why he should which is precisely what the Swedes desire to have emerge. The Swedish character of the Delaware Celebration is thus emphasized without anyone being able to find a justifiable criticism for what has been done: namely the commemoration of the departure of the first Swedish settlers from a Swedish port, on the *Kalmar Nyckel* and *Fågel Grip* has been carried out so as to focus all the attention upon the fact that the expedition was purely Swedish and that what is to be celebrated in the Delaware River Valley next year is Swedish too, and nothing else.[45]

The Pennsylvania visit was consequential for the Swedish commission since they sought to use the commemoration to promote their country's positive image in America. The envoy was thus undoubtedly right in his suspicions. Earle's visit to Sweden was part of the behind-the-scenes power struggle between Sweden and Finland, and Delaware and Pennsylvania. These conflicts centered on which group that had the preferential rights to the commemoration. The Pennsylvania delegation's visit to Sweden became a part of the argument for commemorative primacy; it showed both Finland and Delaware that there was a contemporary bond between Pennsylvania and Sweden that was built on history. The visit demonstrates the political potential of delegation travels in cross-border commemorations and how this potential was understood through the ways in which the travels represented history. As the envoy explained, Sweden's and Pennsylvania's justification for the commemoration's character was emphasized through the celebration of the colonial departure from Gothenburg. The urgency of the situation, as expressed in his letter to the secretary of state, was rooted in the visit's historical message and the fact that its relevance was produced through cross-border interactions.

The idea that the delegation would revisit the routes of Swedish settlers, this time in the interior, also permeated the 1948 Swedish Pioneer Centennial. An article by Nils William Olsson published in a special centennial issue of the *American Swedish Monthly* expanded on this theme. Titled "Swedish Delegation Follows the Path of the Pioneers," the article was illustrated with a map plotting the midwestern routes of the delegation. The map visually underlined the commemorative area of significance: it was cropped around the Midwest and thus geographically excluded the history of seventeenth-century colonization.[46] The Swedish delegation did visit the East Coast, but purely out of necessity. Following an overnight stay after their arrival in New York City on June 1, members went straight to Chicago by train.[47] Even though commemorators on the East Coast did their best to argue for their natural spot on the delegation's itinerary, the core of the 1948 commemoration was the Midwest and so was the focus of the tour.

The choices of where to depart, where to land, and where to go were made with references to historical analogy. To repeat a delegation landing in a modern way or to be at the same spot at which the past unfolded had two seemingly paradoxical functions. On the one hand, it created a bridge to the past that the delegation was there to commemorate. The historical place was thus infused with the utterances of the present, making them more alive and seemingly more important. On the other hand, the contemporary presence of delegations at a historically significant location manifested the distance to the past. This distance bridging was accomplished through ideas about race based on the history of immigration, while the distance manifesting relied on arguments of modernity and technological progress.

Traveling by Blood, Commonalities of Race

The geographical centers of the commemorations were located in different parts of the United States. But even though the tercentenary commemorated a past that played out mainly in the Delaware Valley, it is significant that it also covered the Mississippi Valley, the heartland of the centennial. The 1938 tercentenary delegation began its travels in and around the Delaware Valley, visiting cities such as Wilmington, Philadelphia, and Washington, D.C. They continued north to New England and then set out west for Minneapolis–Saint Paul by way of Detroit and Chicago. On the way back to the East Coast, some delegates visited Pittsburgh before the reunited delegation returned to Sweden from New York.[48] Although the Chicago and Minneapolis–Saint Paul celebrations were the largest and, some would claim, the most successful, they were initially not included in the plans of the Swedish commission. A few months after that commission had been formed, Sigfrid Edström informed Oscar Solbert that the tour to the Midwest "is not even very popular with us."[49] The royals were "not anxious" to visit Illinois and Minnesota and wanted to go home after the celebrations on the East Coast.[50] Going to Chicago and Minneapolis–Saint Paul, Edström believed, would favor some Swedish Americans and thus cause discontent in other parts of the country.[51]

The Swedish position on extending the tour westward was met with counterarguments from Swedish Americans as well as Swedish diplomats in the United States. Solbert tried to persuade Edström that they should (indeed needed to) include Chicago and Minneapolis—"the two centers of the greatest Swedish American population"—on the itinerary.⁵² In Minnesota, the Swedish consul Carl F. Hellström worked intensely toward this end. He maintained that Sweden needed to stop neglecting Minnesota in its relations with the United States. In a letter to the Swedish minister for foreign affairs, Hellström elaborated on the issue:

> Minnesota is generally called "the Swedish state" in the United States, and the Swedish emigrants and their descendants in this state undeniably constitute the largest Swedish population area anywhere in the world outside Sweden's borders. . . . A certain malaise can be noticed in not only Swedish-American but also American circles that Minnesota is not properly considered [by Swedes] . . . who visit America for information, studies, or cultural purposes, or as businessmen, and I am asked all too often why this is the case. . . . From a Swedish point of view Minnesota should be particularly close to heart for Sweden given the large population of Swedish descent and what the Swedes have done to build and develop the state into its present great well-being and general position.⁵³

After continued lobbying, the idea somehow gained traction in Sweden, and it was eventually decided that the royals indeed would travel to Chicago and Minneapolis–Saint Paul.⁵⁴ There were invitations for the delegation to travel to the West Coast as well, but they had to be turned down due to lack of time.⁵⁵ In a letter to the chair of the Los Angeles committee (one of the local committees formed throughout the country), Boström stressed the importance of local interests in the commemoration. This was a crucial component in making the commemoration a "universal celebration" including all Swedish-American organizations: "Although the landing of the first colonists naturally took place in the East, this Tercentenary is a celebration of equal interest to every person with Swedish blood, whether he lives in the East or the West, in the North or the South. . . . I hope to see, as a result of the Tercentenary, a full recognition of what the Swedish race has done towards building up and developing this great country."⁵⁶ The decision to visit the Midwest was based on the argument that it was the area with "the largest Swedish population" in the United States, a group effectively defined through the claimed possession of common bloodlines. Because "full recognition" of the Swedes could not be achieved by having the delegates tour all parts of the United States, the Swedish-American commission encouraged all Swedish Americans to make "a pilgrimage" to Delaware. The Swedish-American committee of Oregon, for example, chartered a train to transport people from cities in the Pacific Northwest to the celebrations in the Delaware Valley.[57] An additional twenty-five states throughout the country appointed committees that traveled to Delaware for the celebrations.[58] Here, blood created a teleological connection to New Sweden. As a destination for the tercentenary pilgrimage, The Rocks was framed as the place for the beginning of Swedishness in America.

Given the influence of Swedish-American organizations during both commemorations, it is not surprising that the 1948 delegation followed a route similar to its 1938 predecessor's. But while the tercentenary delegation traveled to the Midwest in pursuit of the descendants of Swedish pioneers and immigrants, those places and people formed the ethos of the Swedish Pioneer Centennial. "In a nut shell," Nils William Olsson explained, "we hope to stage celebrations in the various Swedish centers in the Middle West to commemorate the coming of the Swedish pioneers."[59]

The 1948 centennial delegation began its travels in New York and quickly proceeded to Chicago, making stops in cities such as Rockford, Detroit, Des Moines, Moline, and Minneapolis–Saint Paul, continuing as far west as Lincoln, Nebraska, before returning to Sweden from New York by way of Philadelphia on July 3.[60] All of the cities visited had formed local committees in accordance with the Swedish-American commission's effort to locate the commemoration in places "where descendants of Swedish immigrants have had a significant role in developing the life of the community."[61] After landing in New York, Prince Bertil told the press that the delegation had "come to this country at the invitation of our kinsfolks [sic] in the Middle West, men and women of Swedish birth and ancestry."[62] An article in the international edition of *Newsweek* published before the start of the commemoration outlined the itinerary of the delegation, explaining that it followed "the westward trail of the pioneers." The article had the headline "The Swedish in America's Blood."[63] This trail, though, did not refer to actual pioneer journeys. Rather, the itinerary, like the headline, was based on a broader and longer history of immigration and emphasized the presence of Swedish blood in the contemporary United States.

Traces of Swedish blood had, on a political level, also been important during the Pennsylvania delegation's visit to Sweden in 1937. Although the tour was influenced by international and interregional tugs-of-war, it also had a more personal dimension for Governor Earle himself. The Swedish-American and Pennsylvanian commissions stated that his decision to travel to Sweden was based on the claim that he had "found Swedish blood in his veins."[64] Upon arriving in Gothenburg in 1937, Earle gave a speech at the unveiling of two plaques commemorating the departure in 1638 of the ships *Kalmar Nyckel* and *Fogel Grip* to the Delaware Valley. "It is," he said, "with proud humility that I, with the blood of these pioneer Swedish forefathers in my veins, come to you in this official manner to present a small token of Pennsylvania's debt of appreciation." Earle pointed out that his delegation's tour was "a return voyage" following the route of the seventeenth-century colonists.[65] He was, in other words, the descendant of a Swedish colonist who, so to speak, was coming home.

But Earle's homecoming was not an actual coming home; this was his first visit to Sweden. In a similar sense, Sweden was not a de facto homeland for most of the people involved in the New Sweden Tercentenary and the Swedish Pioneer Centennial. For the majority of the commemorators, Sweden was the point of perceived bloodlines. This notion was present in the idea of following the steps of immigration to places considered to be Swedish.

To trace genealogy is never simply to know oneself but to establish connections and collective relationships: to family, ethnicity, and nation. The idea of a genealogical diaspora is, in this way, an extension of imagining the nation as a family, adopting biological closeness as the basis for common interests and solidarity.[66] Beginning with the 1845 founding of the New England Historic Genealogical Society, genealogical societies emerged throughout the United States in the decades after the Civil War. The American genealogical interest was spurred by the great societal changes of the late nineteenth century. In the light of urbanization, industrialization, and large-scale immigration, many Anglo-Americans sought to trace their pedigree as a way of legitimizing their social standing. Until World War II, according to François Weil, American genealogy largely served the "belief in racial differences and hereditary virtues, as well as in the superiority of Anglo-Saxon blood above all others."[67]

This way of conceptualizing relatedness and the value of bloodlines in the United States was influenced by a discourse of race. But these notions did not fully correspond to that construction in Sweden, a fact stemming from the countries' widely different historical experiences. Unlike the United States, Sweden did not have a large-scale history of domestic slavery, indigenous dispossession, mass immigration, Jim Crow laws, and institutionalized disenfranchisement. The question of domestic racism was, in short, not considered to be an issue in mid-twentieth-century Sweden.[68] Rather, many Swedes were critical of the racial segregation and discrimination in the United States. The most notable critic was the social scientist Gunnar Myrdal, who, in 1944, published the highly influential *An American Dilemma* about the social, economic, and political conditions of the African American population.[69] Yet while the contexts of race differed markedly between the two countries, Sweden and the United States shared a discourse that connected national belonging and personal character to biological essences. This discourse can be explored through the policies and practices of eugenics.

The concept of race changed profoundly during the mid-twentieth century, greatly affected by the Holocaust and the racism of the Nazi regime. The intellectual background to this change was what the historian Elazar Barkan has called "the retreat of scientific racism." Circling around the discussion of whether human behavior could be explained by biological or social factors, by nature or culture, scholars such as Franz Boas and Robert E. Park had in the early twentieth century begun to critique the scientific emphasis on heredity. Although they laid the groundwork for the wartime introduction of ethnicity as a concept for analyzing cultural differences, ideas of racial biology did not disappear overnight. Despite mounting scholarly criticism, scientific racism had a considerable political impact in the 1930s and 1940s through policies based on eugenics.[70]

In the words of Nancy Ordover, eugenics "has always been primarily concerned with what the nation would look like." The project of monitoring, regulating, and improving the national population was, during the twentieth century, visible in debates about immigration, sexual behavior, sterilization, fertility, and hereditary disabilities.[71] An example with bearing on the commemorations of Swedish settlement was the Immigration Act of 1924, which Matthew Frye Jacobson has called "the high-water mark of the regime of Anglo-Saxon or Nordic supremacy" in the United States. The legislation was strongly influenced by ideas of racial hygiene that deemed certain groups to be less desirable, or even unfit, for admission into the country.[72]

Another eugenicist policy was linked to sterilization laws. Beginning in Indiana in 1907, states throughout the nation would, in the ensuing decades, enact laws regulating its population through sterilization. By 1929, thirty states had enacted such laws, targeted especially at the perceived problem of "inheritable feeblemindedness."[73] In some states, such as Minnesota, the number of sterilizations reached their highest points during the 1930s and 1940s.[74] In the words of Susan Curell, ideas about hereditary human behavior still had "a continuing presence in the public psyche" in the 1930s, visible in both public debates and popular culture.[75]

Eugenics was also institutionalized in Sweden through laws adopted in 1934 and 1941 that regulated the forced sterilization of persons deemed mentally ill or handicapped. According to the historians Gunnar Broberg and Mattias Tydén, the model for the Swedish sterilization program was legislation in the United States. There was an indirect ideological relationship between Swedish social policy, or social engineering, and the sterilization policies. During the 1930s both were connected to the notion that the population was a qualitatively and quantitatively threatened resource—in other words, that there was a population crisis. Even though eugenics sometimes focused on individual ancestry or health, its associated policies and practices fundamentally concerned the well-being of society at large.[76]

These ideas were visible in Sweden in the use of various sociobiological constructs, such as concepts of "the people's body" (*folkkroppen*) and "the people's stock" (*folkstammen*) in describing various social engineering reform projects.[77]

The 1938 and 1948 commemorations were enmeshed in transatlantic discourses that merged biological heredity with identity. Examples appear in Wollmar Boström's 1935 article on the upcoming tercentenary in which he described the contributions of Swedish settlers and immigrants to the United States. "In a purely biological sense," he wrote, "I believe the value of the Swedish stock as a contribution to the population of the United States will be more widely recognized as time goes on. It is not an effervescent froth, but rather the heavy cream that slowly rises to the top."[78]

In this popular understanding of race and ideas about settler and immigrant ancestry, it made sense to think about following in the footsteps of a past defined by blood. Commemorators emphasized that a biological essence united Swedes and Swedish Americans in an imagined transatlantic family. But while bloodlines were at the center of both Swedish and American definitions of racial heritage, commemorators approached the notion from very different contexts. When the Swedes talked about ideas of race, they did not necessarily mean what their American counterparts meant. Different racial hierarchies existed in the United States, always related to the presence and experience of African Americans. In the case of the 1938 and 1948 commemorations, however, statements about race were largely made by commemorators in the United States or by persons from Sweden who had traveled to America. Claims that "the Swedish stock" was "the heavy cream" of the American population and that Swedes and Swedish Americans were "kinsfolks" were intended to be inclusive. Yet they were also exclusive and expressed from a position of privilege, making the more immediate racial contexts of the 1930s and 1940s important.

Explicit racial tensions did surface during the commemorations, though only rarely. They were particularly evident in the plans for the area surrounding The Rocks. In 1936 Amandus Johnson explained that "we dreamed of an area around there of a great many acres made into a park with about three blocks of the slums cleared away and the rubbish and old nigger huts removed."[79] His hoped-for clearances did not happen, and the slums remained. After the end of the commemoration, a Swedish delegation member, Ove Olsson, wrote about his experience of The Rocks and declared that the "surroundings could have been nicer, than in the Negro quarters of Wilmington."[80]

In the 1930s that area was one of the poorest and most dilapidated parts of the city.[81] It also housed the city's largest African American population. More than one-third of Delaware's relatively small black population lived in Wilmington (33,000 out of a state total of 238,000 in 1930 and 36,000 out of 267,000 in 1940). Although African Americans only made up about 10 percent of the city's inhabitants, their largest concentration was in the East Side district bordering the Christina River. The African American population on the East Side increased between 1930 and 1940. In the eighth ward, which immediately surrounded Fort Christina State Park, it grew from 32 to 51 percent.[82] There was a considerable African American population in the area, but calling it a "Negro quarter" was not demographically accurate. During most of the decade, the white population was the majority. It is illustrative that in some of the blocks closest to the park, such as the 900 block of East Seventh Street, located a hundred yards from the park entrance, all tenants in both 1930 and 1940 were white.[83]

The statements by Johnson and Olsson were both racial and socioeconomic markers. Regardless of the fact that the neighborhood in reality was of mixed race, the significant population of African Americans was sufficient to rankle Swedish and Swedish-American commemorators. To them, the black presence was a disturbance. These comments become germane when we consider Delaware's history of slavery and subsequent treatment of populations of color. At the time of the New Sweden Tercentenary, Delaware was a Jim Crow state that systematically discriminated against African Americans, with institutionalized segregation of the school system, restaurants, theaters, and other public spaces.[84] In the light of this history, the statements of the tercentenary commemorators also reveal something about historical belonging. Here, the issue was no longer one of mere "Swedish blood" or "the value of the Swedish stock" but of how a racial discourse was used to legitimize claims to an area that was, to a considerable extent, inhabited by African Americans.

Different Crossings, Shared Technologies

While race functioned to bridge the past and the present of the tours, the delegations' means of transportation served to manifest historical progress. Notions of acceleration and rupture are frequently adopted in commemorations as a way of emphasizing continuity, discontinuity, and change. Ideas about modernization—that is, the movement toward modernity—stand at the center of these conceptions and constitute an important mode through which commemorations are situated in time.[85] The rapid technological developments of the midtwentieth century were reflected in the delegations' different modes of transportation, which included car, train, boat, and airplane. The Pennsylvanian and Swedish delegations of 1937 and 1938 crossed the Atlantic by ocean liners. On both occasions, they traveled with the Swedish American Line, founded in 1915. That line expanded its traffic rapidly with the acquisition of several new ships in the 1920s and became a major carrier of emigrants (until the 1924 Immigration Act), returning migrants, tourists, and mail between Sweden and the United States.[86] Describing his journey with the line's flagship *Kungsholm*, a Swedish delegation member maintained that it was like being on board a "floating luxury hotel."[87] During the first decades of the twentieth century, the ocean liner was not only a technological wonder in its own right but also an evocative image of city planning: it was standardized, with simple geometrical aesthetics, and separated social functions in a limited space. In many ways it was the ultimate symbol of modernity.[88]

Just as the actual technology of transportation manifested modernization, so did the ways in which various transportation methods were described in relation to the past. In his radio speech from Gothenburg, the crown prince emphasized the comfort on board the liner and reassured his listeners that, unlike the situation of the seventeenth-century colonists, "there is no risk connected with our undertaking."[89] The newsletter of the Swedish American Line reported

FIGURE 11. The Swedish delegation in 1948 traveled to the United States by air, landing with a chartered SAS flight at LaGuardia Airport in New York City on June 1, 1948. Courtesy of the Swenson Swedish Immigration Research Center, Augustana College, Rock Island, Illinois.

on the Pennsylvania delegation's "comfortable ten-day crossing" on the ship *Drottningholm*, which "had little in it to compare, outwardly, with the voyage of the first batch of New Sweden settlers."[90]

The Swedish American Line itself related the crossing to even earlier pasts, promoting their ships at the time of the tercentenary as descendants of the Vikings'. The *Kungsholm*, a promotional pamphlet claimed, "retraces the path of Leif Ericson's [sic] toy ship in today's version of adventure. Motor-driven, hence dustless, sootless, smokeless . . . unsurpassed as a perfect means of travel."[91] The Viking imagery appeared several times during the commemorations juxtaposing Viking Age vessels with more modern ships.

In 1948, the development of commercial air travel made it possible for the majority of the Swedish delegation to travel to the United States by plane, flying with the newly formed Scandinavian Airlines System (SAS).[92] The Swedish-American commission stressed the meaning of this event: "Such a flight . . . will dramatize the difference in transportation 100 years ago, when a voyager was fortunate to make the Sweden-America trip in six weeks."[93] Prince Bertil also highlighted the technological progress in a speech he gave upon arrival in New York:

> I cannot help thinking of how different their crossing was from ours. We have travelled speedily and safely in great comfort, even luxury. We know that ahead of us lie some weeks during which friends with open hearts will do their utmost to make our stay in this country and agreable [sic] and easy one. Those others, who came here before us in the search for a new life in a strange country, traveled quite differently: on small and unsafe vessels, jammed together in narrow quarters, with little or nothing that they could call their own—and in their hearts a great feeling of uncertainty of what [the] future might have in store for them.[94]

One airplane had also been used during the 1938 tercentenary. Before the celebration of "Forefathers' Day" in Pennsylvania—commemorating the date of the colonists' landfall—an airplane traveled to the other original twelve states of the Union, carrying invitations from Governor Earle for the celebrations in Philadelphia. The airplane was christened *Kalmar Nyckel* at a ceremony performed by Gertrud Boström, the wife of the Swedish envoy.[95] The trip was, according to Governor Earle, intended to "demonstrate the boon of progress" since the time of the colonists.[96] Unlike the delivery of the Pennsylvania invitations, however, the journey of 1948 was explicitly referred to as replicating the nineteenth-century emigration in a modern way. Sweden, it showed, was one of the nations that had modernized to the extent that the Atlantic crossing not only could be comfortable but also luxurious and fast.

The travels inland followed the same technological trajectory as the overseas crossings did. While the 1938 delegation traveled westward by train, the 1948 delegation used trains, cars, and airplanes for their journeys. Describing the experience of traveling with the delegation through western Illinois in areas where many Swedes had settled in the nineteenth century, a representative of the Illinois commission "could not help . . . compare our existence with that of the pioneers."[97]

FIGURE 12. The 1948 delegation's travels in the American interior were made by airplane and car but mostly by train. En route from Chicago to Minneapolis–Saint Paul, delegation members could relax in the brand-new Skytop Lounge of the railway company Milwaukee Road. Courtesy of the Swenson Swedish Immigration Research Center, Augustana College, Rock Island, Illinois.

The platform of progress created by comparing the delegations with the pioneers was also used to promote the transport businesses. The presidents of the Swedish American Line and SAS wrote articles in the special issue of the *American Swedish Monthly*, contrasting the crossing of the emigrants with the modern alternatives that were now provided by the Swedish-based transportation companies.[98] In a postwar era of reduced travel (a mere 147,000 Americans had traveled to Europe in 1947, compared to a prewar peak of 359,000), this was a clear attempt to gain market share.[99]

The manifestation of modernity through traveling-as-reenactment had precedents in American cultural history. In his analysis of the phenomenon of pioneer-trail reenactments in the turn-of-the-century United States, David Wrobel describes "the tendency to contrast the demands of the past with the luxuries of the present." This was especially done by way of the Pullman Palace Car. The modern train was framed not only as enabling the experience of history—as a way for elderly pioneers to relive their past journeys—but also as a technology limiting the actual old-fashioned pioneering experience.[100] The latter argument was not common in the 1930s and 1940s, probably because the majority of the nineteenth-century settlers by then had passed away. The manifestation of modernity during the tercentenary and the centennial rather served as a tool of contrast. It was present in the composition of the delegations as well as through the framing of transportation technologies. While the delegations displayed sociopolitical dimensions of modernity, the methods of transportation were set against a backdrop of technological and industrial progress.

Since the late nineteenth century, the United States had been a role model for technological modernization in Sweden. For Swedish travelers to America, the modern means of transportation shaped narratives of their traveling to and around the United States.[101] Among many Swedish observers, the United States was considered a technical civilization of engineering ingenuity; it was also criticized, however, for valuing technological prowess at the expense of artistic and spiritual ideals. While the awe for the United States as an economic role model waned during the 1920s and 1930s, admiration for its technology continued.[102]

According to some scholars, America's most tangible influence on Europe has been cultural, even though it certainly has asserted considerable political, economic, and military power as well.[103] Through culture the United States has functioned as a symbol of modernity in Europe. One example is the American car. When cars such as Cadillacs were promoted in Sweden during the 1930s, they were marketed as a social status symbol for the modern upper middle class. In the years following World War II, the American car was associated with a simultaneous hope in the future and in a new Swedish society as manifested in the connection between social mobility and technological consumption.[104]

Cross-border ideas about technological progress that combined social and political modernity were instrumental when commemorators imagined traveling in a modern way. The comfort and luxury of American cars and trains were indeed emphasized, but so was the modernity of Swedish and Scandinavian ships and airplanes. Commemorators thus demonstrated that technological modernization was a transatlantic and shared phenomenon. Touring the history of colonization and pioneering manifested notions of mutual modernity, with the delegations and transportation methods echoing social, economical, political, as well as technological progress. The means of transportation thus accounted for a temporal shift in the tours as reenactments, salvaging the travels from being buried in the past.

༄

No single event is more important to cross-border commemorations than delegation tours. The relationship between the travels of delegations and the celebrations staged during commemorations are dialectic, the former often directing the design and magnitude of the latter. But the delegations are also in themselves commemorative statements. In the cases under study, they represented both the present and the past; they were signs of "nostalgic modernism," to quote Michael Kammen.[105] This duality, it seems, is ingrained in the genre of commemorative traveling, visible in the common notion of following in the footsteps of history. In a literal sense, traveling commemorative delegations are both carriers and producers of memory.

The legitimacy of delegation travels is, however, not always based on following the actual routes of selected people from the past. Rather, commemorators in the 1938 and 1948 celebrations followed the contemporary traces of immigration, which were grounded in claims of persistent and unbroken racial genealogies. By seamlessly connecting the history of New Sweden to that of mass immigration, the reproduction of Swedish blood in America was explained and given historical depth. These two dimensions worked in tandem to demonstrate the contemporary meaning of the settler histories at the foundation of the commemorations.

By declaring the delegations to be modern in their constitution and through their means of transportation, their travels manifested a rupture in time, demonstrating through the persistence of blood in the contemporary United States that the Swedes were the victors of settler colonial history. These tours celebrated the triumphs of settlement; they represented its permanence and the settlers' successful establishment of civilizations that replaced Native American societies. The manifestation of the delegation-as-the-modern-state, traveling in a modern way through the United States, positioned Swedes at the forefront of a historical and a contemporary hierarchy of race in North America. Representations of settlement, in and through the travels, spread across two temporalities, shaping history as well as the acts of the present, thus contributing to the promotion of mutual transatlantic modernities.

CHAPTER 5

Bonds of Swedishness

Festivals and the Mending of Cultural Differences

After the Swedish delegation arrived in Philadelphia in 1938, one of the first items on the program was a Swedish-American parade and festival. Costumed and uniformed Swedish-American societies lined the mile-long route from the Navy Yard down Broad Street to the American Swedish Historical Museum in FDR Park. The parade was followed by a "typical Swedish Lawn Festival" in front of the museum, with participants from across the United States. The event was arranged by the Swedish-American commission specifically as a forum for interactions between visiting Swedes and Swedish Americans. The idea was to "show our friends from Sweden that we have not forgotten the things that we learned in our youths—that we still know how to wear Swedish folk costumes, do the Swedish folk dances, sing Swedish songs and other forms of entertainment." The parade and the lawn festival were, according to the commission, "our big opportunity to show our guests from Sweden how closely we have held to the customs and traditions of our native Sweden."[1] The lawn festival was an occasion for Swedish Americans to demonstrate to Sweden that they had retained cultural traditions of dance, dress, and music. The cultural manifestations drew their strength and meaning from being made at a cross-border celebration, where the members of the Swedish delegation could watch and legitimize the tradition's authenticity.

FIGURE 13. Crown Prince Gustaf Adolf took time to speak to Swedish Americans in the audience during the festival on the grounds of the Minnesota State Fair in Minneapolis–Saint Paul on July 17, 1938. Photo courtesy of the American Swedish Institute.

Festivals are events that resonate with concerns of the community. They are public and participatory and based on individual performance. Generally designed by cultural leaders, they are intended to both cater to and demand participation from the broader community. In the United States, the twentieth-century practice of arranging indoor and outdoor festivals, pageants, and parades had deep roots. After the United States gained independence, festivals became an important means of affirming unity and an emerging American nationalism. By 1777, the citizens of Boston, Philadelphia, and other cities were already taking part in celebrations of Independence Day, and public fêtes—or "ratification celebrations"—were staged, partly as political propaganda and partly to instill national unity, during the ongoing debates over the Constitution in 1788.[2] As immigration from Europe increased in the late nineteenth century, festivals became an attractive tool for manifestations of both ethnic belonging and allegiance to the new American homeland. It seems as if every immigrant group in the United States at some point has arranged such an event, including, for example, repeated Saint Patrick's Day celebrations (which began as Protestant events in 1762 but were taken over by Catholic Irish in the 1820s) and Italian-American Columbus Day parades.[3]

The dominant interpretation of the notion of ethnic festivals in the United States suggests that they are expressions of something "unabashedly American."[4] In recent years, however, an increasing amount of scholarship on immigration and on cultural memory has emphasized the transnational dimensions of ethnicity. Immigrant communities engage in networks and have social and economic ties across borders, thus showing that ethnic maintenance is not nationally confined but a process of hybridization.[5] As Daron Olson has demonstrated in a study of Norwegian-American commemorations and ethnic mythmaking, "Norwegian Americans created myths that were designed for a Norwegian context as well as an American context."[6] Studies by Donna Gabaccia, Dirk Hoerder, and Adam Walaszek have likewise shown that the late-nineteenth and early-twentieth-century mass migrations of Germans, Italians, and Poles were linked to nation building in the homelands. For these countries, emigration was "a vital contribution to national strength."[7]

Proceeding from this transnational understanding of ethnicity, and as demonstrated by the 1938 Lawn Festival in Philadelphia, we can see that commemorative festivals have also been important in the promotion of cross-border relations. The public festivals in 1938 and 1948 were most often organized at indoor or outdoor stadiums and arenas and frequently drew audiences numbering in the tens of thousands. They were celebrations for the people, but they were also forums for physical interactions between local American communities and the visiting representatives of Sweden. Together, Americans, Swedish Americans, and Swedes joined in celebrating a mutual history going back to the seventeenth-century colonists in New Sweden and the nineteenth-century pioneers in the Midwest. Supposedly, these histories had established a link between Swedes in Sweden and Swedes in the United States. This bond contained grains of conflict since Swedishness had developed differently on either side of the Atlantic. Yet everyone could gather around the celebration of transatlantic Swedishness through claims that its essence was harbored in qualities inherent in the allegedly common blood.

So That All Can Come Free to See

Of all the events arranged during the commemorations, the festivals drew by far the largest attendance. They were arranged in every major city that the Swedish delegations visited.[8] The 1938 tercentenary also presented a "water pageant" and fireworks display on the Schuylkill River near Fairmount Park in Philadelphia, an event that drew at least 100,000 people. (Other reports estimated attendance at 400,000, which the Pennsylvania commission termed "one of the largest crowds ever gathered in the history of Philadelphia if not the entire United States.")[9] The largest audiences in both 1938 and 1948 came as the Swedish delegations traveled to the Midwest, with massive crowds gathering at the celebrations in Chicago and Minneapolis–Saint Paul. When the 1938 delegation arrived in the Twin Cities, a quarter of a million people lined the route of the procession, with about 70,000 people attending a celebration at the grounds of the Minnesota State Fair. In the words of the Swedish crown prince, it was "by far the largest and finest reception I have had in America."[10] The public festivals were a chance for all Americans—not only those of Swedish descent—to see European royalty.[11]

Crown Prince Gustaf Adolf, Crown Princess Louise, Prince Bertil, and the other delegation members were the honored guests at every

FIGURE 14. Roughly 70,000 people gathered at the grounds of the Minnesota State Fair to see pageantry and to hear the Swedish crown prince speak at the lectern. Less than a third of the audience is visible in this picture. Photo courtesy of the American Swedish Institute.

festival they attended. The royals were pictured at the center of the poster for the 1938 festival at Chicago's Soldier Field, and the names of Prince Bertil and the Swedish delegation appeared ahead of the names of any local organizer or official in the 1948 Minnesota State Fair souvenir program.[12] These details demonstrate both the centrality of royals in the manifestation of Swedishness in the United States and the important role of the Swedish representatives during these events.

In many festivals, the Swedish delegations were the focus of the entire event. In Minneapolis–Saint Paul and Chicago, for example, organizers seated the delegations and royalty on stages in front of the audience. At the Chicago Stadium in 1948, the delegation was literally seated at center stage, along with President Truman and members of the Swedish-American commission. The stages for the pageant performances were placed on the far sides of the platform. At a 1938 religious

FIGURE 15. The Chicago committee of the American Swedish Tercentenary Association advertised its main activity, a festival at Soldier Field Stadium, with pageantry, military parades, and—most importantly—Swedish royals. Source: Swedish National Archives in Arninge.

meeting in Minneapolis–Saint Paul, a newspaper reported that "as many eyes were on the royal party as on the ministers."[13]

The festivals were opportunities for every interested person to participate in the celebration. The intent was that no one should be excluded based on class or economic standing, which meant that admission prices were kept at a minimum.[14] The discussions about the celebration to be arranged in New York City in 1938 provide a good illustration of the fundamental idea behind the festivals. The initial plans for that celebration included the unveiling of a monument to the Swedish-American Civil War engineer John Ericsson's warship, the ironclad *Monitor*, in Greenpoint, Brooklyn. It soon became clear, however, that the monument would not be finished in time for the commemoration. Instead, organizers suggested replacing the unveiling ceremony with a stadium concert.[15] This idea was supported by the Swedish commission but questioned by Oscar Solbert, the chair of the Swedish-American commission. According to him, it would be an insufficient substitute for the unveiling ceremony: "In each Swedish American Day on the tour, one outdoor mass meeting is planned so that all Swedish Americans and Americans can come free to see and hear the Crown Prince." Organizers needed to create such an opportunity; and the concert, though it was a good idea, could "not take the place of a daytime mass meeting."[16] Unlike the more exclusive indoor events, such as luncheons and banquets, the festivals were events for the average citizen.

After the two commemorations had ended, organizers emphasized the ways in which they had strengthened transatlantic relationships. According to Conrad Bergendoff, the chair of the 1948 Swedish-American commission, the Swedish Pioneer Centennial showed that "a new day has dawned for the relationship" between Sweden and Swedish America.[17] The Swedish embassy in Washington, D.C., referring to a statement by an unnamed American scholar, emphasized that "the jubilee has had its greatest significance for the first, second and third generation Swedish Americans" and declared that "this was in his [the scholar's] opinion almost the most important [aspect], for the youngest generation, who no longer has any memories or other personal bonds, connecting them to Sweden."[18]

In lengthy reports, Swedish-American newspapers marveled at the scale of the celebrations and their successful performance. According to the Minneapolis-based *Svenska Amerikanska Posten*—which detailed the program, speeches, and scenes of thousands of Swedish Americans in attendance—the Twin Cities celebration was "the world's largest Swedish fete." (The newspaper also praised the Swedish-American character, noting that "despite the massive crowds we did not observe a single intoxicated" person.)[19] The festivals were opportunities for the Swedish-American community to come together in grand manifestations that boosted their ethnic pride, celebrating Swedishness with representatives of their (or their ancestors') old homeland.

The ideological foundation for these celebrations of Swedishness was located in American nationalism. In the often-quoted words of Richard Hofstadter, "it has been our fate as a nation not to have ideologies, but to be one."[20] The civic nationalism of the United States means that the nation consists of all people who voluntarily subscribe to the idea of a national political creed.[21] These often abstract ideas—of freedom, equality, justice, and the pursuit of happiness—are exemplified in the Declaration of Independence and the Constitution. This form of nationalism made it possible for European immigrants and their descendants to voluntarily assert and express belonging to old homelands without challenging their allegiance to America. As long as they embraced the American political creed, they were free to express other cultural, linguistic, and historical belongings.[22]

Of course, American civic nationalism has, since the dawn of the republic, been paired with racial nationalism, as epitomized by the Naturalization Act of 1790, which granted citizenship only to free white persons. During Reconstruction, the Fourteenth Amendment of 1868 extended citizenship to African Americans, but they were soon disenfranchised again in the South through measures such as grandfather clauses and polling taxes. Non-white immigrants remained ineligible for citizenship. With the Chinese Exclusion Act of 1882, Chinese immigrants were barred from entering the country. The demarcation of whiteness continued in the early twentieth century with the U.S. Supreme Court decisions *Ozawa v. the United States* (1922) and *United States v. Thind* (1923), which labeled Japanese Americans and

Indian Americans as racially nonwhite and thus ineligible for naturalization. Although eastern and southern European immigrants in the 1930s and 1940s were eligible for immigration and naturalization, they suffered discrimination on the American labor market. As David Roediger has shown, Italians, Poles, Hungarians, and others—the object of racial slurs such as *dagos, guineas, greasers,* and *hunkies*—were racialized as "inbetween peoples" during the early years of the twentieth century. They were seen as white legally but not socially.[23] Yet even as the fulfillment of the ideal of American civic nationalism was complicated for many people in the United States, and outright impossible for others, it had since the late-nineteenth century been relatively easy for Swedish Americans.

The commemorative landscape was also more challenging for groups whose homelands were at war with the United States or were controlled by totalitarian regimes. This included Germany during both world wars, Italy in the 1930s, and all nations of the Eastern Bloc during the Cold War. When members of a German-American association in 1915 erected a statue of Continental Army general Baron Von Steuben at Valley Forge, public pressure soon forced them to remove it.[24] During the Cold War, the Assembly of Captive European Nations, a coalition of representatives from countries in central and eastern Europe that were under Soviet domination, proclaimed fiftieth anniversaries of independence in the Baltic States in 1967–68 and in Czechoslovakia and Poland in 1968–69. These observances, supported by members of the U.S. Congress, were specifically organized as Cold War manifestations against the ancestral homelands.[25] Similar public sentiments or political situations were, unsurprisingly, not a factor in the Swedish and American commemorations.

Unlike earlier Swedish-American celebrations, the festivals of the 1930s and 1940s involved cooperation between local committees and the visiting delegations. Their interactions permeated festival performances. A parallel to these celebrations was the 1939 visit of Norway's Crown Prince Olav and Crown Princess Märtha, for which Norwegian Americans arranged festivals throughout the country. The two-month tour drew massive turnouts, and the royals used those occasions to promote "greater recognition of the ties between Norway and Norwegian Americans," emphasizing that Norwegians on both sides of the Atlantic shared history and core values.[26] As in the Norwegian case, the Swedish representatives were always the festivals' promoted guests of honor: they were the center of attention, and their speeches constituted the main attraction of the programs. The festivals would have been qualitatively different events without their presence.

Swedishness and the Frictions of Modernity

The programs at the majority of commemorative festivals in 1938 and 1948 focused on performances of Swedish folk dances and songs. Several festivals during the tercentenary featured repertoires with a Swedish national romantic theme, including songs by the Swedish composers Hugo Alfvén and Gunnar Wennerberg—especially Wennerberg's "Hear Us, Svea" (*Hör oss, Svea*), which was a recurring piece.[27] Such patriotic Swedish songs expressed passionate feelings for the homeland and were commonly sung in Swedish America. This pattern was repeated during the centennial, when the majority of the stadium festivals centered on Swedish dance and choral music.[28]

When the 1938 delegation appeared at the Minnesota State Fair in Minneapolis–Saint Paul, a banner over the stage read, "*Sverige Sverige, Våra Fäders Land: Välkomna till Svenskarnas Dag och Minnesota*" (Sweden, Sweden, Our Father's Land: Welcome to the Swedes' Day and Minnesota).[29] This greeting was aimed more at the foreign guests than at the large Swedish-American crowd who faced the stage, most of whom did not need to be welcomed to Minnesota in the Swedish language. For many—perhaps the majority—who attended this event, Sweden was the land of their parents or grandparents, not the land of their own birth.[30] The festivals reflected the separation that had arisen between Sweden and Swedish America as a result of the mass migration.

Beginning in the 1920s, the large-scale influx of people immigrating to the United States who had come of age in Sweden was on the decline. By 1938, the majority of the Swedish-American community was separated from Sweden through what the historian H. Arnold Barton has called "the great divide." The end of the mass migration made Swedish ethnicity in America a matter less of lived experience and more of conscious construction—through, for example, participation in ethnic organizations and celebrations. By the 1920s, as Barton writes, "Swedish Americans appeared in Swedish eyes increasingly as relics of the past, ever more out of touch with modern Sweden."[31] Traditional music and costumed folk dancers were common in ethnic parades and festivities in Swedish America, but they corresponded more with the nineteenth-century country that the emigrants had left than they did with the Sweden of the mid-twentieth century.[32] This difference was more marked for Swedish Americans than for many other ethnic groups. An example is Norwegian-American ethnicity. While being culturally similar, Norwegians on both sides of the Atlantic retained a stronger folkloristic and national romantic dimension in the twentieth century, a fact largely explained by a more fervent Norwegian nationalism spurred by the country's 1905 independence from Sweden.[33]

In writing about the latter part of the twentieth century, Barbro Klein has noted that the popularity of folk dance and folk music in the United States prompts many people in Sweden to say that Swedish Americans "are more Swedish than in Sweden." Meanwhile, some Swedish Americans see the erosion of cultural traditions in Sweden as signs of cultural deterioration.[34] While cultural traditions informed by national romanticism—such as folk dancing and folk costumes—continue to be central aspects in the maintenance of Swedish ethnicity in the United States, they became increasingly marginalized in Sweden by the 1920s. The prevalent nationalism in Sweden since the nineteenth century had been romantic and patriotic, focusing on the nation's glorious history, sacralized images of its nature, and the preservation of folk culture. This traditionalist culture would in subsequent decades persist among cultural conservatives. Following the societal changes of the 1920s and the political success of social democracy in the 1930s, another form of nationalism developed that soon became dominant.[35] It emphasized national integration and progress, epitomized by the concept of "the People's Home" (*Folkhemmet*). The nation of the People's Home was a place that could be improved through, for instance, interventions of social hygiene, and it was inhabited by a racially defined people.[36] This was a representation of the nation that focused on modernity rather than a romantic and patriotic past.

The different notions of Swedishness in Sweden and the United States were expressed in diverging ideas about the cross-border commemorative festivals. For instance, at the 1948 parade in Rockford, Illinois, a local newspaper declared that this was an event in which "Parade Units Display Old Country Lore for Visitors from Sweden."[37] In the words of a Swedish journalist, however, the parade made a "hilarious impression with bearded Vikings and Wild West cowboys in an anachronistic mixture." It was interesting to observe, the journalist continued, that "the taste of the [18]80s still lives on among the Swedish Americans despite the modernization."[38] The changes of Swedish nationalism underscore the differences of the romantic and patriotic historical representations that dominated the festivals. When representatives of Sweden were part of these performances, they participated in legitimizing ideas about Swedishness common in Swedish America. Although different notions of cultural modernity were a factor defining the great divide, the commemorative festivals were events that significantly downplayed these differences.

Religion was another prominent feature of the festivals, which likewise was defined through different ideas about modernity. Several festivals began and ended with religious invocations, while some of the more secular programs were preceded by religious services. In Minnesota in 1938, a separate religious service was held in the State Fair Hippodrome, an indoor arena, and performed by ministers from several Protestant denominations: Baptists, Evangelicals, Methodists, Covenants, and Lutherans.[39] A similar multidenominational service was arranged during the centennial in the large Moody Church in downtown Chicago. This "Centennial Memorial Service" was intended to display "a serious aspect in recognition of the spiritual heritage that has been left us by the pioneers."[40]

The religiously informed festivals were intended to commemorate the spiritual legacies of the Swedish settlers, whether they were seventeenth-century colonists or nineteenth-century pioneers. At an All-Lutheran convention arranged by the Augustana Synod in

FIGURE 16. The Swedish delegation, President Truman, members of the Swedish-American commission, and other dignitaries were seated at center stage at the Chicago Stadium festival on June 6, 1948. Seated behind the lectern, the dignitaries were surrounded by the orchestra and flanked by pageantry scenes on the far left and far right. A massive choir of 1,600 people filled the stands behind the stage. Courtesy of the Swenson Swedish Immigration Research Center, Augustana College, Rock Island, Illinois.

Philadelphia in 1938, Conrad Bergendoff, adhering to his idea about the inseparability of Swedish heritage and Lutheranism, maintained that the importance of the New Sweden colony should be understood through its religious significance: "The Delaware Tercentenary celebrates ultimately a *religious* power, and commemorates a people gathered around their churches." For Bergendoff, it was "as a chapter of American church history that the full meaning and glory of the Delaware settlement are revealed."[41] The fact that this religious dimension was downplayed in the tercentenary was what eventually prompted the Augustana Synod to arrange the Pioneer Centennial. As a consequence, the spiritual legacy of the Swedish pioneers was front and center at several centennial festivities.[42]

The most elaborate festival program of the centennial was the celebration at Chicago Stadium. The show centered on musical performances, a historical pageant, and speeches by prominent people, who included, in addition to President Truman and Prince Bertil, the renowned poet and author Carl Sandburg. At least 2,000 participants performed in the show, including a choral group of about 1,600 people. The Chicago Symphony Orchestra under the leadership of the Swedish director Hilding Rosenberg performed Rosenberg's own opera *The Voyage to America*. The show ended with "The Hallelujah Chorus" from Handel's *Messiah*.[43]

In a newspaper interview before the festival, Vilas Johnson, the chair of the local organizing committee, commented on the program. The show, he said, would center on "the different aspects of Swedishness from 1848 onwards." He told the reporter that he did not want the popular Wennerberg song "Hear Us, Svea" on the program because it "belongs irrevocably to a time with a sense for the bombastic." Instead, Johnson preferred to have "A Mighty Fortress Is Our God" conclude the festival.[44] This was not a national romantic song but a religious and specifically Lutheran one. The song that organizers eventually chose to end the festival—from the *Messiah*—fulfilled the same demands and underlined the importance of Protestantism to the centennial organizers. In short, the history represented through songs and pageantry at the Chicago Stadium festival focused less on national romantic character and more on the spiritual aspects of Swedish settlement.

The religious dimension of the festivals was affected by different ideas among Swedish and Swedish-American commemorators. Since the late nineteenth century, Sweden had become increasingly secularized, as evidenced by the abolition of the teaching of Lutheranism in elementary schools as well as a decrease in church attendance. With few exceptions, every Swede was still automatically enrolled in the Lutheran state church at birth, but the midcentury pattern was, according to the sociologist Richard Tomasson, "belonging but not believing."[45] Yet while secularization was increasing in Sweden in the 1930s and 1940s, religious values and practices remained important among Swedish Americans. From the start, religion had been a significant element of the Swedish mass emigration to the United States. Compulsory membership in the Church of Sweden as well as laws that until 1858 outlawed religious meetings outside of the church created an additional impetus—or, for some people, a primary one—to emigrate to a land of religious freedom. In the nineteenth and early twentieth centuries, the maintenance of Swedish-American ethnicity continued to be greatly influenced by the work of religious denominations, of which the most important was the Augustana Synod. Before World War I, the synod included half of all Swedish Americans who were involved in any ethnic organization.[46] By the 1920s, the relation between religion and ethnicity had become less prominent in many Swedish-American organizations. Still, the ethnic denominations had influence over the Swedish-American community to a degree that exceeded their membership rates.[47] At the opening of the Swedish Pioneer Centennial, there was, in other words, a marked religious divide between Swedish America and Sweden. As a consequence, it was primarily representatives of Swedish America who nurtured the religious aspects of the commemorations.

One of the critics of the pioneers' spiritual legacy was a Swedish delegation member named Gunnar Hirdman, the vice-chancellor of the Workers' Educational Association and a prominent figure in the adult education movement in Sweden. In a newspaper interview Hirdman expressed his views of the Chicago Stadium festival. The program was much too long, he thought, and the organizers had included "too much religion" in the celebration.[48] It is noteworthy that except for the Swedish archbishop Gunnar Westin, who was a professor of church history and a good friend of the Augustana Synod, no member of the Swedish delegation officially expressed any appreciation of the pioneers' spiritual legacy.

The Chicago Stadium program also included a performance by a Swedish gymnastic troop, the Sofia Girls (*Sofiaflickorna*), whom the Swedish commission had dispatched to the United States. The all-women group specialized in performances that, in contrast to nineteenth-century preferences for militaristic and mechanical moves, focused on rhythmic and organic movements. Commenting on their performance at Chicago Stadium, Hirdman said that it had been "everything but appropriate to let the Sofia Girls promote physical culture in a smoky venue in the middle of the night."[49] His conception of nighttime aside (the program had begun at 8 P.M.), it is clear that the Swedish commission members saw the Sofia Girls as an extended representation of the modern Swedish state, describing it as "excellent propaganda for Swedish physical education."[50] The display of physical fitness corresponded to the prevailing idea that physical education was an important aspect of the country's modernization.[51] Hirdman's praise of modern physical culture and criticism of religious legacies illustrate the frictions involved when commemorators joined in cross-border celebrations of pioneer history. There was no stated opposition to the performance of national romantic dance and music, but the emphasis on the pioneers' religious character highlighted the different notions of Swedish and Swedish-American modernity.

The Migration as a Legacy and a Thing of the Past

Since the nineteenth century, many immigrants and their descendants in the United States had celebrated histories that they believed would validate their ethnic group's rightful place in their new homeland. Some of these histories showed that the immigrant group "was here first," or took part in the founding of the United States, or had a deep ideological relationship to the new homeland. The myths comprised a range of pre-Columbian histories, including Scandinavian-American myths about Leif Erikson's landfall in Vinland in the year 1000 (which, some proponents claimed, was located in New England), Mexican-American legends of Aztlán, and stories about the Polish explorer John of Colno. Anglo-Americans also had such mythical stories, of which the *Mayflower* was most influential. The Pilgrim mythology inspired other ethnic groups to promote similar narratives of foundational exodus, including the Jewish-American story of *St. Catarina*'s arrival in New Amsterdam in 1655 and, of course, the 1638 arrival of *Kalmar Nyckel* to the Delaware Valley.[52]

In the celebrations of Swedish settlement in America, the claims of individual migrant contributions to the United States—and, by inference, to contemporary Swedish and American relations—were largely made as settler colonial legacies. The actual connection between the seventeenth-century New Sweden colony and the nineteenth-century immigration was feeble, as the crown prince noted in his speech at the Minnesota State Fair in 1938. He maintained, however, that there had nonetheless been connections, of which the most important was a history of land claims. "The North American soil," he said, "has to a not insignificant extent been cultivated by Swedes, who have built their homes and hearths, roads and cities. In hundredfold greater numbers, they have continued the Delaware Swede's cultivation of the new land."[53] In other words, while a variety of successful people had contributed their individual sacrifices and achievements to the nation, Swedish immigrants as a collective had contributed the process of land taking and settlement.

Although most centennial histories included narratives about "Virgin Lands," commemorators also made a point of including representations of Native Americans and their interactions with the Swedish settlers. A 1948 pageant in Rockford began with a scene in which "The friendly Indian," greeted the first Swedish settlers in the Midwest.[54] According to the Swedish commission, the scene represented a history of "the first settlement and the arrival of the first pioneers and [their] battles with Indian tribes."[55] A parade in Des Moines some days later included traditional American sections such as parade queens and drum corps, girls in folk costumes and Swedish scout leaders on a visit to the United States, but also "an honest-to-God Indian chief."[56] As the historian David Glassberg has shown, it was common for parades and pageants to begin with a scene depicting the meeting between Natives and the first white settlers, and it was likewise common for these scenes to be played by all-white casts.[57] The Des Moines parade's inclusion of an actual representative from a tribal community (albeit under unknown circumstances) was an exception. With or without Native American participants, the representation of encounters between indigenous peoples and Swedish pioneers in the nineteenth-century Midwest anchored the histories of a Swedish presence in America.

It was true that the Swedish settlers who moved into the Midwest in the decades after 1840 lived in close proximity to Native Americans. Their relationship was sometimes shaped by conflict but often by exchanges. An influential encounter took place during the 1862 U.S.-Dakota War. Forced onto a reservation in southern Minnesota where they faced starvation, members of the Dakota tribe attacked white settlers throughout the Minnesota River Valley in August 1862. The war ended with their surrender to the U.S. army in late September and the subsequent mass execution of thirty-eight Dakota men in Mankato, Minnesota. It is estimated that five hundred settlers were killed during the war—some of them Swedish immigrants—together with an unknown number of Dakotas.

Generally, however, everyday encounters between white homesteaders and Native American were not violent but often shaped by cooperation, trade, and the sharing of food.[58] An example of the complexities of the encounters took place at the Spirit Lake Dakota Indian Reservation in North Dakota. The reservation, established in 1867 in the aftermath of the U.S.-Dakota War, was the home of the tribe's Sisseton and Wahpeton bands. In 1887, it was opened to white homesteaders through the General Allotment Act, also known as the Dawes Act. The reservation was divided into individual properties allotted to the Dakotas, while the "surplus" land was made available to white settlers. In the coming decades, immigrants, most of them from Sweden and Norway, flowed onto the reservation and soon outnumbered the Dakotas. By 1929, tribal members owned only a quarter of the land. As a consequence of the settlers' land taking, Swedish Americans and Dakotas came to live, quite literally, next door to one another on the reservation. Although their social and cultural lives initially were segregated, they engaged and mingled with each other through trade, agricultural labor, land leases, and intermarriages.[59] Thus, the realities of the past were considerably more complex than the commemorative representations of friendly greetings or Native battles.

Commemorators represented history as not only a continuing legacy but also a contrast to the present; they asserted that emigration really belonged to the past. A prominent feature of many Swedish delegation speeches was the juxtaposition of contemporary Sweden with nineteenth-century Sweden, the country that the migrants had left. Yet even as this contrast was emphasized, the delegates also stressed that the country was fundamentally the same. This was the gist of Prince Bertil's 1938 speech in Avon, Massachusetts: "Much has changed since You or Your forefathers left Sweden. We have had a lot of work done [in Sweden] during the last decades. Sweden is a state in progress. But the Swedish country itself is the same, with its vast forests, its clear lakes, and sea-surrounded coasts. And in a thousand Swedish homes warm thoughts are sent to relatives and friends in the country beyond the ocean."[60] The nature and the people in Sweden, according to the prince, were the same as when the immigrants had left their old homeland. What had changed was Swedish society.

The crown prince's addresses in Chicago and Minneapolis–Saint Paul elaborated on this theme. The Sweden of today offered rich opportunities, he said at the Minnesota State Fair, and had in some areas even surpassed progress in the United States: "But I know very well that this was not nearly the situation during the 1800s, when the flow of the emigration to America was at its strongest." Gustaf Adolf spoke extensively about Sweden's improvements in farming, a topic that reflected the character of the supposed audience. Moreover, according to him, Sweden's democratic institutions had developed, and its current school system ensured that "each and everyone nowadays has the opportunities to reach as far as possible on the social scale"—an explicit contrast between contemporary Sweden and the nineteenth century. Sweden today was, Gustaf Adolf said, "really something in which we all can feel pride and satisfaction."[61]

It is significant that the parts of these speeches that concerned Sweden's modernization—including the quotations from the Massachusetts and Minnesota events—were delivered in Swedish, not English. Swedish was, in fact, woven into the delegates' speeches in several cities throughout the United States, most often in places that had significant Swedish-American communities, such as New York, Chicago, Omaha, and Rockford. The choice to incorporate Swedish should be understood in light of the festivals' general celebration of Swedishness in the United States. Use of the language had, by the 1930s, declined significantly in many areas of America. There had been seventy-two Swedish-language newspapers in the United States in 1915 with a combined circulation of more than 650,000 copies; by 1930, forty-three newspapers remained with a circulation of about 360,000. The same pattern was clear in Swedish-language church services, which began disappearing from the early 1900s through the 1930s.[62] But while the use of Swedish in official settings declined, a substantial number of people in the United States claimed the language as a mother tongue at least until the mid-1900s.[63] Likewise, Sweden maintained an interest in promoting Swedish abroad—for example, through government-sponsored lectureships in Swedish at U.S. universities.[64] Language maintenance was an important aspect in the Swedish-American community; and though interest in this maintenance differed, the cross-border commemorations enabled Swedes from both sides of the Atlantic to celebrate their mutual heritage language.

The crown prince's speech at Soldier Field in Chicago was similar to the one in Minnesota, with the majority of it given in Swedish. Instead of farming, he focused on the iron and steel industry, the forest industry, and waterpower as well as on improved infrastructure and increased salary levels. These were topics that, again, resonated with the expected audience. Without holding back on the superlatives, Gustaf Adolf claimed that "a more democratic country [than Sweden] . . . can hardly be found anywhere else on earth."[65] Such statements from the leaders of the delegation centered on representations of Swedish modernization, on the movement from the desolate darkness of the nineteenth century to the progressive light of the contemporary welfare state.

These kinds of representations had been part of a critique of Swedish society since the early 1900s, one aimed at correcting the shortcomings that had encouraged people to emigrate. Although Swedish conservative and liberal reformists differed in their proposed solutions, the majority agreed that the country did need to modernize. Industrialization was said to have caused increased mortality and drunkenness, miserable living and working conditions, famine and poverty. In the words of the historian Martin Alm, the narrative about the causes of emigration was "a question about progress vis-à-vis regression, which only could be solved through Swedish modernization."[66] This was also the narrative promoted by the Social Democratic Party, which dominated Swedish politics for most of the twentieth century, beginning in the 1930s. According to this narrative—a history that eventually became part of the nation's self-image—the social, political, and economic destitution of the nineteenth century came to an end in the 1930s when it was replaced by the welfare state.[67] The representation of Sweden's modernization thus rested on a rupture between the old and the new society and on the idea of a steady progress. The history of emigration was used to epitomize this rupture.

Ten years later, in 1948, the Swedish delegation made similar statements in several festivals throughout the Midwest. In his speech at Chicago Stadium, Prince Bertil acknowledged that there had been "compelling reasons to force a man to give up his home and his country." Many who emigrated might have felt bitterness toward Sweden, but the emigration was now "a thing of the past" and luckily the feelings of resentment had not prevailed in Swedish America:

> Sweden of the last century was a poor country. Of course there were, as in most European countries, much social and economic injustice, an uneven distribution of wealth and education, class barriers, political inequalities. . . . [The emigrants] went because there was not enough arable land for them, because industry was in its infant stage and could not give them work and income, because modern technic [sic] had not enabled the nation to mobilize the natural resources that still slumbered in the forests, in the mountains, in the waterfalls, in the brains of unborn scientists and engineers. . . . We know that the emigration, however painful a process it was, served to carry Sweden over a crisis of poverty and overpopulation that might otherwise have proved impossible to overcome by peaceful means and legal reforms. It was a safety valve, if such a one was needed.[68]

The emigration had forced many in Sweden to think constructively about how Swedish society could be developed. The letters migrants sent back to Sweden had influenced religious movements, temperance movements, and the course of democratization. In this process, as Prince Bertil explained, the emigration had benefited the building of modern Sweden. This was an image of Sweden's modernization that was also promoted by American commemorators. "Sweden's generous contributions to America of the cream of her manpower has made both countries stronger," U.S. Senator Edwin C. Johnson of Colorado said in a speech in Detroit. Sweden had become one of the most progressive democracies in the world, and the senator claimed that it was the "influence on Sweden of the migrants she sent forth [that] helped accomplish this fortunate phenomenon."[69]

Commemorators claimed that Sweden had progressed through a break with the past and had now become modern. The message was that the nineteenth-century seeds of modern Sweden finally were in bloom. While the crown prince's speeches in 1938 had underlined how Sweden was now different from the Sweden that was familiar to the immigrants, commemorators from both Sweden and the United States in 1948 emphasized that this change actually had occurred thanks in part to the Swedish immigrants in America. The American festival audiences were in this way included as key agents in the modernization of Sweden. By 1948, the emigrants and their ancestors received full acknowledgment from the land of their ancestors—along with suggestions that it nowadays was a pleasant country to which one, presumably, could return.

These statements, aimed directly at the Swedish-American community, stood in stark contrast to the anti-emigration discourse proliferating in Sweden at the turn of the twentieth century. Although there were differences between notions of Swedishness among homeland Swedes and Swedish Americans, possible frictions were downplayed in the attempt to mend cultural differences. Swedish Americans had been described as a national problem, been reframed as overseas assets, and were now represented as a link between Swedish and American modernity.

The Qualities of Blood Lineage

When President Roosevelt spoke at The Rocks in 1938, his address immediately struck a personal tone. He described his own association with the New Sweden colony: his ancestor, William Beekman, had in 1658–63 been a governor with jurisdiction over the colony's remaining residents. This statement was followed by applause, but the loudest cheers came after the president said that he descended from a New Sweden colonist, Martinus Hoffman, and declared, "I am also proud that Swedish blood runs in my veins."[70] Although Roosevelt was not present at the festivities in order to embody an actual ancestor from New Sweden, he did stress his Swedish genealogy, his personal connection to the colony, and thus his investment in the commemorated history.

The representations of Swedishness and of Swedish contributions to America received a different and deeper meaning in a context in which the organizers, the audience, and most of the participants were either immigrants or immigrant descendants. Festival speakers frequently addressed their comments directly toward the audience of Swedish Americans, emphasizing how "you" had made contributions to the United States. Talking to his "countrymen" in Chicago, the crown prince opened the Swedish part of his Soldier Field speech by stating, "It is sometimes so wonderfully easy to speak, namely, when one has many and significant [things] in common with those to whom one is speaking." He then addressed the audience directly, describing how "you" (*ni* and *eder*) had contributed to the development of the United States: "I represent the public opinion of Sweden as a whole when I tell you how pleased we are over there every time we hear of your success and loyalty in your adopted country."[71]

The point of these statements was to emphasize how specific audience members or their specific ancestors had contributed to the building of America through settlement and immigration. These were not general, sweeping declarations but ones intended directly for the ears of the listeners. "I have been told," Gustaf Adolf said in the Swedish portion of his Minnesota State Fair speech, "that the Swedish emigrants and their descendants in the United States and Canada have cleared as much land as the Swedes [did] in their own country." This fact, he claimed, united Swedes and Swedish Americans and was a testament to the "constructive cultural work that the Swedish stock" had done in America.[72] In this statement, the Swedish Americans in the audience were represented as embodying a successful settler colonial legacy. They were present in the 1930s and 1940s as builders of a society that had not existed a century earlier in the Midwest.[73]

The notion of historical embodiment was exemplified by fictional and factual individuals. In a 1948 speech at an outdoor stadium in Rockford, Prince Bertil told a joke about an immigrant man from a small village in southern Sweden. The Swede arrived in Rockford and was met by "a big Negro" who spoke to him in Swedish. When asked how he could speak Swedish, the man replied that "in this town we come from Sweden all of us. But it's very hot, you know. Just wait a year or two and you'll look as I do." The Swede was "scared stiff" and quickly returned to Sweden. (This ending, Bertil added, might have been invented, as the Swede possibly stayed to run a successful farm or business.) After looking around the stadium, Bertil concluded that the fear of the immigrant man was unnecessary as the people looked "very much the same" as in Sweden.[74] His racialized description of the immigrant man served to circumscribe the physical features of what a Swede is, thus representing a biological dimension of Swedishness.

The audience at some of the centennial festivals did not have to merely visualize the physical pioneer legacy. In cities such as Minneapolis–Saint Paul, Omaha, and Moline, the pioneers were also represented by actual immigrants. The Omaha program featured a presentation involving the "Oldest Pioneers" and in Moline thirty of the area's "oldest Swedish settlers" were seated on stage.[75] The *Minneapolis Sunday Tribune* advertised for a "typical Swedish pioneer" who would be the newspaper's guest at the celebrations and be seated on stage during the Minnesota State Fair festival. The paper requested information about when the person had come to Minnesota (the requirement was before 1900), where he or she had settled, as well as the "hardships" and "advantages" of pioneer life.[76]

The bonds of Swedishness expressed in the celebrations of Swedish settlement were contained within ideas about a particular blood lineage. This idea has been widely nurtured in the United States. It was, for example, present in President Roosevelt's 1944 proclamation of Leif Erikson Day, announced in remembrance of the Viking explorer said to have encountered North America in the year 1000. The proclamation, which was released during the Nazi occupation of Norway, stated, "We hail the Norwegians as our fellow fighters in the sacred cause of democracy. . . . And we greet our own fellow citizens of Leif Erikson's blood, fighting in the battle lines and on the home front."[77] As in the Swedish case, the shared history and values of Norwegians and Americans were framed as a consequence of genealogy.

The discursive source of the connection between ancestry and ethno-racial belonging is the relation between what Werner Sollors refers to as "consent" and "descent."[78] The idea that ethnicity is a consequence of ancestral origins, as opposed to a culturally and socially informed choice, is visible in present-day population estimations of U.S. ethnic groups—for example, in the common statement that there are 40 million people of Irish origin in the United States. As Catherine Nash has pointed out, this figure is based on ethnicity as defined by descent. Nash situates the idea of a connection between blood lineage and character traits in political, social, and cultural discourse in the late nineteenth century as well as in present-day practices and discourses of genetics. Like notions of blood, race, and spirit in the nineteenth century, genes "are commonly understood as the set of inherited instructions that determine all life as well as individual identity."[79] The essentialism of genetics that was present at the turn of the twentieth century remains an influential mode of explanation, enabling the idea of nations as corporeal entities. Although scientific practices have changed from those of anthropometry to those of genetics, from blood to genes, a nearly perpetual notion connects personal character to ancestry.[80]

One of the more unusual of such representations was President Truman's speech at the June 4, 1948, Chicago Stadium festival, where he balanced contemporary politics with an emphasis on the ideological legacy of the pioneers. The chair of the local Chicago committee later claimed that the 1948 centennial was "carried out with no political overtones," yet it ought to have been clear to everyone in the stadium that the president's speech had a political character.[81] Truman's appearance was part of an eighteen-day "non-political inspection tour" around the country; but as the *New York Times* noted, "its obvious purpose was to put Mr. Truman's candidacy for re-election before the grassroots voters in a series of homey back-platform contacts."[82] The event was held at a venue that drew a primarily Republican audience.[83]

Truman began by describing the Swedish immigrants who had been denied a future in Sweden: "To the land-hungry immigrants, the tough prairie sod seemed a golden opportunity and they conquered

FIGURE 17. The speeches by President Truman and Prince Bertil were the main attraction at the 1948 Chicago Stadium festival. Vilas Johnson, the chair of the Chicago committee of the Swedish-American commission, is seated next to Truman, while Conrad Bergendoff and Gösta Oldenburg sit to the right of Prince Bertil. Courtesy of the Swenson Swedish Immigration Research Center, Augustana College, Rock Island, Illinois.

it through hard work." According to him, the Swedish nineteenth-century immigration was one of the "great epics in our history," a reminder of the strength of the nation. The United States had been "a beacon of hope to the oppressed everywhere," a place where people could find democracy, individual liberty, and freedom. Emphasizing how important it was for the United States to stay this way, Truman criticized the Republican Congress for not enacting legislation to admit immigration of Europeans who had been displaced after the war.[84] Two days earlier, the Senate had voted to pass the bill that would eventually become the Displaced Persons Act of 1948. Truman had argued that a "substantial number" of the 800,000 displaced persons in Europe should be admitted to the United States, but the bill allowed the admittance of only 200,000 people during a two-year period. In addition, it included what the president called "crippling amendments" concerning eligibility, such as the requirement that half of those admitted should have agriculture experience, something that effectively excluded most Jews.[85] Referring to the bill in his Chicago speech, Truman exclaimed, "Look at the reward these people are getting for their opposition to communism!" There was, according to him, no danger that these displaced persons would include foreign communist agents or political activists. Rather, the danger of communism lay "in those areas of American life where the promise of democracy remains unfulfilled." It was a belief in freedom and equality that made America strong, and he underlined that Americans "inherit that belief from the pioneers—Swedish and others—who settled this great Nation. . . . Here on the prairies of the Middle West is a living example of the truth of this philosophy. The abundance we enjoy here was created out of the riches of the soil and out of the labor of the men who work it, and, above all, out of American faith."[86]

John Bodnar has argued that Truman's main message was that "the immigrants who began arriving from Sweden a century ago were ultimately nation builders."[87] The majority of the president's address, however, did not concern the Swedish immigrants or pioneers. Its focus was on displaced persons and, at the dawn of the Cold War, a message of anti-communism. Indeed, a day earlier, Secretary of State George Marshall had sent Truman a memorandum in which he had criticized Sweden's neutrality as being of greater advantage to the Soviet Union than to the West.[88] The different dimensions of the speech need to be understood in relation to one another. By acknowledging how the notion of the pioneer was circulated through the contemporary political messages of the president, we see that a somewhat different pioneer emerges—one who was not only a nation builder but also the carrier of a belief in democracy, freedom, and equality.

Thus, it is important to acknowledge that Truman spoke to a national American audience via newspaper reports and radio broadcasts as well as to a particular audience at a cross-border commemorative festival. The cross-border character of the pioneer as a carrier of Swedishness rather than as the builder of a nation made this historical representation relevant outside a U.S. context. Clearly, Truman did not intend to manifest a sense of Swedishness. His interest was in contemporary U.S. politics, in arguing for a generous admittance of displaced persons (a project that eventually failed as, "with great reluctance," he signed the Displaced Persons Act on June 25), and in being reelected in the fall.[89] For these purposes he used the pioneer as a patriotic symbol. But by talking about the Swedish pioneers in this specific setting, by directly addressing an audience of Swedish Americans and high-profile representatives of Sweden, he charged his message with meanings beyond the patriotic. Given Marshall's memorandum, we may even speculate that he intended to coax the Swedes out of their staunch neutrality and shift them toward the American sphere of interest. The forum was, after all, not a domestic political rally but a commemoration of Swedish pioneering in the presence of representatives from different countries who had appropriated that history as their own.

The fundamental connection between Truman's representation of pioneers and immigrants and a more profound level of Swedishness involved notions of racial lineage. Commemorators emphasized that the Swedish Americans were, first and foremost, American citizens. At the same time, the festival attendees and the people of Sweden were united by the idea of common bloodlines. As Prince Bertil said at the Chicago Stadium, "it was only human if at this moment you of Swedish stock wish to recall for yourselves and to remind your friends and neighbors of other racial background of your share in the common achievement."[90] According to Carl Sandburg, the audience's presence at the stadium could be explained by a "love of a breed and a blood that made a name for itself all over the world." The descendants of the pioneers, according to the *Chicago Daily Sun Times*, enjoyed "every reference to the deeds of their blood kin."[91] These were expressions of racial solidarity that rested on the assumption that biological connections account for moral interest in another person and that these connections form "the natural expressions of feelings of community."[92] Through historical and biological connections linking the qualities of the pioneers, their contribution to the building of America, and ideas about transatlantic racial solidarity, President Truman's message became charged with dimensions of Swedishness.

The immediate racial context of the Chicago Stadium festival was complex. Like other cities in the Northeast and the Midwest, Chicago had changed considerably as a result of the Great Migration. From 1900 through the 1970s, large numbers of African Americans relocated from the South to industrial centers in the North, dramatically altering the nation's racial distribution. During the first wave of the migration, between 1910 and 1930, Chicago's African American population grew from 44,000 (2 percent of the total population) to 234,000 (6.9 percent of the total).[93] Although the influx slowed during the Great Depression, it picked up speed again in the 1940s as wartime production increased the demand for labor. Between 1940 and 1950, Chicago's black population grew from 278,000 (8.2 percent of the total) to 492,000 (13.6 percent of the total), with the majority of the migrants moving to the city's South Side.[94]

The city's social landscape also changed between the 1890s and the 1930s due to a large influx of immigrants from southern and eastern Europe. After 1930, the largest white ethnic group in Chicago was Polish. If we include both the first and the second generations, Polish Americans numbered more than 400,000, or 12 percent of the city's population.[95] By 1940, foreign-born residents in the Chicago metropolitan area constituted more than 18 percent of the population. Of these, the largest groups were Polish (16.6 percent of the foreign-born), German (12.5 percent), Italian (9.7 percent), Russian (8.7 percent), and Swedes (6.8 percent).[96] The Swedes, with a population of 56,000, remained the fifth-largest foreign-born group in Chicago into the following decades, but their numbers steadily declined, dropping to fewer than 17,000 in 1960.[97] The celebration of Swedish settlers and immigrants took place in the context of these demographic changes. They were statements made by a shrinking ethnic population in a thoroughly multicultural and multiracial city. Because the right to the city's foundational history was conditioned by racial belonging, it effectively excluded the majority of the city's present-day population from taking pride in the making of Chicago.

The idea that history should be embodied in individuals representative of the past was particularly visible during the festivals, where almost everyone present claimed to have a personal relation to the histories commemorated. The importance of Swedish pioneering and immigration was emphasized by contributions to both the building of the United States (through settlement) and to Sweden (through modernization). Ideas about blood bonds and racial solidarity were the glue that made it possible for everyone at the festivals to jointly embrace these histories.

Through the presence of foreign delegations in events chiefly organized by American commemorators, the festivals became forums for the celebration of common histories and the mending of cultural differences. Although the festivals did focus on culture, in a broad sense, and on Swedish contributions to the United States, I do not want to overemphasize the nationalistic dimension. Rather, the commemorations showed how ethnicity in the United States stretches outside American borders in both its maintenance and its contents. The festivals are a lens into the transcultural dimensions of Swedishness. History and culture were negotiated and asserted by Swedish Americans and homeland Swedes but also by people—most tellingly, President Truman—who clearly did not think of themselves as belonging to either of those categories.

A factor that enabled commemorators to share in these histories was the dual idea that the people at the stadiums and the arenas were related and that historical belonging was conditioned by ancestry. This was the essence of Prince Bertil's fictional story about the immigrant man and "the Negro," of the choice to seat living representatives of "the oldest pioneers" on stage, of President Roosevelt's claim that Swedish blood ran in his veins, and of Prince Bertil's and President Truman's representation of the pioneers as carriers of an ideology of freedom and liberalism. Ideas about racial solidarity—that constructed *we* at the festivals—made it possible for commemorators to accept a wider range of cultural expressions. Their conception of Swedishness clearly differed; but they shared a belief that everyone still belonged to the same family, and that all were carriers of the same history.

CHAPTER 6

Perpetual Friendships

Business and Politics in Commemorative Dinners

On leaving the United States in 1938, the Swedish crown prince delivered a radio speech in which he summed up the past few months of travel and commemorative events. "Friendship," he said, "is the word I would choose as the keyword to these Swedish American celebrations."[1] After the celebrations, letters between the crown prince and Secretary of State Cordell Hull, as well as between Hull and the Finnish minister for foreign affairs, all expressed how the commemoration had strengthened and renewed "old bonds of friendship" between the countries.[2]

Considering the connotations of dining together and breaking bread, we should not be surprised that the concept of friendship was evoked abundantly at tercentenary and centennial dinners. While banquets and luncheons are common events at commemorations, they are often analytically overlooked.[3] But these festive and usually lavish gatherings are not primarily intended to serve the metabolic needs of hungry guests; they are commemorative occasions in their own right. Their guests sometimes number more than a thousand. These invitation-only events thus function as social arenas in which selected people from the groups participating in the celebrations can meet to network but also to commemorate history. Dinners are, in other words, replete with cultural meanings and significance. The food and the dinner settings are part of "a code that can be seen to express patterns about social relationships."[4]

In his research on modern and ancient international relations, the historian Paul Burton makes a fruitful analytical distinction between friendship as a concept in the domestic sphere and friendship as a concept that anthropomorphizes state relationships. Even though states cannot be friends in a literal sense (since friendships are always personal relationships), the word is often used to describe state relations. Friendship rests on the fulfillment of mutual expectations and is thus a potentially fragile bond, more so than what Burton terms "ascribed relationships" such as kinship. While friendship is an emotional relation, kinship is a relation defined by blood. Kinship relations carry a different set of expectations and are more resistant to frictions and conflicts. Regardless of the nature of the relation, friendships rely on a network of meetings in which every meeting is a confirmation of the friendship. Applying this logic to commemorations in general and to dinners in particular, we see that they can, in and of themselves, be regarded as performances of selected friendships.[5]

The exclusivity inherent in commemorative dinners is important in understanding how such luncheons and banquets frame the social groups that commemorate history and the history that these groups commemorate. In reports about a 1938 tercentenary luncheon hosted by the state of New Jersey, newspapers called it an event for the "crème de la crème," open only to "the select and elite."[6] However, the elitism of commemorational dinners is sometimes contested. Precisely because they are events for prominent people, the considerations and politics that affect choices about whom to include and on what basis often permeate their organization.

Because commemorative dinners regularly include business leaders and politicians, they serve as a lens into the ways in which such festivities relate to issues of trade and diplomacy. The histories of Swedish settlement in America were charged with political and commercial meanings but augmented their impact through claims that the two nations' friendship would be perpetual because it was based on ideas about racial connections. By exploring the tension between friendship as a personal affiliation, friendship as a metaphor for state and institutional relations, and the biologically determined concept of kinship, a study of commemorative dinners suggests how these relations were bound up with the histories of the colonists, the pioneers, and the immigrants.

Cross-Border Settings

The luncheons and banquets supplied organizers, delegation members, and dinner guests with opportunities to meet in formal and informal settings, both during and outside the dinner programs. The commemorative dinners were politicized and commercialized events tailored as forums for social networking in which guests could initiate, manifest, and promote relations within their own nations and across the Atlantic. Dining in public is a social activity shaped by its setting, and both architecture and cultural customs become part of the dinners as performances.[7] The ways in which the dinners were designed and performed are thus relevant to an understanding of their social and commemorative functions.

The culture of elite public dining in the United States changed considerably in the decades before the 1938 and 1948 commemorations. In the late nineteenth century, the American elite displayed its social standing by eating French cuisine, and French-style restaurants spread throughout the United States. The quintessential fine-dining establishment of the time was Delmonico's in New York City, which served French cuisine (sometimes prepared by French chefs) that diners ordered from extensive and elaborate French-language menus. In the 1910s, as a growing urban middle class made its way into establishment restaurants, the culture of food and public dining began to change. Instead of ostentatious multi-course French dining, both critics and costumers demanded simpler, more wholesome food. As Helen Zoe Veit has shown, this change of preference was connected to the wartime Americanization of immigrants and ethnic culture as well as to racialized thinking about cross-cultural mingling. Instead of "mixing" different ingredients, diners wanted "purity": that is, they had "the sense that real American food was by nature plainer, simpler, and more honest, and less convoluted than food from other countries." Both the middle and the upper class consumed these plain American meals. As a consequence, class distinction was determined, in the words of the historian Harvey Levenstein, by "*where* one ate, not what one ate." By the 1930s, as the middle class began to frequent restaurants, the elite had shifted to dining at men's clubs, university clubs, luncheon clubs, and country clubs. As a testament to this new American culture of public dining, Delmonico's lavish French-style establishment closed in 1923.[8]

The notion that the setting of the dinners was more important than the gaudiness of the food held sway in 1938 and 1948. While most of the commemorative luncheons took place at social clubs or country clubs, most of the evening banquets were held in the great ballrooms of luxury hotels, such as the Palmer House in Chicago and the Waldorf-Astoria in New York. Through ballroom decorations,

FIGURE 18. The luncheon at Hotel du Pont in Wilmington, Delaware, was held hours after the opening of the 1938 tercentenary. The head table (on the right) included Prince Bertil, Secretary of State Cordell Hull, and Governor Richard C. McMullen of Delaware. Courtesy of the Delaware Public Archives.

the design of the programs, and the framing of menus and food, the dinners seemed to embody cooperation and mutuality. The banquet and luncheon venues carried both Swedish and American national symbols; walls, tables, and backdrops were adorned with Swedish and American flags and garlands, and sometimes the flag of the host state. In the East Coast celebrations of 1938, the national colors also included Finland. Most dinners followed a standardized structure. They began and often ended with blessings from Protestant pastors, a toastmaster presented the hosts and the foreign guests, and a musical program included national anthems and occasionally patriotic songs. Through their decorations and programs, the dinners retained a noticeably American character while linking to the international dimension of the commemorations.[9]

The 1938 banquets arranged in Pennsylvania exemplify the ways in which cross-border relations were channeled through local contexts. As fall elections loomed and the unemployment rate reached 15 percent, state organizers thought it would be unwise to have "Bacchanalian feasts and revels" in which they were "wining and dining royalty."[10] Therefore, no liquor was served at the Pennsylvania dinners. On April 8, 1938, the state commission and the Swedish Colonial Society arranged a Forefathers' Day banquet at the Benjamin Franklin Hotel in Philadelphia.[11] The organizers included both national and regional elements in the dinner. In addition to the unofficial state song "Pennsylvania," the Swedish folk song "Värmland," and "The Star Spangled Banner," the program included speeches by U.S. Senator Ernest Lundeen of Minnesota, Governor George Earle, and the Swedish envoy Wollmar Boström.[12] The dinner had been scheduled so that thirty minutes of speeches and musical performances could be broadcast live via radio to listeners in Pennsylvania, Sweden, and Finland, as well as to Swedish and Finnish organizations in the United States.[13] This was a common arrangement at the time and had also been used at Norwegian-American celebrations.[14] Meanwhile, in Stockholm, about 1,200 people had gathered at an event at City Hall arranged by the Swedish commission to hear the broadcast and speeches by, among others, the Swedish crown prince and the U.S. envoy to Stockholm.[15] Through the broadcast, the Forefathers' Day banquet was detached from the local (liquor-free) Pennsylvania context. The history of Swedish and American connections reached far beyond the Benjamin Franklin Hotel's ballroom.

The relation between the dinners' attachment to American culinary culture and their cross-border performances was also visible in the choice of food and the design of menus. In general, the majority of commemorative menus followed the same format. The dinners generally began with fresh fruit (often a halved grapefruit or melon) as well as celery, salted almonds, and olives. Ham and chicken were popular main dishes across the United States in 1938; a Swedish delegate reported that it had been tedious to eat chicken "ten times during the first week" of celebrations.[16] At the post-Depression dinners in 1948, steak, particularly filet mignon, was the preferred dish.[17]

None of these foods was chosen to represent Swedish-American culture or history. They were not the products of immigrant enclave businesses, common in the nineteenth and early twentieth centuries, where both producers and consumers were part of a specific ethnic food culture.[18] Nor were they common to Sweden, where French cuisine dominated among the social elite.[19] Rather, they were representative of American upper-class restaurant cuisine of the 1930s and 1940s. The ways in which food was consumed and prepared changed very little during these decades. According to Levenstein, the preferred dinner, for both middle- and upper-class Americans, consisted of "meat, a starch, a vegetable, a salad, and dessert." Beef, steak, pork, veal, lamb chops, and chicken were mainstays on restaurant plates, and the favored accompaniments were potatoes, carrots, and peas.[20] There is, in fact, a striking similarity between the 1938 and 1948 menus and those of other festive dinners of the era, which also consisted of a piece of meat or (less often) fish, accompanied by sides of potatoes and vegetables (often peas and lettuce hearts) and topped off by a modest dessert such as ice cream.[21]

An exception to the homogenous American banquet fare, albeit a minor one, was the 1948 banquet in Chicago at which the guests experienced a Swedish and American crossover, with "Swedish lingon berries . . . served in the supreme of melon cocktail and a Swedish Spring salad . . . served with the broiled filet mignon."[22] But while the cross-border performances of the dinners did not come from foods consumed, the elaborate ways in which the dishes were presented reflected the commemorative occasion.

Like guest lists, decorations, and speeches, the menus were commemorative displays in their own right.[23] For example, the 1938 menu at the Hotel du Pont offered "Delaware Asparagus Hollandaise" and "Ice Cream duPont," and the guests at the University Club in New York City had "Buffet Suedoise" and "Sorbet Gothenburg."[24] During the 1948 centennial, the Chicago banquet served "Illuminated Bombe Cardinale Suédoise," while the Rockford dinner ended with "Swedish Pioneer Centennial Ice Cream."[25] At the Pennsylvania Forefathers' Day banquet, planners initially intended to serve the guests a menu consisting of "Tomato Surprise / Celery, Almonds, Olives / Potage Mongole aux Croutons / Shrimp Mexican / Broiled Boneless Shad and Roe / Duchesse Potatoes / New String Beans / Hearts of Lettuce, Lorenzo Dressing / Coupe St. Jacque au Cointreau / Petits Fours, Demi-Tasse, After Dinner Mints."[26] After revisions, the menu read:

Tomato Surprise Delaware
Celery / Almonds / Olives
Swedish Potage with Croutons
Shrimp Tinicum
Broiled South River Shad and Roe
Finnish Potatoes / Wicaco Peas in Butter
Hearts of Lettuce / Printzhof Dressing
New Gothenburg Fruit Cup
Rambo Cakes / Coffee Tankard / Mints Kingsessing[27]

The duchesse potatoes and French-style fruit cup were reframed to represent Finland and the settlement of New Gothenburg. The potage became Swedish, the "tomato surprise" Delawarean; and the Mexican shrimp, Lorenzo dressing, petits fours, and after-dinner mints were renamed after New Sweden places and people: the settlements of Wicaco and Tinicum, New Sweden governor Johan Printz's house Printzhof, the area of Kingsessing in present-day Pennsylvania, and the colonial family of Rambo. The Forefathers' Day banquet menu was made not simply to be consumed but to be pondered as a commemorative statement.

The renaming of dishes emphasized both geographical distance and colonial-sounding origins. The interchangeable names belonged, after all, to dishes that already carried non-American monikers. Together with decorations and performances, the menus—which in themselves were collectable tokens to be brought home and archived—became signifiers of transatlantic, historical friendships.

Political Friendship

"Never in the history of the United States and of Sweden has there been any time when peace and friendship did not reign between us," Prince Bertil declared at the Pennsylvania Commonwealth banquet on June 28, 1938. His audience in the Benjamin Franklin Hotel ballroom was predominantly made up of state and federal politicians and administrators, some seated according to instructions from the U.S. State Department. In addition to the Swedish and Finnish delegations, the roughly 1,000 guests included out-of-state delegates and leaders of Swedish-American societies.[28] The mutual peace and friendship that Prince Bertil described was a fact of great value in a climate of global political unrest.

> Traditional friendship between two countries like ours cannot fail to be an asset of special value in troubled times. We are going through an historic age, rich in conflicts between nations and within nations. I believe it would be difficult to find an historical epoch, where, alas, unrest, strife and hatred have been more prominent. At such a time great importance must be attached to the fact that two nations are imbued by the same ideals. As you stand for law and order and tolerance in this Commonwealth of Pennsylvania and in the United States, and as you cherish the ideals of international understanding and friendship, so do we in Sweden. And may I say with some pride that we have done so for a long time.[29]

This theme of peace and freedom was reiterated numerous times during the commemorations, most often when the guest list consisted of political representatives, and it was championed by American and Swedish commemorators alike. Speaking on behalf of the court system at the Commonwealth banquet, the state's chief justice claimed that the presence of the visiting Swedish and Finnish delegations was a sign of the peaceful relations that were missing in so many places around the world. While many nations suffered aggression and enmity, Sweden and Finland were "secure in the traditions of religious freedom and democracy more ancient than our own, [and we] may look with a sense of security to the friendship built up for 300 years in America."[30]

These themes and their opposites—conflict and hatred—were eerily familiar at the time. On June 18, 1938, readers of the *Chicago Daily Tribune* saw this headline on the front page: "Crown Prince of Sweden Off for U.S. Fete." In block letters above the article, however, another headline ominously declared, "Smash Berlin Jews' Shops." The *Tribune* reported on a "Night of Terror" during which Jewish stores in Berlin had been looted and 143 Jews arrested. The Nazi regime, the article continued, was planning to build two new concentration camps to contain the increasing number of detained Jews.[31] In the weeks preceding the start of the tercentenary, readers of the *New York Times* also got a sense of the tumultuous political situation. On the newspaper's front pages were articles about "Civilian Bombings in Spain and China Condemned by U.S."; "700 Slain, 1,300 Wounded by Bombings in Canton"; "Vienna Nazis Widen Drive on Jews; Every Family Reported Suffering." On June 26, the day before the beginning of the celebrations, the *Times* reported, "Italy Sends War Warning as Loyalists Talk of Raids on Bombers' 'Home Bases.'"[32] As the crown prince talked about shared Swedish and American ideals of law, order, tolerance, and religious freedom, these headlines formed the backdrop.

On July 3, 1938, the federally appointed U.S. Delaware Valley Tercentenary Commission arranged a dinner at the Mayflower Hotel in Washington, D.C. Included among the 160 guests were Secretary of State Cordell Hull, Secretary of War Harry Hines Woodring, and Attorney General Homer S. Cummings.[33] Two days earlier, newspapers had declared, "Roosevelt Warns Nations All Must Keep Peace; Extols Our Civic Liberties."[34] Now, in this politically charged setting, the crown prince delivered a speech in which he emphasized that the New Sweden settlers and the subsequent immigrants "will for ever constitute a lasting link of friendship between our two countries."

"This is all the more important," he continued, "at the present time when we seem to hear of nothing but war and rumours of war and dissension amongst the people of the world." He claimed that modern society had made the world interdependent and connected and that it was therefore vital to promote peace and international cooperation.[35]

The crown prince's speech illustrates how history was adapted in service of diplomacy. Leaders from both nations repeatedly echoed these themes. Hull said in Wilmington that "there is need today, perhaps a greater need than ever before, in relations among individuals and among nations, for those same qualities and principles which characterized the colonizers of New Sweden."[36] Through these speeches and in light of the high-ranking politicians in attendance, the histories of New Sweden and Swedish immigration were constructed as the root of present-day peace and friendship.

The timing of the 1938 commemoration was clearly advantageous for national commemorators who were grappling with mounting geopolitical tensions and the rise of totalitarian regimes in Europe and Asia. Although U.S. foreign policy during most of the 1930s was isolationist, President Roosevelt believed that the best way for the country to stay out of war was to prevent it. After Italy's attack on Ethiopia in 1935, he began to actively encourage resistance to totalitarian regimes and to promote negotiations between conflicting nations. At the same time, the State Department began to acknowledge the importance of cultural relations for foreign policy. According to the historian Frank Ninkovich, the department in the mid-1930s increasingly considered "mutual understanding [to] form the basis of peaceful international relations." The escalation of crisis and warfare in Europe and Asia was the beginning of the end of American isolationism.[37]

In 1938, Roosevelt used the New Sweden Tercentenary to demonstrate his country's good relations with Sweden and Finland. In his opening address at The Rocks, the president welcomed the foreign delegations by saying that they represented "a true friendship under which we have lived from the earliest times unmarred by any rift, unbroken by any misunderstanding." Sweden, Finland, and the United States, he declared, "will continue their service in the days to come in the cause of friendship and of peace among the nations of the world."[38] These statements were not only courteous platitudes; they were also a way of showing that Sweden and Finland were part of the democratic orbit. For Sweden, a country with a historically strong economic and cultural orientation toward Germany, Roosevelt's remarks were intended to bring the country closer to American interests. Alongside the development of U.S. foreign relations, such comments underlined the commemorations' function as forums for public diplomacy.[39]

A set of royal visits in the 1930s were another step toward the end of U.S. isolationism. The visits of Great Britain's King George VI and his wife Elizabeth in 1935 and Norway's Crown Prince Olav and Crown Princess Märtha in 1939 were, from Roosevelt's point of view, arranged with "the aim of building alliances that could further combat totalitarian governments."[40] In a key moment during the British visit, he treated the royals to a hot dog picnic at his Hyde Park estate while assuring King George of American support in case of war. In 1938, while Sweden's crown prince was still at a New York hospital being treated for his renal colic, Crown Princess Louise and a few members of the Swedish delegation also visited Hyde Park and received a taste of Roosevelt's "Hot Dog Diplomacy."[41] The *New York Times* reported, "Roosevelts Treat Guests to Hot Dogs: First Lady Insists on Serving the Roadside Fare at Picnic for Crown Princess Louise." Although the Roosevelts had sought to appease the Swedish guests by also bringing a smorgasbord of hors d'oeuvres to the picnic site, the main attraction was "hot dogs, dripping with mustard, [that] were tucked into the familiar rolls" and "washed down by beer."[42] The commemoration, and the practice of formally and informally dining together, was an opportunity to manifest allegiances without explicitly declaring alliances.

The reiteration of peaceful relations carried different meanings after World War II. Given Sweden's neutrality during the war and its nonaligned military position after 1945, the implications of such statements had become greater. Sweden's national image had been compromised due to its wartime concessions to Germany; and by the late 1940s, during the ongoing Marshall Plan negotiations, America was eager for it to pick sides in the dawning Cold War. The 1948 centennial gave Sweden a way to raise its profile in the United States. From the U.S. standpoint, however, the commemoration was less necessary as a platform for international relations. The State Department showed little interest in the event, which took place as the United States was turning toward a foreign policy of unilateralism.[43]

The important exception was President Truman's participation in the celebrations in Chicago. At the Chicago Stadium festival, he emphasized that the countries' "friendship is heightened by the fact that Sweden today is one of the most prosperous and progressive democracies in the world." This, he seemed to imply, had not always been the case. "When I think of the great epics in our history, like the Swedish immigration of a century ago, I am reminded again of the source of our strength as a nation." The immigrants had escaped restrictions in Sweden to find economic opportunity, personal freedom, and a democratic way of life in the United States. "We must fight today," Truman continued, "to see that America stays that way." This task was important for handling pressing contemporary challenges: for instance, helping Europe's displaced persons and protecting American citizens from the threat of communism.[44] This was neither the first nor the last time that the president would use commemorations in an effort to conquer the spread of communism. Truman had, for example, fostered an alliance with Mexico through the memory of the U.S.-Mexican War: in 1947 he had laid a wreath at the memorial of the Boy Heroes at Chapultepec, and in 1950 he would repatriate Mexican flags captured by U.S. troops. The speech's juxtaposition of democracy and communism echoed the language of the 1947 Truman Doctrine and the State Department's ongoing propaganda campaigns against the Soviet Union.[45] At a banquet on the following day, Prince Bertil reiterated the president's sentiments, saying that Sweden and the United States "stand united in our firm decision to maintain and defend our freedom and independence, as well as our democratic way of life."[46]

The commemorators' mutual expressions of peaceful relations rested on the notion that both countries were modern nations who shared democratic and liberal values. This commonality was emphasized in multiple speeches during both the 1938 and 1948 celebrations. At a 1948 banquet in Omaha, Prince Bertil told a story about "Peterson," a name that he had encountered during his visit to Nebraska, along with other Swedish names such as Swenson, Larson, and Lundberg. Peterson, he asserted, was not only a name but also a description of something greater: "of the pioneer, of the average Swedish immigrant to Illinois, Minnesota, Nebraska, and the other Middle Western states."[47] His speech's theme was likely to satisfy the primarily Swedish-American businessmen and professional leaders present at the banquet—including Val Peterson, the governor of Nebraska.[48]

But who was the Peterson in the prince's speech? "He was one of the unknown soldiers in a great, peaceful but very hard battle," Bertil claimed, "which gradually transformed an immense area of prairies, forests and swamps into the most highly civilized lands on this earth." He was hardworking, courageous, and resourceful; he had integrity and a deep sense of justice and decency. He built churches, hospitals, and schools and produced descendants (the prince did not mention the involvement of any women) who played prominent roles in business and industry. But he was also, Bertil said, "an agent which made possible the fusion of two cultures . . . which were not too different in basic principles." To understand the good relations between Sweden and the United States, we must, according to the prince, give much of the credit to the pioneers, these "great ambassadors of good will."[49]

Bertil's description of the Swedish pioneers as intercultural agents and peaceful soldiers reveals the dual function of the Swedish Pioneer Centennial: it promoted international relations while simultaneously commemorating the history of pioneering. Even though commercial interests also influenced this particular speech, Bertil used the representation of successful settler colonial legacies to argue for a broader political friendship between Sweden and the United States. Swedish pioneers had helped to build America using virtues and characteristics they had transplanted from Sweden. The rendering of friendship manifested in the microcosm of the banquet thus incorporated the benevolence of the pioneers. Even the conquering of uncivilized land became a nonviolent battle in which the guests at the Omaha dinner could find common ground. The commemoration of the pioneers was interpreted as an incentive for future friendly relations.

Claims that pioneer ideals were modern, liberal, and democratic were part of the construction of "Nordic democracy," a concept fashioned in the 1930s and 1940s to demarcate the Scandinavian countries as harbingers of democracy in a totalitarian age.[50] Both within and outside those countries, the concept was imbued with an ancient character. The construction relied in part on notions of a specific Nordic culture that was characterized by homogeneity, continuity, adherence to the rule of law, and a shared sense of liberty. Yet, in fact, modern democracy in the region was still relatively young.[51]

Until the 1860s Sweden was governed by the king and the Riksdag of the Estates (*ståndsriksdagen*), which had origins in the fifteenth century and was composed of members of the nobility, the clergy, burghers, and peasants. After a constitutional reform in 1866, the country introduced a bicameral assembly called the Riksdag. Although the reform gave parliamentary representation to new social classes, such as the growing middle class, voting rights were still heavily restricted. The First Chamber of the Riksdag was elected indirectly by county and city councilors, and only men older than thirty-five and with sizable real estate assets and incomes were eligible. In all, only about 6,000 citizens fulfilled these requirements. For the Second Chamber, voting rights were restricted to men older than twenty-one who did not have outstanding taxes and who owned real estate, leased a large agricultural property, or had considerable taxable income. Before 1909, when a constitutional change granted greater voting rights to men, only 9.5 percent of the Swedish population had de facto voting rights. Equal suffrage was not extended to both men and women until the 1921 election. The democratic principles of Sweden were, in short, not as ancient as the 1930s and 1940s commemorators claimed; on the contrary, its suffrage reforms came later than those of many other European nations.[52] Nonetheless, in an effort to extend the temporality of democracy, the peaceful, freedom-loving, and law-abiding Swedish pioneers were represented as agents who twined the historical roots of Swedish democracy with the archetypal democracy of the United States.

Commercial Friendship

The commemorations were democratic manifestations, but they were also celebrations arranged by market economies. This function played out within and outside commemorative events. During their 1938 tour, the leaders of the Swedish delegation were invited to dinners and parties with members of the American social and economic elite, held at places such as Pierre S. du Pont's Longwood Gardens in Pennsylvania, Henry du Pont's Winterthur estate in Delaware, Robert Wood Bliss's Dumbarton Oaks in Washington, D.C., and Hiram Edward Manville's yacht *Hi-Esmaro* off the New England coast.

Although many of the commemorative dinners were arranged by local Swedish-American associations, the ethnic dimension frequently collapsed into a business one since many events were organized or co-organized by chambers of commerce.[53] In Minneapolis in 1938, the Swedish consulate and the city's chamber of commerce worked together to arrange a tercentenary luncheon at the Minneapolis Club. According to the consul, Carl F. Hellström, this was not a "comprehensive citizen luncheon" but an informal "business men's luncheon" with 150 to 200 guests. It was to be open only to chamber of commerce members from other Minnesota cities and to "the city's most prominent citizens . . . that have commercial relations with Sweden or those . . . open [to] such relations, who at the moment are fairly numerous." Hellström believed that the luncheon would "serve an excellent purpose for still furthering commercial relations in the future."[54] The business dimension and the emphasis on cross-border connections not only permeated the commemorations but also informed the ways in which the history of Swedish settlement was represented.

At a 1938 dinner arranged by the International Chamber of Commerce (ICC) at the Union Club in New York, the crown prince emphasized "the primordial importance of abolishing, wherever it may be possible, the barriers which hamper the free flow of international trade." He supported his description of Swedes as "staunch advocates" of free trade by evoking the 1783 Treaty of Amity and Commerce between Sweden and the United States. Signed before the end of the Revolutionary War, it had established an alliance of free commerce and navigation and explicitly called for peaceful and friendly relations between Sweden and the new American republic. The crown prince indicated that this old treaty had been confirmed by the nation's more recent reciprocal trade treaty, signed in May 1935. Such statements harkened back to the question of democracy and peace: "Sound trade relations are conducive to good political relations. Where trade is expanding, friendship also will flourish. It seems to me therefore that in striving for sound commercial relations between the nations of the world we are at the same time working in the interest of peace. Much of the present unrest in the world is no doubt due to unwisely restrictive trade policies."[55]

The crown prince's speech at the ICC luncheon stands in contrast to his speech at the U.S. Delaware Valley Tercentenary Commission dinner in Washington, D.C. The latter was strongly informed by politics, the former by business. This difference resonated with the dinner setting. In the words of the historian David Ellwood, the ICC was "a businessmen's league of nations" that promoted world peace through free trade.[56] Before this audience, "a large group of prominent business executives," the crown prince stressed a mutual history of commercial friendship.[57]

By evoking friendship in terms of free trade, commemorators adhered to capitalist notions of freedom common in U.S. foreign policy and predominant since the presidency of Woodrow Wilson. American territorial expansionism after the Spanish-American War of 1898 had been replaced by policies of intervention to protect U.S. interests abroad. While the Wilson administration presumed, in the words of the historian Thomas Bender, that "global commodity, goods, and financial markets should always be at the disposal of the United States," it also realized that colonies "were not necessary to [its] global ambitions."[58]

In reality, however, free trade had not been the leading principle for long. A 1920s neo-mercantilist trend had led up to the Great Depression and the subsequent collapse of world trade. The introduction of high-tariff trade policies reached a peak with the Tariff Act of 1930, commonly known as the Smoot-Hawley Act, which was later blamed for causing a wave of international trade tariffs and drastically decreasing U.S. trade. The Smoot-Hawley Act has been described as "a diplomatic affront." It made countries around the world react with hostility toward the United States and contributed to the spread of protectionist trade policies during the early 1930s.[59] After their victory in the 1932 elections, Roosevelt and the congressional Democrats began initiating changes to this domestically and internationally criticized trade policy. The result was the Reciprocal Trade Agreement Act of 1934, which authorized the executive office to make trade treaties in negotiations with foreign countries. It has been described as the economic side of Roosevelt's Good Neighbor policy in foreign relations.[60]

As Donna Gabaccia has shown, the end of U.S. protectionism was related to contemporary changes in the restriction of immigration. After 1935, when immigration had declined and its role in connecting the United States to a global world diminished, "free trade and the lowering of tariffs worldwide became the official U.S. formula for global peace and international cooperation."[61] When, in 1935, Sweden signed a treaty with the United States based on the Reciprocal Trade Agreement Act (it was one of the first countries to do so) the two nations set forth on a path of lowered tariffs and increased trade volumes.[62]

The patterns of trade were changing at the time of the commemorations. The value of U.S. imports from Sweden had a record year in 1938 with a value of more than 58 million dollars, while U.S. exports to Sweden had climbed well above their pre-Depression level, reaching 64 million dollars. Although overall American trade with Sweden was a fraction of the U.S. total (in 1938, both import and export to all of the Nordic countries amounted to only 4 percent), the United States had become Sweden's third-largest export country after England and Germany. However, U.S. trade with Sweden carried a significant weight when it came to certain specific goods. By the late 1930s, Sweden was exporting considerable quantities of paper pulp, iron ore, and ball bearings to the United States and had become one of the world's biggest importers of American cars. Close to 14,000 cars were exported to Sweden in 1938—a massive increase since 1932, when only 1,400 cars were exported. Although Australia (16,400 cars), Argentina (19,000 cars), and South Africa (23,800 cars) were the largest importers of

U.S. automobiles, Sweden's purchases were greater than, for example, Canada (12,000 cars), Belgium (11,000 cars), and the United Kingdom (4,200 cars).[63] Swedish and American businessmen and officials certainly wanted to build on this trend. Thus, in the aftermath of the Depression and international protectionism, commemorators used the 1938 tercentenary as a forum for promoting increased commerce and mutually manifesting a newly reinstated trade agreement based on histories of free trade.

In 1948, fewer references were made to historical treaties on the national level. Instead, the focus was on Swedish industrial and economic development and the contributions of Swedish Americans to U.S. progress. At a banquet in Rockford sponsored by the city's chamber of commerce, Prince Bertil devoted his speech to comparing the industrial economies of the two countries. He hailed Rockford (a bit hyperbolically) as one of the leading industrial cities in the United States and said that it reminded him of "a typical, progressive industrial community in Sweden." Even though Sweden had been economically struggling during the past few years, the future was bright for its large industries and its hundreds of thousands of small businesses. Therefore, celebrating the history of Swedish immigration and its contribution to American industry and commerce was "much more than a gesture in commemoration of a great past."[64] In New York City, Bertil maintained—without citing specifics—that Sweden in fact owed America for its industrialization, foreign trade, and democratization: "Not only were some of the savings of the immigrants sent back to parents and other relatives in Sweden whose material lot was thus improved, American ideas and inventions also helped to modernize our own country."[65]

The progress and modernity of Sweden were, in this way, presented as inseparable from the hard work, success, and contributions of Swedish pioneers and immigrants to the United States. The emphasis on Sweden as a democratic country of business and commerce was attached to a contemporary discourse exemplified by the Truman Doctrine. The idea that all freedom depended on freedom of enterprise became a fundamental premise for U.S. anti-communism during the Cold War.[66] When Swedish commemorators underlined their adherence to commercial friendship with the United States, they demonstrated their participation in the capitalist market ideology of the West. The portrayal of economic progress was thus linked with the emphasis on political friendship.

As international trade resumed after the end of the war, American exports to Sweden continued to grow, reaching a new peak in 1947 when more than 31 percent of Sweden's total imports came from the United States. Swedish exports to America had a harder time regaining their prewar foothold. In the late 1940s, the country's trade deficit with the United States amounted to about $358 million.[67] The Swedish delegations thus had a concrete, perhaps even pressing, reason to stimulate American interest in Swedish business and industry.

During their tours, the delegations visited six of the eight largest industrial centers in the country, cities whose economies depended on world markets: Chicago, Detroit, Philadelphia, and New York in 1938 and 1948, as well as Pittsburgh and Boston in 1938. Their itineraries in these cities included visits to industries and businesses. For instance, in Detroit, the 1938 delegation toured the General Motors and the Ford Motor Company factories. Ten years later, the 1948 delegation was treated to a business luncheon at the Detroit Athletic Club. The guests included the presidents, vice-presidents, general managers, and chairmen of companies such as General Motors, Ford Motor Company, Michigan Bell Telephone Company, Great Lakes Steel Corporation, and the Detroit Board of Commerce.[68] The Swedish minister of commerce—who because of ongoing Marshall Plan negotiations did not end up taking part in the tour—had been scheduled to meet with American representatives of business and industry.[69] His speech at the Chicago banquet would have centered on the theme of "Sweden's foreign trade and general economic problems, our involvement in the Marshall Plan and Swedish opinions on the economic recovery work etcetera."[70] These dimensions of the celebrations were clearly not commemorative but were specifically intended to encourage trade.

In 1948 the business interests were so apparent that critics sometimes complained that they were diverting attention from the actual reason for celebration. Before the start of the centennial, an organizer in Escanaba, Michigan, informed the Swedish-American commission executive, Nils William Olsson, that he was "afraid [that] some attempt would be made to use the Prince's visit more or less as an advertising stunt for Escanaba."[71] This maneuvering did not go unnoticed in Sweden. Days into the celebration, Swedish newspapers began to reflect on the elitism of the program. "The Swedish-American tycoons are crowding around Prince Bertil during the great jubilee festivities in Swedish America," reported one newspaper, "but it seems as if the simple pioneer, who should have been celebrated, has been completely forgotten."[72] The newspapers leveled similar criticisms against a stadium festival in Detroit, which local politicians had exploited as a venue for election speeches, thus neglecting both the Swedish delegation and the history of the pioneers.[73]

The centennial became a platform for demonstrating commercial allegiances between free-trading western countries. The lowering of trade tariffs, international military aid, and programs such as the Marshall Plan were all connected to U.S. national security policies and the containment of communism.[74] By the late 1940s, with their international treaties in place, the Swedish government was encountering the United States through its corporate representatives, not its federal administration. As the Cold War world dawned, this marker showed that the two countries occupied very different positions in the geopolitical order.

Friendship as Kinship

As the 1938 Swedish delegation traveled to the Midwest, the history of immigration was framed as a way to make the area feel like home. Noting in Chicago that the delegates had not come "to a foreign country but to friends," the crown prince echoed the oft-stated statistic that Chicago's Swedish-American inhabitants were numerous enough to match the population of the second-largest city in Sweden.[75] This statistic was mentioned again at a 1948 banquet in Chicago, when Governor Dwight H. Green of Illinois claimed that it was the foundation of the "close bonds of kinship and affection which our people feel toward Sweden."[76]

The representations of successful settler colonial histories, from the New Sweden colonists to the Swedish immigrants of the nineteenth and twentieth centuries, were conflated during commemorative dinners. "We are proud," Prince Bertil said at a 1938 dinner with federal representatives in Washington, D.C., "to think that our northern race should thus have contributed through their respect for law and order, their love of freedom and their industriousness to the upbuilding of their adopted country." He claimed that New Sweden and the nineteenth-century immigration had produced 2 million individuals "of pure Swedish origin or of mixed Swedish descent." They were primarily Americans but also "kith and kin" of the people of Sweden.[77]

At a welcome banquet for Pennsylvania's governor during his 1937 visit to Sweden, the governor of Gothenburg, Malte Jacobsson, passionately expressed the strength of this kinship and the mutual political ideals: "Blood unites us, water divides us, but—blood is thicker than water! You, Governor Earle, in whose veins the blood of the old Swedish settlers on the Delaware is running, you come to us not as a stranger but as one of our own."[78]

The blood that ran in Governor Earle's veins was construed as a source of friendship and, more profoundly, of shared values and ideologies. In Stockholm, the city council chair stressed that "order, law, and right" were based on "values of an ancient national culture" that Sweden had brought to North America. His message to Earle emphasized that democracy and peace were not only part of an ancient history in Sweden but also ran in the Swedish blood: "The fact that in your veins there runs blood derived from the Swedish pioneers of those early days adds to the pleasure we feel in now welcoming you to the old country which faithfully guards and preserves the free constitution, the democracy, which our fathers, during the course of thousands of years, created and watched as one of their most cherished human rights."[79]

The significance of blood, measured as either "pure" or "mixed," was brought full circle in Prince Bertil's final speech of the 1948 centennial, at a banquet in New York. During its travels in the Midwest, the delegation had seen the accomplishments of the Swedish pioneers and their descendants in all walks of American life, people with whom Sweden shared history, ideals, and traditions. The emigration from

Sweden had created a great loss of people, but the material and ideological contributions relayed back across the ocean had helped Sweden modernize.

In a copy of the speech that differs from a printed version in the report of New York State, the pioneers are described as "the best foreign investment Sweden ever made." Touring the United States (and, as the copy states, seeing the blue-eyed, blond-haired people with "typical, open Swedish faces"), Prince Bertil had asked himself, "Where in the whole world today does my country Sweden, outside of Scandinavia, have more or better friends than right here in the United States?" There was hardly a Swede that did not have a known relative in the United States, and there was hardly a country where the people were more pro-American. A paragraph in the copy of the speech, which for unknown reasons was omitted in the printed version, underlined the significance of this friendship. Whether uttered at the Waldorf-Astoria Hotel or not, it signifies the weight of the connection between kinship and friendship.

> It was to celebrate the memory of men like that [the pioneers], humble workers from Sweden, who helped develop this mighty land from the ground up, that this jubilee has been held. That we as representatives of Sweden were invited to participate is, of course, a new proof of your unbroken regard for our country. . . . Such personal friendship, mutual respect and esteem are, it seems to me, the soundest foundations for what is known as international relations. States and governments represent, after all, only the people who support them. I wish it were possible to apply this formula in wider circles. We would then have enduring peace.[80]

The international friendship between Sweden and the United States was framed as a foreign investment, an asset of a racial family. The transatlantic genealogies, Bertil explained, "give us courage . . . to persevere in our resolve to maintain our national independence, our democratic institutions, our own individuality, come dark days, come bright." This message—which appeared the next day in the *New York Times*—sent a clear signal to the United States about Sweden's Cold

War allegiance and emphasized that its connection to Sweden was innate. The genealogical bonds that supposedly stretched across the Atlantic had created a stable foundation for the common ideologies of democracy, freedom, and free trade. There was, according to Harry Truman, "scarcely a family in Sweden which does not have relatives in this country." And this, he said, "is the kind of personal tie which strengthens friendly international relations."[81]

⌇

The friendship so frequently mentioned in the commemorational dinners, one denoting both state relations and personal affiliations, was not and could not be fragile. Although international affinity was portrayed as inherent in the very soul of nations, states, and companies, its stability was founded in the histories that the two commemorations so heavily relied on. The migration was a shared experience that linked Sweden and the United States, but it also established genealogical bonds. The ideas of Swedish-American kinship rested on notions of common bloodlines and were directly related to the delegation travels. During the dinners, however, this idea was transposed from the bodies of Swedes and Americans—which were at the core of the indoor and outdoor festival celebrations—to descriptions of interstate relations. Considering the immediate contexts of the commemorations, they should be regarded as high-profile events of public diplomacy, both political and commercial, as businesses and government representatives sought to historically legitimize their push for increased trade.

Importantly, the notion of friendship during the dinners worked in two ways. It was reiterated because it served diplomatic and commercial purposes, functioning as a statement of political allegiance at two crucial geopolitical moments. In 1938 Sweden, Finland, and the United States manifested their mutual adherence to democracy, peace, and free trade, whereas in 1948 the centennial helped Sweden to reinstate itself as an ally who shared those values with the American superpower. But ideas about friendship also informed the histories commemorated and thus, in a circular fashion, strengthened contemporary relations. Commemorators described Swedish settlement and immigration as a peaceful and tolerant process: civilizing parts of North America, helping to build the United States, and laying the foundations of economic, social, and cultural prosperity. The representations of benign colonial relations with Native Americans, the peaceful conquering of the midwestern wilderness, the religious tolerance and humanitarian values all served the contemporary interests of manifesting international goodwill—the common adherence to peace through democracy and trade. The colonists and the pioneers were represented as role models for contemporary society and, indeed, for the entire world.

Conclusion
The Resilience of History

In recent years few people have had access to Fort Christina State Park. After closing for a decade due to problems with vandalism and loitering, it reopened in 2016. Eighty years after the park's inauguration, its focal point is still the monument by Carl Milles. Hidden within that monument is a box that both literally and metaphorically attests to the resilience of the 1938 New Sweden Tercentenary. In the spring of that year, as the monument was being erected in Wilmington, the Swedish commission shipped a gift across the Atlantic: a copper box decorated with the Vasa sheaf—the symbol of the royal dynasty of King Gustavus Adolphus and Queen Christina—as well as medallions and insignia recalling Sweden's seventeenth-century Age of Greatness.[1] The Swedish commission chair, J. Sigfrid Edström, told his Delaware counterpart, Christopher Ward, about the significance of the gift and gave him instructions on what to do with it:

> I send in the Swedish diplomatic pouch a copper box containing a written statement on parchment, signed by myself, concerning the monument, also Swedish coins, medals, etc. as well as newspapers. This copper box is sent to the Swedish Minister Mr. Wollmar Boström. He may add some mementos in the box whereupon he ought to turn the box over to you so that you can add what you think desirable, for instance the Delaware medal and the American coin, etc. After this has been done, please have the top of the box soldered on to the box itself. This box shall be put into the foundation under the monument.[2]

CONCLUSION 177

After receiving the box, Boström added a copy of the *Washington Star* dated May 9, 1938, which contained an article about the tercentenary. (Oddly, he also reported to Ward that the box had been "a little damaged in the corner.")[3] Eventually, it was inserted into the monument in the presence of Delaware's governor, Richard C. McMullen.[4]

It is worth pondering the function of the copper box. Inside the monument, it is physically invisible to present-day visitors. More striking, however, is that it also seems to have vanished from memory; its presence is not highlighted anywhere in the park today, and I have not encountered any mention of it in accounts of the commemoration. As a time capsule, the box's presence inside the monument fixes time and literally harbors history. But what time? And what history?

The copper box is a fitting metaphor for the relation between the New Sweden Tercentenary and the history that it commemorated. The Rocks is, on the one hand, the site of the colonists' landfall in the spring of 1638. On the other hand, it is the site inside Fort Christina State Park at which the Swedish delegation landed and the New Sweden Tercentenary began three hundred years later. The items inside the box do not relate to the object of the commemoration—that is, to the New Sweden colony. Rather, they are memorabilia of the event in itself: a statement from the chair of the Swedish commission, tercentenary medals, and newspaper articles. The copper box was intended as a commemorative self-reference. In contrast to the monument that encases it, the box was not supposed to represent the past; it was created to make history.

The cross-border commemoration of 1938 profoundly shaped and influenced subsequent celebrations of Swedish settlement in America. The celebration made history in and of itself; it has been seen as a historical highwater mark in relations between Sweden and the United States.[5] Like the monument's entombed artifact, the extent of the celebration's effect might be hard to detect. Yet before 1938, there was no established place at which to commemorate New Sweden. The tercentenary created a set of sites that have since become the only conceivable venues for commemorations of the colony. While the 1948 Swedish Pioneer Centennial had fewer lasting effects than the New Sweden Tercentenary did (that is, in terms of material culture and established commemorative practices), it did resonate with the practices of the 1938 event, thus ensuring that histories of Swedish settlement would continue to be celebrated through cross-border commemorations.[6]

The New Sweden Tercentenary and the Swedish Pioneer Centennial created patterns that have been reproduced in subsequent celebrations of Swedish people in the United States. One such pattern concerns movement: delegations, led by Swedish royalty, have continued to revisit commemorative places in the Delaware Valley and the Midwest—not only cities such as Wilmington, Philadelphia, Chicago, and Minneapolis–Saint Paul but also specific sites such as The Rocks, Governor Printz Park, and the Jenny Lind Chapel in Andover, Illinois. All major commemorations of the colony, including those at the 350th and 375th anniversaries, have staged a reenactment of the colonial landing. In 1938 the delegation landed at The Rocks "in a modern way," using military longboats; and in 1988 Sweden's King Carl XVI Gustaf and Queen Silvia stepped ashore from a rowboat.[7] In 2013, Swedish royalty again arrived at The Rocks, but this time on a full-scale replica of *Kalmar Nyckel,* which, since the 1990s, has been moored at the docks of the Kalmar Nyckel Foundation, next to Fort Christina State Park.

Several contemporary motivations explain the visits to these places, but the practice of going there can be traced back to the tercentenary. As in 1938, later commemorations of New Sweden have also included participants from Finland. Their involvement has always, however, remained in the shadow of the Swedes'—partly because the colony has been framed as a project of the Swedish state, partly because of the public appeal of royalty, which the republic of Finland lacks. Finnish influences have mostly been isolated to specific ceremonies and have not shaped the overall celebrations.

Like most cross-border commemorations, the power relations involved in planning the tercentenary and the centennial were decidedly asymmetrical: commemorators in the United States principally controlled decisions about travel, the festivals, and the dinners. While Swedish officials did not cede all decision making to U.S. commemorators, they made most of their decisions with an awareness of how they might be perceived in America. Clearly, these officials cared deeply about what people in the United States thought about their actions, often going out of their way to make sure their projects would be positively received there. American organizers, however, did not seem to care nearly as much about opinions in Sweden. Swedish Americans continued to perform national romantic music and folk dances and to emphasize the spiritual legacies of the pioneers, regardless of the Swedes' reactions and opinions. This imbalance was coupled with asymmetries of dominance within the United States: on the one hand between the federal government and the states and, on the other hand, between the states and Swedish Americans.

The 1938 and 1948 commemorations were organized jointly by several groups precisely because they provided a forum for the promotion of cross-border relations. Their impetus involved different contemporary interests—some local or regional, others international. The celebrations were fundamentally formed by the dual forces of historical disposition—the long history of Swedish settlement and immigration and the advantageous social and racial status of Swedes in America—and geopolitical circumstance. Neither commemoration would have been initiated without the ambition and energy of local and regional Swedish-American leaders and state officials. But the celebrations became nationally significant because of transatlantic ideas about the formation of modern democratic states, the rise of totalitarian regimes and the threat of war in the 1930s, and the changing geopolitical order of the late 1940s. These contemporary incentives were informed by a set of transatlantic connections: ideas about mutual technological, social, and economic modernity; bonds of Swedishness founded on perceptions of common bloodlines and shared ideological beliefs; and notions about perpetual friendships within social, political, and commercial arenas. The tropes of modernity, Swedishness, and friendship shaped the 1938 and 1948 commemorations. These dimensions were, during both celebrations, manifested through shared claims that Swedish settlers had contributed to the civilizing of America. To an even greater extent than commemorative practices, these representations have continued to affect subsequent celebrations of Swedish settlement in America.

Changing Circumstances, Malleable Histories

Even though the commemorative context has changed dramatically since the mid-twentieth century, the ways in which Swedish settler history has been celebrated across the Atlantic remains remarkably consistent. Commemorators have charged history with varying meanings while retaining the central dimensions of the narrative. From President Franklin D. Roosevelt in the 1930s, to Vice-President Lyndon B. Johnson in the 1960s, to Swedish and American politicians in the 1980s, stakeholders have reiterated the claim that the history of the New Sweden colony is a history of friendship.[8] This theme also dominated the most recent cross-border commemoration of the New Sweden colony, the 375th anniversary in 2013. During a banquet at the riverside Chase Center in Wilmington, Delaware—in front of an audience of businesspeople, Swedish Americans, Governor Jack Markell, and Vice-President Joe Biden—King Carl XVI Gustaf declared that "the early migrants planted the seeds of a deep-rooted partnership among our countries."[9] As the dominant way of framing the relevance and legacy of the colony, friendship continues to be at the forefront of Swedish settler commemorations.

At the time of New Sweden's 325th anniversary in 1963, the colony was still usually described as the first permanent Swedish settlement in the United States. Its historical significance was based on a presumed settler colonial impact. As Prince Bertil said at a Swedish Colonial Society dinner in Delaware, "while New Sweden was founded primarily to promote commerce, it turned, instead, into an agricultural community." In his view, it was this characteristic, containing "all the fundamental ingredients of western civilization," that "gave the settlement a permanent significance."[10] When the U.S. Congress adopted a resolution designating 1988 as the "Year of New Sweden," it described the colony as "the first permanent settlement of Swedes in North America" and the settlers as "instrumental in the founding of our Nation."[11] The resolution did not elaborate on the so-called civilizing significance of the colony. Yet this dimension has been integral to the celebrations.

A persistent part of the historical representation of the colony has been the friendly relations between settlers and Native Americans. One example among many was a 1988 traveling exhibit, *The Fabric of A Friendship*, produced by the American Swedish Historical Foundation of Philadelphia in cooperation with the state-owned Swedish Tobacco Company. It focused specifically on the relationship between Swedish colonists and Native Americans, with emphasis on their friendliness and their trade—characterizations of the colony that at the time were common in both scholarly and popular literature. The exhibit was intended to "broaden the appeal" of the commemoration, to increase opportunities for trade relations, and to "add critical 'historical' credibility" by including "important Indian artifacts and displays." The artifacts, which included farming tools and ceremonial pieces, were secondary to the displays, which incorporated visuals, sound, and staged settings. The exhibit featured a life-sized replica of a colonial log house and a Lenape dwelling as well as a twenty-eight-minute film about New Sweden's governor, Johan Printz, narrated by the Hollywood actor Max von Sydow. The Swedish Tobacco Company explicitly sought to gain "important support from the American Indian community."[12] Yet rather than seeing the tribal community as a potential customer base, the notion of friendly Native relations primarily gave credence to the commemorative activity and legitimacy to the tobacco company's business ventures.

The major historical exhibit of the 1988 celebration, however, was *Before Penn: Swedish Colonists in the Land of the Lenape* at the American Swedish Historical Museum. This new permanent exhibition was partly funded by the National Endowment for the Humanities and included artifacts on loan from, among other institutions, the Nordic Museum in Stockholm. Paying special attention to the relation with the Dutch, English, and Lenape, the exhibit interpreted "the Swedish colonial experience in the Delaware Valley prior to William Penn's arrival."[13] In conjunction with the exhibition opening, the director of the museum proposed a historical reenactment. The plan involved "using the descendants of the Colonial Swedes and the Lenni Lenape Indians to greet King Carl XVI Gustaf and Queen Silvia."[14] The museum would "stage reenactments of Indians (represented by two

FIGURE 19. The 1988 commemoration of New Sweden featured a reenactment in front of the American Swedish Historical Museum in Philadelphia. James "Lone Bear" Revey of the New Jersey Sand Hill Band of Lenape and Cherokee Indians presented Sweden's Queen Silvia with gifts supplied by the museum. Courtesy of Erhan Güner, from *New Sweden '88: 350 Years of Friendship*.

living Lenni Lenape chiefs) giving tobacco to the Swedish settlers (represented by the King and Queen)."[15] The director of exhibitions, Zoriana Siokalo, discussed the idea with James "Lone Bear" Revey, a leading member of the New Jersey Sand Hill Band of Lenape and Cherokee Indians. In a letter to him she instructed:

> We would like you to greet the Royal Couple (no more than one minute!) with a word or two on behalf of the Lenape descendants. The Museum will supply you with a beaver pelt and a tobacco leaf to "trade" with the King. I would also like to ask you to present them with some small gift (perhaps one of your handmade crafts, such as a beaded pouch or the strand of shell wampum beads on your list [of crafts supplied by the museum]). The Museum will cover the cost of this gift.[16]

Judging from the correspondence between Lone Bear and Siokalo after the event, the reenactment was a success. The weather was beautiful, and everything had proceeded according to plan. While Siokalo called the reenactment one of the highlights of the day, Lone Bear called it "one of the high lights in my life."[17]

It is easy to point to the uneven power relations in this event, as the museum provided both instructions and artifacts for Lone Bear to use in the reenactment, thus circumscribing the tribe's agency. The event was informed by a settler colonial legacy that made it a representation of dispossession and replacement. In the official Swedish report of the celebration, a picture of Lone Bear and Queen Silvia was described as a "colorful interlude in the packed schedule for the anniversary of the landing."[18] Yet if we look at the event from a different perspective, it is possible to conceive of it as empowering the Lenape in the Delaware Valley. The New Jersey Sand Hill Band is not recognized by the state of New Jersey as an indigenous nation, in contrast to the Nanticoke Lenni-Lenape Tribal Nation of New Jersey and the Lenape Indian Tribe of Delaware, who both took part in the 2013 reenactment and who have received state recognition from New Jersey and Delaware. Thus far, however, none of these three groups has been successful in obtaining federal recognition. For the Lenape of the Delaware Valley, participating in a cross-border commemoration in which tribal members appeared with foreign heads of state might serve as leverage in their struggle for sovereignty and recognition. An oral history of the Nanticoke nation describes that "the Swedish government and royal family visit occasionally, and Sweden even considers the tribe to be a sovereign nation."[19] Clearly, the commemorative participation of the Swedish government can also be regarded as acts of symbolic tribal recognition.

To understand how the history of Swedish settlement continues to be celebrated as a positive experience among representatives of both the settlers and the dispossessed, we must understand how that history has been discursively framed. Since the late nineteenth century, it has been common to describe the colonists and the pioneers as immigrants. This conceptualization continued throughout the twentieth century, as demonstrated by the Swedish commission's report on

FIGURE 20. On May 11, 2013, the landing of the Swedish colonists received its most vivid reenactment to date. King Carl XVI Gustaf stepped ashore from the replica of *Kalmar Nyckel* and was greeted at The Rocks by Principal Chief Mark "Quiet Hawk" Gould of the Nanticoke Lenni-Lenape Nation. Photo by David Sica, courtesy of StellaPictures.

the 1988 commemoration, which declared, "The Swedish descendants from this first wave of immigrants are today estimated to be a couple hundred thousand. Subsequent immigration from Sweden, from the 1840s onwards, to other parts of the continent, has been of significantly greater scale. The celebration of the first Swedish settlement on the Delaware is therefore intimately connected to the immigration a few centuries later."[20]

By proceeding from a description of the New Sweden colonists as immigrants, the Swedish commission could conflate the representation of the colony with that of immigration history without actually explaining this connection (that is, without expounding on the "therefore"). In the process, the report bypassed any discussion of colonialism and framed the colony as an ephemeral episode in a context of peaceful immigration and trade. This representation of New Sweden as the precursor of the Swedish mass immigration to America, first suggested by Swedish Americans as a late-nineteenth-century homemaking myth, was incorporated, through the 1938 commemoration, into the national mythology of Sweden. Today it is standard fare in representations of the colony.

While the New Sweden colonists are still sometimes described as settlers, the Swedish pioneers of the nineteenth century are nowadays framed as immigrants. The Migration Jubilee of 1996 was a sesquicentennial celebration of both emigration and immigration in Swedish history, from 1846 to 1996. It was staged as an initiative of the Swedish Ministry of Culture and arranged in cooperation with local Swedish-American organizations. From Sweden's point of view, the commemoration was intended to strengthen the country's interest in national history.[21] Although organizers explicitly sought to celebrate postwar immigration to Sweden, the event became primarily a commemoration of 150 years of emigration to the United States. Its point of departure was Erik Jansson's religious settlement Bishop Hill in western Illinois, which organizers described as having "triggered the first modern 'mass emigration' from Sweden to North America."[22]

The 1996 commemoration showed that representations of nineteenth-century emigration to America could easily be juxtaposed with twentieth-century immigration to Sweden. This juxtaposition was made possible by detaching the history of Swedish emigration to America from a settler colonial significance. The year 1846, which was chosen as the commemoration's opening date, did indeed signify a moment of settlement. Unlike previous commemorations, however, this one frequently downplayed settler colonial representations of, for instance, virgin lands; Native contact; the building of "the first" churches, schools, and houses; and the cultivation of farmland. Rather, it focused on the emigrants' dream of a better life in America, on successful Swedes in U.S. history, and on the cultural peculiarity of Swedish America as viewed from a Swedish perspective. The representations of contributions to U.S. nation building—and, by implication, to Sweden's—had become part of the immigrant pursuit of the American dream.

In 1963 Prince Bertil had maintained that as "a purely commercial and political venture, the colony would not have been able to exist for very long."[23] Since then, the increased involvement of corporations has made the trade dimension a predominant representation of Swedish settlement. In the words of the Swedish commission in 1988, the New Sweden colony was "a trading station."[24] The increased emphasis on New Sweden as a trading post has gone hand in hand with an increased interest in cross-border commemorations among Swedish businesses and enterprises. This shift dovetails with a trend in the United States, where commemorations in the decades after the 1976 bicentennial of the American Revolution became shaped by consumerism.[25] Corporations had been involved in Swedish settlement celebrations in the 1930s, but by the 1980s they had taken charge of the commemorative project. The commemorations staged since then have been visibly affected by neoliberal contexts.[26] The 2013 celebrations in Wilmington commenced with a seminar called "Making It in America," which focused on the success of Swedes and Finns in the United States. "Many of the Swedes who migrated to the United States became successful entrepreneurs," the king said in a speech later that day—from Civil War engineer John Ericsson to the people behind "the Greyhound bus, the Coca Cola bottle and the zipper."[27]

Since the mid-twentieth century, Swedish settlement in America has been continuously described in terms of historical friendship, signifying both political and commercial relations. Vice-President

Johnson captured these sentiments at a luncheon speech in Wilmington in 1963, when he—in a Cold War context, merely a few months after the Cuban Missile Crisis—talked about 325 years of "unbroken history of peaceful and friendly relations." He described the settlers of New Sweden and, after alluding to the 1783 Treaty of Amity and Commerce and the nineteenth-century immigration, declared that "our mutual devotion to peace is no less than theirs."[28] The friendship has also been given a deeper meaning by being framed as a kinship, a representation still established by conflating colonialism with migration history. The friendship between Sweden and the United States, according to Prince Bertil in 1963, was "strengthened by millions of family ties" that offered "great opportunities for increasingly active mutual relations."[29] The Swedish immigrants and their descendants have "bound our transatlantic community together," Carl XVI Gustaf said in 2013, making "our relations today as strong as ever" on both a state and a grassroots level.[30]

These transatlantic ties are no longer described in terms of common "blood," "stock," or "race," as they were in the 1930s and 1940s. But notions of biological essence ingrained in the racial family are still at the core of the genealogies that bind Swedes in the United States with Swedes in Sweden, and they continue to be charged with certain values. "I think all of those early immigrants [in New Sweden] shared the same values," the king explained in 2013: "hard work, strong faith and a belief in the opportunities of their new homeland." These values had become "a vital part" of the United States and, in the king's view, still influenced the countries' relations.[31]

Histories of Swedish settlement continue to be celebrated because they have become entangled across national borders. They do not concern only one group of people. The practice has been stimulated by the fact that Sweden and the United States have generally had amiable relations during the twentieth century. U.S. foreign policies have often been criticized in public debates in Sweden, and relations were strained during the Vietnam War; the U.S. ambassador to Sweden was, for example, called back to Washington, D.C, in 1972 when Prime Minister Olof Palme compared the U.S. bombings in Hanoi with the atrocities at Guernica, Babij Jar, and Treblinka. Nonetheless, the two countries have remained close partners. Throughout the postwar period, American popular culture has wielded a major impact in Sweden, with American music, television, and literature remaining popular also during periods of political anti-Americanism. In the United States, Sweden has been used as both a positive and negative example, depending on political outlook. Its image there has been informed by social progressivism and modernism—including Swedish design and architecture, promoted under the moniker "Swedish Modern"—and by notions that the country's socialist policies, lack of traditional social values, and secularization have created a sexually unbridled country with abnormal suicide rates.[32] But despite being appropriated under changing circumstances on two sides of an ocean, interpretations of the histories of Swedish settlement and immigration have been remarkably similar. They have been malleable and resilient, characterized by adaptability and thus longevity. Their resilience is exemplified by the lingering assertion that Swedish colonists and pioneers have contributed by civilizing the continent, either through explicit references to the replacement of Native Americans or by ignoring the continental context of settler violence. This notion gives depth to contemporary cross-border relations. Its legitimizing function is the principal appeal of histories of Swedish settlement in America.

Leaving the National Paradigm

While memories of colonialism, pioneering, and immigration have generally been marginalized in Sweden, the opposite is true in the United States. These histories—along with memories of independence, certain national leaders, and wars—constitute the core of national and regional American mythologies. Memories of East Coast colonial settlements thrived during the early twentieth century, as seen in such diverse expressions as regional commemorations and the colonial revival movement, yet their significance as a national American myth of origin eventually diminished. As Matthew Frye Jacobson has shown, during the 1960s the story of Plymouth Rock as the origin of whiteness in America was replaced by the story of Ellis Island, highlighting the idea of America as a nation of immigrants.[33]

Yet histories of settlement in America have continued to be important, albeit not generally as a myth of origin for the nation as a whole. An exception is the history of pioneering and the idea of the frontier as a thoroughly American experience, which have remained influential, not least through popular culture.[34] Stories of the pioneers have been part of the idea of the American dream in which the self-made man strives for freedom and success. At the regional or local level, colonial histories continue to be viable in an assortment of public settings. Toward the end of his magnum opus on Plymouth Rock, John Seelye reminisced about his visit to Plymouth in 1995 for the 375th anniversary of the Pilgrim landing, an event that was "different only in degree" from the Rock's heyday in the nineteenth and early twentieth centuries. Although no longer considered the point of origin for Americans in general, Plymouth Rock is still important regionally, especially for local business and tourism.[35]

The same holds true of The Rocks in Wilmington. In 1939, the General Assembly of Delaware adopted a resolution authorizing the governor to "each year" proclaim March 29—the claimed date of the colonists' landing—as "Delaware Swedish Colonial Day."[36] Delaware governors proclaimed the day in every year until 1963 and in most years during the following decade. In 1961, Fort Christina State Park was designated as a National Historic Landmark. President Barack Obama declared it a National Monument in 2013, and in 2015 it became one of seven Delaware sites in the First State National Historic Park. Since the park's public reopening in 2016, its interpretation has been managed by the Kalmar Nyckel Foundation and the Old Swedes Foundation, who also manage the nearby late-seventeenth-century Old Swedes Church. These developments show that The Rocks has retained some level of public historical interest in Delaware as the state's foundational site. This regional dimension, however, has continuously been promoted and upheld by Swedish-American organizations—most notably, the Delaware Swedish Colonial Society. Delaware Valley regionalism has thus been paired with sustained claims that the site constitutes the beginning of Swedishness in America. The latest major commemoration of the colony in 2013 was organized by New Sweden Alliance, Inc., an organization consisting of seventeen associations and institutions, including the American Swedish Historical Museum and the Swedish-American Chamber of Commerce.[37]

Settler memories have also been activated repeatedly in the twentieth and twenty-first centuries in the service of international relations. An example is the 350th and 400th anniversaries of the Jamestown Colony. Its commemoration in 1957 was grandly celebrated as a Cold War heritage, with ample state and federal funding for the refurbishment of Colonial Williamsburg, and the participation of dignitaries such as President Dwight D. Eisenhower, British royalty, and the commander of the North Atlantic Treaty Organization (NATO). Commemorators built a full-sized replica of the 1607 vessel *Susan Constant* and organized a naval review of 114 ships from NATO allies and nations that had links to the settling of America. At a gala dinner in New York City, Britain's Queen Elizabeth II emphasized the shared history of England and the United States, which, she said, "illustrates these two stories, yours and ours . . . , both stories of experiments and adventure in freedom." President Eisenhower concurred: "The English-speaking people march forward together, to stand steadfast behind the principles that made the two nations great."[38] Fifty years later, in 2007, the Jamestown Colony was again commemorated across borders. The celebration, named "America's 400th Anniversary," had been initiated by the Virginia General Assembly and was organized by a foundation that included members from the public and private sectors. The explicit objective was to arrange a regional celebration that had national and international significance. The event was eventually organized through a partnership between British companies operating in Virginia and Virginia-based businesses working in the United Kingdom. Attendees included President George W. Bush and—again—Queen Elizabeth II.[39]

The mythological character of settler histories in the United States helps explain why scholars generally have continued to study memories of colonization, pioneering, and immigration within a national paradigm. But the 1938 and 1948 commemorations show that settler histories have significances that far exceed the confines of the United States. It is not possible to understand the meaning of

Swedish settlement in America by solely considering how it relates to U.S. patriotism, American regional identities, or Swedish nationalism. Such frameworks only reiterate national mythologies by treating history as nationally circumscribed. To acknowledge the presence of different commemorators and the organizational involvement of different—and often non-national—groups is to be sensitive to how interactions across borders change commemorations. These changes might occur on different spatial and temporal levels: affecting some groups and contexts more than others and influencing both the dynamic of contemporary relations and the ways in which history is represented through the interests of the present.

This book would have arrived at different answers if it had relied on methodologies and frameworks of the national paradigm. To subscribe to the notion that "we are what we remember" encourages us to assume that a specific social group commemorates a specific history, one that allegedly belongs to that group, in order to create a specific identity or memory. This book challenges that idea. Instead, it contributes to an ongoing discussion about "how public memorial symbols and commemorations, though they occupy physical places, in fact symbolise hybrid narratives about past events."[40] To leave the national paradigm is to adopt a way of seeing and a set of methods that do not take the nation as their point of departure or make it the natural endpoint of analysis. This approach requires us to analyze the movements and interactions of commemorators, and the various forms and contents of celebrations, while being sensitive to the transnational and transcultural dimensions of the exchanges. This is, perhaps, most germane when we consider commemorations of histories that are not confined within the borders of nation-states. Studying them only in specific places means localizing, and thus often nationalizing, histories that cannot be meaningfully circumscribed in that limited framework.

The importance of leaving the national paradigm might be most pressing for commemorations of "difficult pasts," including that of settlement. Celebrations of indigenous dispossession have long been fiercely contested in the United States and elsewhere.[41] In 1992, organizers of the quincentenary commemoration of Christopher

Columbus's landing in America were forced to abandon a history that celebrated a chauvinistic history of "discovery." Instead, they decided to focus on less Eurocentric "encounters." Eventually they emphasized "not the epic story of feats beyond compare but the tragic tale of invasion and loss."[42] Although the colonial landing was reenacted at Jamestown in 2007, the commemoration also included a program devoted to discussions and displays of African American and Native American experiences of the colony. In 2010 the organizers of the 400th anniversary of Santa Fe, New Mexico, likewise created space for Native voices. One result of the Native cooperation was a publication that included accounts of "the struggles, strife and challenges created, both past and present, by imperialistic colonial influences and, of course, the Native Americans themselves, as well as thought provoking commentaries and personal pieces, some told in the tradition of Native storytellers."[43] These are examples of what the memory studies scholars Louis Bickford and Amy Sodaro see as "a new, future-oriented paradigm of commemoration that seeks to use knowledge of the past—and especially its traumas and violence—to create a better present and future."[44] Such aspects have been absent in celebrations of Swedish colonialism and pioneering. The protests and critical discussions of the late twentieth century that have accompanied colonial commemorations in the United States and beyond have not had any visible effect on celebrations of Swedish settlement.

In recent years, studies have shed light on the exceptionalism of the Nordic countries, contesting the notion that they are more humanitarian, less inherently racist, and ostensibly unaffected by colonial legacies.[45] As Ylva Habel has argued in Sweden, there seems to be a "lingering attachment to collectively held conceptions of political, historic and cultural innocence vis-à-vis racial issues."[46] These dimensions of Swedish exceptionalism have hampered critical discussions about race and postcolonialism. "Swedish scholarship, and popular understanding," writes Gunlög Fur, "has gone from no colonialism to post-colonialism without stopping at the in-between."[47] The lack of a postcolonial overhaul and the notion of Swedish racial innocence relates to the increased descriptions of the New Sweden colonists as immigrants. This reframing allows for the otherwise complicated historical process of colonialism to be embedded within an allegedly more benign narrative of immigration: as the former is a state project imbued with power and racism, the latter is an individual venture associated with freedom. More than a way of describing the past, this discourse has been a precondition for the continual framing of settlement as a positive legacy.

The New Sweden colony was, during the twentieth century, gradually detached from an American myth of origin. Although recent events show that it once again is being appropriated as a foundational history of the Delaware Valley, its commemorative potential has for decades been primarily activated by Swedish-American organizations or whenever an overseas delegation comes to town. Since the early twentieth century, repeated cross-border commemorations have been instrumental in maintaining that version of its memory. By way of these celebrations, the historical representations of Swedish settlement in America have increasingly been informed by Swedish innocence.

The New Sweden Tercentenary and Swedish Pioneer Centennial drew much of their strength from the notion that the Swedish settler colonial ventures lacked all of the negative and violent aspects of the Dutch and British colonies or the American West. They were presented as innocent projects, without warfare or hostility, steeped in a love of freedom. This representation has been reaffirmed by the postwar image of Sweden as a humanitarian, noncolonial country, allegedly lacking a history of racism and violent conflicts. The history of Swedish settlement in America continues to be represented within a narrative that was cemented in the 1930s and 1940s. It is still reiterated in service of transatlantic profit and pride.

NOTES

ABBREVIATIONS

AKC	Allan Kastrup Collection, MSS P:308, Swenson Swedish Immigration Research Center, Augustana College, Rock Island, Illinois.
ASI 1938	Scrapbook Svenskarnas Dag 1938, American Swedish Institute, Minneapolis, Minnesota.
ASI 1948	Scrapbook Svenskarnas Dag 1948, American Swedish Institute, Minneapolis, Minnesota.
CBP	Conrad Bergendoff Papers, MSS 5, Augustana College Special Collections, Rock Island, Illinois.
BNS	Bestyrelsen för firandet av Nya Sverigeminnet, U14, Utställningsbestyrelsen, National Archives in Marieberg, Stockholm, Sweden.
DE 325th	Swedish 325th Anniversary, General Files, 1963, Delaware Public Archives, Dover, Delaware.
DEC	Temporary Commemorative Commissions, Delaware Tercentenary Commission/Delaware Swedish Tercentenary Commission, Delaware Public Archives, Dover, Delaware.
DoS	Department of State, Decimal File 1930–39, RG 59, National Archives and Records Administration, College Park, Maryland.
DoS Sthlm	Records of the Foreign Service Posts of the Department of State, Stockholm Legation and Embassy, RG 84, National Archives and Records Administration, College Park, Maryland.
HRR	Handlingar och räkenskaper avseende resorna, Royal Palace Archives, Stockholm, Sweden.

NS '88	New Sweden '88 Collection, American Swedish Historical Museum, Philadelphia, Pennsylvania.
NWOP	Nils William Olsson Papers, Swenson Swedish Immigration Research Center, Augustana College, Rock Island, Illinois.
PAC	Pennsylvania Three Hundredth Anniversary Commission, Commemorative, Monument, and Exposition Commissions, Bureau of Archives and History, Records of Special Commissions, RG-25, Pennsylvania State Archives, Harrisburg, Pennsylvania.
SI	Svenska institutet, Hemmamyndigheten, FIIa, National Archives in Arninge, Stockholm, Sweden.
SPCA	Swedish Pioneer Centennial Association, MSS 5, F. M. Johnson Archives, North Park University, Chicago, Illinois.
TC	1938 Tercentenary Collection, American Swedish Historical Museum, Philadelphia, Pennsylvania.
UD 1920	Utrikesdepartementet, 1920 års dossiersystem, P66, National Archives in Marieberg, Stockholm, Sweden.
UD Chi	Utrikesdepartementet, Konsulatarkiv, Chicago, F1g, P66, National Archives in Arninge, Stockholm, Sweden.
UD Mpls	Utrikesdepartementet, Konsulatarkiv, Minneapolis, F1g, P66, National Archives in Arninge, Stockholm, Sweden.
UD Wash	Utrikesdepartementet, Beskickningsarkiv, Washington, P66, F1g, National Archives in Arninge, Stockholm, Sweden.

PREFACE

1. On the ethics of cross-border commemorations, see Adam Hjorthén, "Global Histories and Cross-Border Commemoration," in *Commemoration: The American Association for State and Local History Guide*, ed. Seth C. Bruggeman (Lanham, M.D.: Rowman and Littlefield, 2017), 63–64).
2. The American mythology about the Kensington Runestone is discussed in David M. Krueger, *Myths of the Rune Stone: Viking Martyrs and the Birthplace of America* (Minneapolis: University of Minnesota Press, 2015). On the exhibitions of the runestone at the Swedish History Museum and the Runestone Museum in Alexandria, see Adam Hjorthén, "Displaying a Controversy: The Kensington Rune Stone as Transnational Historical Culture," *Swedish-American Historical Quarterly* 62, no. 2 (2011): 78–105.

INTRODUCTION: AN ENTANGLED HISTORY OF SETTLER COMMEMORATIONS

1. Amandus Johnson, letter to Wollmar Boström, December 14, 1936, F3, vol. 231, UD Wash.
2. See the special issue of *Sverige & Amerika* 45–46, no. 1–2 (2013). The commemoration was organized by the New Sweden Alliance, Inc., https://www.newswedenalliance.org.
3. The symbolism of the handshake was adopted in acts of settler colonial conciliation during the eighteenth and nineteenth centuries. The clasped hands of a Native American and a U.S. soldier were, for example, pictured on Thomas Jefferson's Indian Peace

Medals, distributed to Natives in the midst of dispossession. The symbolism also appears in contemporary performances of indigenous and non-indigenous reconciliation. See Penelope Edmonds, *Settler Colonialism and (Re)conciliation: Frontier Violence, Affective Performances, and Imaginative Refoundings* (Basingstoke, U.K.: Palgrave Macmillan, 2016), 19–23.

4. Museums and historic sites in Europe located at the settlers' point of departure testify to the importance of American settler histories outside the United States. They include the Mayflower Museum in Plymouth, England; the American Pilgrim Museum in Leiden, the Netherlands; and the Muelle de las Carabelas (the Wharf of the Caravels) in Palos de la Frontera, Spain.

5. *America's 400th Legacy Site,* http://www.jamestown2007.org; "2009 Annual Report of the Santa Fe 400th Anniversary Committee, February 2010," http://www.sfreporter .com (no longer available online); Jason Dearen, "King of Spain and His Wife Cheered during Their Visit to St. Augustine," *Orlando Sentinel,* September 18, 2015; Consulate General of France in Miami, "Celebrating 450 Years of French History in Florida," http://www.consulfrance-miami.org.

6. *Mayflower 400,* http://www.mayflower400uk.com.

7. Currently about 4.3 million people in the United States claim Swedish ancestry. See U.S. Census Bureau, "B01003: Total Population," Race/Ancestry: Swedish (089–090)," *2006–2010 American Community Survey,* http://factfinder.census.gov.

8. The 1938 commemoration was also called the Delaware Tercentenary, the Pennsylvania 300th Anniversary, and the Swedish-American Tercentenary. Its most common name, however, was the New Sweden Tercentenary.

9. Geoffrey Cubitt, *History and Memory* (Manchester, U.K.: University of Manchester Press, 2000), 219.

10. Theories of cultural memory, which have been most vigorously developed by Aleida Assmann, are more fluent and more open to transnational analyses than collective and social memory are, which are impeded by their links to specific collective or social groups. See Aleida Assmann, "Transformation between History and Memory," *Social Research* 75 (Spring 2008): 49–72; and Assmann, *Cultural Memory and Western Civilization* (Cambridge: Cambridge University Press, 2011).

11. John Gillis, *Commemorations: The Politics of National Identity* (Princeton: Princeton University Press, 1994), 3.

12. Brian Conway, "Local Conditions, Global Environments, and Transnational Discourses in Memory Work: The Case of Bloody Sunday (1972)," *Memory Studies* 1, no. 2 (2008): 189. See also Daniel Levy, "Changing Temporalities and the Internationalization of Memory Cultures," in *Memory and the Future: Transnational Politics, Ethics, and Society,* ed. Yifat Gutman, Adam D. Brown, and Amy Sodaro (New York: Palgrave Macmillan, 2010), 17–18.

13. Jeffrey Lee Meriwether and Laura Mattoon D'Amore, eds., *We Are What We Remember: The American Past Through Commemoration* (Newcastle upon Tyne, U.K.: Cambridge Scholars Publishing, 2012). An illustrative example is H. V. Nelles's study of the 1908 Quebec Tercentenary, which included both British- and French-speaking, local and federal, Canadian commemorators, as well as representatives from France, the United States, Great Britain, and several First Nations. Still, Nelles framed the celebration as a project of nation-building (*The Art of Nation-Building: Pageantry and Spectacle at Quebec's Tercentenary* [Toronto: University of Toronto Press, 1999], 317). Another example is Kirk Savage's overview of American scholarship on commemorations, which includes no discussion about cross-border topics and only reference

literature that study memory in America. This fact is worth emphasizing because the overview covers close to sixty books ("History, Memory, and Monuments: An Overview of the Scholarly Literature on Commemoration" [2006], https://www.nps.gov).

14. Astrid Erll, "Travelling Memory," *Parallax* 17, no. 4 (2011): 8.

15. See, for example, Daniel Levy and Natan Sznaider, *The Holocaust and Memory in the Global Age* (Philadelphia: Temple University Press, 2006); Udo J. Hebel, ed., *Transnational American Memories* (Berlin: Walter de Gruyter, 2009); Michael Rothberg, *Multidirectional Memory: Remembering the Holocaust in the Age of Decolonization* (Stanford: Stanford University Press, 2009); Aleida Assmann and Sebastian Conrad, eds., *Memory in a Global Age: Discourses, Practices and Trajectories* (Basingstoke, U.K.: Palgrave Macmillan, 2010); Julia Creet and Andreas Kitzmann, eds., *Memory and Migration: Multidisciplinary Approaches to Memory Studies* (Toronto: University of Toronto Press, 2011); Irial Glynn and J. Olaf Kleist, eds., *History, Memory and Migration: Perceptions of the Past and the Politics of Incorporation* (Basingstoke, U.K.: Palgrave Macmillan, 2012); Chiara De Cesari and Ann Rigney, eds., *Transnational Memory: Circulation, Articulation, Scales* (Berlin: Walter de Gruyter, 2014); and Lucy Bond and Jessica Rapson, eds., *The Transcultural Turn: Interrogating Memory Between and Beyond Borders* (Berlin: Walter de Gruyter, 2014).

16. Michael Rothberg, "Multidirectional Memory in Migratory Settings: The Case of Post-Holocaust Germany," in De Cesari and Rigney, *Transnational Memory*, 130.

17. My definition of entangled history is inspired by the French-German concept of *histoire croisée*. See Jürgen Kocka and Heinz-Gerhard Haupt, "Comparison and Beyond: Traditions, Scope, and Perspectives of Comparative History," in *Comparative and Transnational History: Central European Approaches and New Perspectives*, ed. Jürgen Kocka and Heinz-Gerhard Haupt (New York: Berghan, 2009); and Michael Werner and Bénédicte Zimmerman, "Beyond Comparison: Histoire Croisée and the Challenge of Reflexivity," *History and Theory* 45, no. 1 (2006): 30–50.

18. For a discussion of these concepts, see Steven Vertovec, *Transnationalism* (London: Routledge, 2009), 3. There is a tendency among historians and other scholars to situate the transnational as an identifiable object—describing, for example, transnational identities, spaces, or moments. Transnationalism does not necessarily overthrow national trajectories and can still produce exceptionalist standpoints and narratives. See the critique in Donald E. Pease, introduction, in *Re-Framing the Transnational Turn in American Studies*, ed. Winfried Fluck, Donald E. Pease, and John Carlos Rowe (Hanover, N.H.: Dartmouth College Press, 2011), 16–26.

19. I understand the concept of historical representation through the fundamental difference between the past as reality and historical writing as a representation of the past and as a substitute for something absent that is no longer directly available to us in itself. See Frank R. Ankersmit, *Historical Representation* (Stanford: Stanford University Press, 2001), 11–17, 39–49.

20. For previous research on the New Sweden Tercentenary, see Max Engman, "The Tug of War over 'Nya Sverige' 1938," *Swedish-American Historical Quarterly* 45, no. 2 (1994): 69–117; Melvin G. Holli, "1938 Delaware Tercentenary: Establishing a Finnish Presence at the 300th Anniversary Celebration," in *Finnish Identity in America*, ed. Auvo Kostiainen (Turku: Turku Historical Archives 46, 1990); and Orm Øverland, *Immigrant Minds, American Identities: Making the United States Home, 1870–1930* (Urbana: University of Illinois Press, 2000), 179–83. On the Swedish Pioneer Centennial, see John Bodnar, *Remaking America: Public Memory, Commemoration, and Patriotism in the Twentieth Century* (Princeton: Princeton University Press, 1992), 47–52.

21. For exceptions, see Michael Scott Van Wagenen, *Remembering the Forgotten War: The Enduring Legacies of the U.S.-Mexican War* (Amherst: University of Massachusetts Press, 2012); Joep Leerssen and Ann Rigney, eds., *Commemorating Writers in Nineteenth-Century Europe* (Basingstoke, U.K.: Palgrave Macmillan, 2014); Philip Mead, "Lest We Forget: Shakespeare Tercentenary Commemoration in Sydney and London, 1916," in *Celebrating Shakespeare: Commemoration and Cultural Memory*, ed. Clara Calvo and Coppélia Kahn (Cambridge: Cambridge University Press, 2015); and Martin Klatt, "Dybbøl 2014: Constructing Familiarity by Remembrance?," in *European Borderlands: Living with Bridges and Barriers*, ed. Elisabeth Boesen and Gregor Schnuer (New York: Routledge, 2017), 30–46. Although his focus is on Cold War practices in the United States, see also Richard M. Fried's discussion of the 1957 celebration of the Jamestown colony and the 1959 Hudson-Champlain commemoration, which "bristled with international themes" (*The Russians are Coming! The Russians Are Coming! Pageantry and Patriotism in Cold-War America* [New York: Oxford University Press, 1998], 112–16).
22. Ronald Reagan, "Proclamation 4928–Dutch American Friendship Day, 1982," April 12, 1982, in *Public Papers of the Presidents of the United States, Ronald Reagan, January 1 to July 2, 1982* (Washington, D.C.: U.S. Government Printing Office, 1983), 453. See also J. W. Schulte Nordholt and Robert P. Swierenga, *A Bilateral Bicentennial: A History of Dutch-American Relations, 1782–1982* (Amsterdam: Octagon, 1982).
23. "The German-American Friendship Garden: A Comprehensive History," *German Missions in the United States*, http://www.germany.info; Ron Alexander, "German-Americans Mark Tricentennial," *New York Times*, August 15, 1983.
24. Stephen J. Summerhill and John Alexander Williams, *Sinking Columbus: Contested History, Cultural Politics, and Mythmaking during the Quincentenary* (Gainesville: University of Florida Press, 2000), 127–78. Compare the framing of Columbus as an American memory in Timothy Kubal, *Cultural Movements and Collective Memory: Christopher Columbus and the Rewriting of the National Origin Myth* (New York: Palgrave Macmillan, 2008).
25. I believe that this methodology needs to be actor-centered, in contrast to the sometimes more structural focus of global history and world history. For an insightful argument for the microhistorical approach to cross-border studies, see Angelika Epple, "The Global, the Transnational and the Subaltern: The Limits of History beyond the National Paradigm," in *Beyond Methodological Nationalism: Research Methodologies for Cross-Border Studies*, ed. Anna Amelina, Devrimsel D. Nergiz, Thomas Faist, and Nina Glick Schiller (New York: Routledge, 2012), 155–75.
26. I have translated into English all of the archival sources in Swedish (and some secondary literature) that I quote in the book. In doing so, I have tried to follow the vernacular as closely as possible while retaining modernized English grammar and spelling.
27. W. J. T. Mitchell, "There Are No Visual Media," *Journal of Visual Culture* 4 (August 2005): 257–61.
28. Victoria J. Freeman, "'Toronto Has No History': Indigeneity, Settler Colonialism, and Historical Memory in Canada's Largest City" (Ph.D. diss., University of Toronto, 2010), 130. See also Annie E. Coombes, ed., *Rethinking Settler Colonialism: History and Memory in Australia, Canada, Aotearoa New Zealand, and South Africa* (Manchester, U.K.: Manchester University Press, 2006).
29. On the memory of Plymouth Rock, see John Seelye, *Memory's Nation: The Place of Plymouth Rock* (Chapel Hill: University of North Carolina Press, 1998), 1–4; Udo J. Hebel, "Historical Bonding with an Expiring Heritage: Revisiting the Plymouth Ter-

centenary Festivities of 1920/21," in *Celebrating Ethnicity and Nation: American Festive Culture from the Revolution to the Early 20th Century*, ed. Jürgen Heideking, Geneviève Fabre, and Kai Dreisbach (New York: Berghahn, 2001); and Anne C. Reilly, "The Pilgrimization of Plymouth: Creating a Landscape of Memory in Plymouth Massachusetts, During the Pilgrim Tercentenary of 1920–1921," in Meriwether and Mattoon D'Amore, *We Are What We Remember*, 244–66. Another foundational history in the late nineteenth century was the Anglo-American mythology about Leif Erikson's Viking settlement in Vinland in about the year 1000, which some writers located in New England. See Annette Kolodny, *In Search of First Contact: The Vikings of Vinland, the Peoples of the Dawnland, and the Anglo-American Anxiety of Discovery* (Durham, N.C.: Duke University Press, 2012).

30. Bodnar, *Remaking America*, 41–77; Øverland, *Immigrant Minds*, 54–86; Kathleen Neils Conzen, "Ethnicity as Festive Culture: Nineteenth-Century German America on Parade," in *The Invention of Ethnicity*, ed. Werner Sollors (New York: Oxford University Press, 1989), 68; April R. Schultz, *Ethnicity on Parade: Inventing the Norwegian American Through Celebration* (Amherst: University of Massachusetts Press, 1994).

31. David M. Wrobel, *Promised Lands: Promotion, Memory, and the Creation of the American West* (Lawrence: University of Kansas Press, 2002), chap. 4. A Swedish-American example is the Bishop Hill Old Settlers' Association of western Illinois, founded in 1896.

32. See, for example, Jeremy Silvester, "'Sleep with Southwester': Monuments and Settler Identity in Namibia," in *Settler Colonialism in the Twentieth Century: Projects, Practices, Legacies*, ed. Caroline Elkins and Susan Pedersen (London: Routledge, 2005), 271–86; Coombes, *Rethinking Settler Colonialism*; Freeman, "Toronto Has No History"; Katrine Barber, "Shared Authority in the Context of Tribal Sovereignty: Building Capacity for Partnerships with Indigenous Nations," *Public Historian* 35 (November 2013): 20–39; Ashley Glassburn Falzetti, "Archival Absence: The Burden of History," *Settler Colonial Studies* 5, no. 2 (2015): 128–44; and Edmonds, *Settler Colonialism and (Re)conciliation*. Although it does not adopt the concept of settler colonialism per se, Leslie Witz's *Apartheid's Festival: Contesting South Africa's National Pasts* (Bloomington: Indiana University Press, 2003) is an important study that analyzes processes of settler celebrations.

33. Daiva Stasiulis and Nira Yuval-Davis, *Unsettling Settler Societies: Articulations of Gender, Race, Ethnicity and Class* (London: Sage, 1995), 20–21.

34. Inscription on the New Sweden monument (by Carl Milles, 1938) in Wilmington, Delaware; Nils William Olsson, "Pioneer Centennial to Be Observed Throughout Middle West in 1948," *American Swedish Monthly* (November 1947).

35. Lorenzo Veracini, *Settler Colonialism: A Theoretical Overview* (Basingstoke, U.K.: Palgrave Macmillan, 2010), 75–94.

36. On Swedish settlers and immigrants' relation with Native Americans, see Maria Erling, "Wrestling with the Mission Mantle: Matthias Wahlstrom, Failed Missionary to the Comanche, and the Relation between the Augustana Synod and the Covenant Church," *Swedish-American Historical Quarterly* 63, nos. 2–3 (2012): 135–57; Karen V. Hansen, *Encounter on the Great Plains: Scandinavian Settlers and the Dispossession of Dakota Indians, 1890–1930* (New York: Oxford University Press, 2013); Gunlög Fur, "Indians and Immigrants: Entangled Histories," *Journal of American Ethnic History* 33, no. 3 (2014): 55–76; and Gunlög Fur, "Jakobsson upptäcker Amerika: Svenskar möter kiowaindianer 1915–2015," in *Årsbok MMXV: Kungl. Vitterhets Historie och Antikvitets*

Akademien (Stockholm: Kungl. Vitterhets Historie och Antikvitets Akademien, 2015), 131–44. On literary and nonfictional representations of Native American and Swedish immigrant encounters, see Ulf Jonas Björk, "Stories of America: The Rise of the 'Indian Book' in Sweden, 1862–1895," *Scandinavian Studies* 75, no. 4 (2003): 509–26; Ulf Jonas Björk, "The Dangerous Prairies of Texas: The Western Dime Novel in Sweden, 1900–1908," *Swedish-American Historical Quarterly* 55 (July 2004): 165–78; and Gunlög Fur, "Colonial Fantasies: American Indians, Indigenous Peoples, and a Swedish Discourse of Innocence," *National Identities* 18, no. 1 (2016): 11–33. See also related works on Norwegian immigrants: Betty A. Bergland, "Norwegian Immigrants and 'Indianerne' in the Landtaking, 1838–1862," *Norwegian American Studies* 35 (2000): 319–50; and Orm Øverland, "Norwegian Americans Meet Native Americans: Exclusion and Inclusion in Immigrant Homemaking in America," in *Postcolonial Dislocations: Travel, History, and the Ironies of Narrative*, ed. Charles I. Armstrong and Øyunn Hestetun (Oslo: Novus, 2006), 109–22.

37. Gunlög Fur, "Romantic Relations: Swedish Attitudes towards Indians during the Twentieth Century," *Swedish-American Historical Quarterly* 55, no. 3 (2004): 150.
38. Hansen, *Encounter on the Great Plains*. On the Homestead Act as a de facto immigration legislation, see Blake Bell, "America's Invitation to the World: Was the Homestead Act the First Accommodating Immigration Legislation in the United States?" (n.d.), https://www.nps.gov.
39. Hansen, *Encounter on the Great Plains*, 5.
40. Aziz Rana, *The Two Faces of American Freedom* (Cambridge: Harvard University Press, 2010), 3; James Belich, *Replenishing the Earth: The Settler Revolution and the Rise of the Anglo-World, 1783–1939* (Oxford: Oxford University Press, 2009).
41. Jean M. O'Brien, *Firsting and Lasting: Writing Indians Out of Existence in New England* (Minneapolis: University of Minnesota Press, 2010).
42. Matthew Frye Jacobson, *Roots Too: White Ethnic Revival in Post–Civil Rights America* (Cambridge: Harvard University Press, 2006), 7–9.
43. Unlike some scholars, I do not see nationalism and transnationalism as opposites or as contradictory. For an argument that research on transnationalism somehow obscures the role of nation-states, see Jeremy Black, *Contesting History: Narratives of Public History* (London: Bloomsbury, 2014), ix–xiii. As I will make clear in the subsequent chapters, national actors, narratives, and mythologies have also been central to cross-border commemorations. Through a transnational approach, however, nationalism becomes a part of the analysis, not its governing principle.

CHAPTER I: MOMENTS OF OPPORTUNITY

1. Sten Dehlgren, "The American Tercentenary Celebrations," in *Sweden's Participation in the U.S. Celebration of the New Sweden Tercentenary*, by Fritz Henriksson (Stockholm: Bonnier, 1939), 142–46.
2. John Gillis, introduction to *Commemorations: The Politics of National Identity* (Princeton: Princeton University Press, 1994), 8.
3. Benedict Anderson, *Imagined Communities: Reflections on the Origin and Spread of Nationalism* (London: Verso, 1983); Eric Hobsbawm and Terence Ranger, eds., *The Invention of Tradition* (Cambridge: Cambridge University Press, 1983). In the United States, patriotic commemorations have paid particular attention to histories of European colonial settlement, U.S. independence, and wars. See, for example, Michael

Kammen, *Mystic Chords of Memory: The Transformation of Tradition in American Culture* (New York: Knopf, 1991); William M. Johnston, *Celebrations: The Cult of Anniversaries in Europe and the United States Today* (New Brunswick, N.J.: Transaction, 1991), 39–61; John Bodnar, *Remaking America: Public Memory, Commemoration, and Patriotism in the Twentieth Century* (Princeton: Princeton University Press, 1992), 169–244; Lynn Spillman, *Nation and Commemoration: Creating National Identities in the United States and Australia* (Cambridge: Cambridge University Press, 1997); Robert Cook, *Troubled Commemoration: The American Civil War Centennial, 1961–1965* (Baton Rouge: Louisiana State Press, 2007); Tammy S. Gordon, *The Spirit of 1976: Commerce, Community, and the Politics of Commemoration* (Amherst: University of Massachusetts Press, 2013); and Thomas J. Brown, *Civil War Canon: Sites of Confederate Memory in South Carolina* (Chapel Hill: University of North Carolina Press, 2015). In Sweden, a nation that has not experienced domestic upheavals such as a revolution or a civil war, commemorations in the nineteenth and early twentieth centuries emphasized the country's seventeenth-century Age of Greatness (when it geographically encircled the Baltic Sea) as well as memories of kings and national heroes. See, for example, Ulf Zander, *Fornstora dagar, moderna tider: bruk av och debatter om svensk historia från sekelskifte till sekelskifte* (Lund: Nordic Academic Press, 2001); Magnus Rodell, *Att gjuta en nation: Statyinvigningar och nationsformering i Sverige vid 1800-talets mitt* (Stockholm: Natur och kultur, 2002).

4. Scholars often pair descriptions of "contested" memories, remembrances, and commemorations with the spatial metaphor of a "terrain" or a "site." For example, see Alan Gordon, *Making Public Pasts: The Contested Terrain of Montreal's Public Memories, 1891–1930* (Montreal: McGill-Queen's University Press, 2001); Jo Roberts, *Contested Land, Contested Memory: Israel's Jews and Arabs and the Ghost of Catastrophe* (Toronto: Dundurn, 2013); Benjamin Ziemann, *Contested Commemorations: Republican War Veterans and Weimar Political Culture* (Cambridge: Cambridge University Press, 2013); Paul A. Pickering and Alex Tyrell, eds., *Contested Sites: Commemoration, Memorial, and Popular Politics in Nineteenth-Century Britain* (New York: Routledge, 2016); and Catharina Raudvere, *Contested Memories and the Demands of the Past: History Cultures in the Modern Muslim World* (Basingstoke, U.K.: Palgrave Macmillan, 2017).

5. Bodnar, *Remaking America*, 13–14.

6. On ethnicity, memory, and commemoration, see Martha K. Norkunas, *The Politics of Public Memory: Tourism, History, and Ethnicity in Monterey, California* (Albany: State University of New York Press, 1993); April R. Schultz, *Ethnicity on Parade: Inventing the Norwegian American Through Celebration* (Amherst: University of Massachusetts Press, 1994); Jürgen Heideking, Geneviève Fabre, and Kai Dreisbach, eds., *Celebrating Ethnicity and Nation: American Festive Culture from the Revolution to the Early 20th Century* (New York: Berghahn, 2001); and Frances Swyripa, *Storied Landscapes: Ethno-Religious Identity and the Canadian Prairies* (Winnipeg: University of Manitoba Press, 2010). On indigenous peoples' political use of commemorations, see, for example, Ronald Rudin, *Remembering and Forgetting in Acadie: A Historian's Journey through Public Memory* (Toronto: University of Toronto Press, 2009), 176–78; Penelope Edmonds, *Settler Colonialism and (Re)conciliation: Frontier Violence, Affective Performances, and Imaginative Refoundings* (Basingstoke, U.K.: Palgrave Macmillan, 2016); Katrine Barber, "Shared Authority in the Context of Tribal Sovereignty: Building Capacity for Partnerships with Indigenous Nations," *Public Historian* 35 (November 2013): 20–39.

7. Seth C. Bruggeman, "Introduction: Conundrum and Nuance in American Memory," in *Commemoration: The American Association for State and Local History Guide*, ed.

Seth C. Bruggeman (Lanham, M.D.: Rowman & Littlefield, 2017), 3–4. On how commemorations are shaped by political changes, see Daniel J. Walkowitz and Lisa Maya Knauer, eds., *Memory and the Impact of Political Transformation in Public Space* (Durham, N.C.: Duke University Press, 2004).

8. Scholars who previously have used the concept of "moments of opportunity" include Rudy Koshar, *From Monuments to Traces: Artifacts of German Memory, 1870–1990* (Berkeley: University of California Press, 2000), 8; Timothy Kubal, *Cultural Movements and Collective Memory: Christopher Columbus and the Rewriting of the National Origin Myth* (New York: Palgrave Macmillan, 2008), 33; and Layla Renshaw, *Exhuming Loss: Memory, Materiality, and Mass Graves of the Spanish Civil War* (Walnut Creek, C.A.: Left Coast, 2011), 29.

9. On the colonial context of the New Sweden colony, see Magdalena Naum and Jonas M. Nordin, "Introduction: Situating Scandinavian Colonialism," in *Scandinavian Colonialism and the Rise of Modernity: Small Time Agents in a Global Arena*, ed. Magdalena Naum and Jonas M. Nordin (New York: Springer, 2013), 3–16.

10. Jean R. Soderlund, *Lenape Country: Delaware Valley Society before William Penn* (Philadelphia: University of Pennsylvania Press, 2015), 1–85, 48; and Mark L. Thompson, *The Contest for the Delaware Valley: Allegiance, Identity, and Empire in the Seventeenth Century* (Baton Rouge: Louisiana State University Press, 2013), 12–65.

11. My account of New Sweden's history is based on John A. Munroe, *Colonial Delaware: A History* (Millwood, N.Y.: KTO, 1978), 13–40; Clinton A. Weslager, *New Sweden on the Delaware: 1638–1655* (Wilmington: Middle Atlantic, 1988); Gunlög Fur, *Colonialism in the Margins: Cultural Encounters in New Sweden and Lapland* (Leiden: Brill, 2007), chaps. 3 and 4; and Carol E. Hoffecker, Richard Waldron, Lorraine E. Williams, and Barbara E. Benson, eds., *New Sweden in America* (Newark: University of Delaware Press, 1995).

12. See, for example, Israel Acrelius, *A History of New Sweden: or, the Settlement on the River Delaware*, trans. William M. Reynolds (Philadelphia: Historical Society of Pennsylvania, 1874), 90; Amandus Johnson, *The Swedish Settlements on the Delaware: Their History and Relation to the Indians, Dutch and English, 1638–1664* (Philadelphia: University of Pennsylvania, 1911), 1:375–9; Christopher Ward, *The Dutch and Swedes on the Delaware 1609–64* (Philadelphia: University of Pennsylvania Press, 1930), 125–26; Alf Åberg, *The People of New Sweden: Our Colony on the Delaware River* (Stockholm: Natur och kultur, 1988), 66, 72–5; and Nils Erik Baehrendtz, "Nybyggarnas indianska grannar," in *Det Nya Sverige i landet Amerika: Ett stormaktsäventyr 1638–1655*, ed. Rune Ruhnbro (Höganäs: Wiken, 1988).

13. Fur, *Colonialism in the Margins*, 125; Gunlög Fur, *A Nation of Women: Gender and Colonial Encounters among the Delaware Indians* (Philadelphia: University of Pennsylvania Press, 2009), 139, 203–4. Terry Jordan and Matti Kaups have argued that certain similarities between Finnish settlers and the Lenape contributed to their friendly relations because the Finns came from a culture of forest shamanism, which resembled Lenape culture, and had previous experience of living in proximity to another indigenous people, the Sámi (*The American Backwoods Frontier: An Ethnic and Ecological Interpretation* [Baltimore: Johns Hopkins University Press, 1989], 87–92).

14. Gunlög Fur, Magdalena Naum, and Jonas M. Nordin, "Intersecting Worlds: New Sweden's Transatlantic Entanglements," *Journal of Transnational American Studies* 7, no. 1 (2016): 4–6. Although decidedly biased, a description of the Swedish congregations in the Delaware Valley appears in Conrad Bergendoff, *The Church of Sweden on the Delaware, 1638–1831* (Rock Island, I.L.: Augustana Historical Society, 1988).

15. John Bodnar, *The Transplanted: A History of Immigration in Urban America* (Bloomington: Indiana University Press, 1985), 1.
16. My overview of Swedish emigration history is based on the final volume of the monumental Uppsala Migration Research Project, which engaged thirty scholars between 1962 and 1976: Sten Carlsson, "Chronology and Composition of Swedish Emigration to America," in *From Sweden to America: A History of the Migration,* ed. Harald Runblom and Hans Norman (Minneapolis: University of Minnesota Press, 1976), 116–32. For a Nordic comparison, see Hans Norman and Harald Runblom, *Transatlantic Connections: Nordic Migration to the New World after 1800* (Oslo: Norwegian University Press, 1987).
17. Roger Daniels, *Guarding the Golden Door: American Immigration Policy and Immigrants Since 1882* (New York: Hill and Wang, 2004), 27–58; Matthew Frye Jacobson, *Whiteness of a Different Color: European Immigrants and the Alchemy of Race* (Cambridge: Harvard University Press, 1998), 83.
18. H. Arnold Barton, *A Folk Divided: Homeland Swedes and Swedish Americans, 1840–1940* (Carbondale: Southern Illinois University Press, 1994), 302; and H. Arnold Barton, "After the Great Migration: Swedish America and Sweden Since 1940," *Swedish-American Historical Quarterly* 46, no. 4 (1995): 332–58.
19. Mark Wyman, *Round Trip America: The Immigrants Return to Europe, 1880–1930* (Ithaca, N.Y.: Cornell University Press, 1993), 7–12.
20. Norman and Runblom, *Transatlantic Connections,* 107–11; and Lars-Göran Tedebrand, *Västernorrland och Nordamerika 1875–1913: Utvandring och återinvandring* (Uppsala: Studia Historica Upsaliensia, 1972), 223–29.
21. Dag Blanck, "'Very Welcome Home Mr. Swanson': Swedish Americans Encounter Homeland Swedes," *American Studies in Scandinavia* 48, no. 2 (2016): 114. On the social and economic life of the returnees in Sweden, see Magnus Persson, *Coming Full Circle? Return Migration and the Dynamics of Social Mobility on the Bjäre Peninsula, 1860–1930* (Lund: Sisyfos, 2007), 233–38; John Johansson et al., eds., *En smålandssocken emigrerar: En bok om emigrationen till Amerika från Långasjö socken i Kronobergs län* (Växjö: Långasjö bokcirkel, 1967), 814–19; and Hans Lindblad, "Impulser som förändrade Sverige," in *Tur och retur Amerika: Utvandrare som förändrade Sverige,* by Ingvar Henricson and Hans Lindblad (Stockholm: Fischer, 1995).
22. There was also a high concentration of Swedish Americans in smaller cities such as Rockford, Moline, and Rock Island in Illinois. In Jamestown, New York, first- and second-generation Swedes in 1930 constituted 37 percent of the total population. See Helge Nelson, *The Swedes and the Swedish Settlements in North America* (Lund: Gleerup, 1943), 43–53; and Sture Lindmark, *Swedish America, 1914–1932: Studies in Ethnicity with Emphasis on Illinois and Minnesota* (Uppsala: Studia Historica Upsaliensia, 1971), 27–33.
23. Orm Øverland, *Immigrant Minds, American Identities: Making the United States Home, 1870–1930* (Urbana: University of Illinois Press, 2000), 8.
24. Catherine Nash, *Of Irish Descent: Origin Stories, Genealogy, and the Politics of Belonging* (Syracuse, N.Y.: Syracuse University Press, 2008), 49; Bénédicte Deschamps, "Italian Americans and Columbus Day: A Quest for Consensus between National and Group Identities, 1840–1910," in Heideking et al., *Celebrating Ethnicity and Nation,* 124–39; Schultz, *Ethnicity on Parade*; Øverland, *Immigrant Minds,* 93–97. On celebrations of ethnic heritage in a local community, see Martha K. Norkunas, *Monuments and Memory: History and Representation in Lowell, Massachusetts* (Washington, D.C.: Smithsonian Institution Press, 2002), 16–66.

25. Other examples include the memory of Taras Shevchenko and celebrations of Irish-American heritage. See Kirk Savage, "Between Diaspora and Empire: The Shevchenko Monument in Washington, D.C.," in *Transnational American Memories,* ed. Udo J. Hebel (Berlin: Walter de Gruyter, 2009), 333–49; and Mick Moloney, "Irish-American Festivals," in *Making the Irish American: History and Heritage of the Irish in the United States,* ed. J. J. Lee and Marion R. Casey (New York: New York University Press, 2006), 426–42.
26. Dag Blanck, "'A Mixture of People with Different Roots': Swedish Immigrants in the American Ethno-Racial Hierarchies," *Journal of American Ethnic History* 33, no. 3 (2014): 51. The Scandinavian literacy rate in 1900 for immigrants over age fourteen was 99.2 percent, the highest for all immigrant groups. See Paul Spickard, *Almost All Aliens: Immigration, Race, and Colonialism in American History and Identity* (New York: Routledge, 2007), 230.
27. Benjamin Franklin, *Observations Concerning the Increase of Mankind, Peopling of Countries, etc.* (Tarrytown, N.Y.: Abbatt, 1918), 10.
28. Madison Grant, *The Passing of the Great Race, or the Racial Basis of European History,* rev. ed. (London: Bell, 1919), 167, 263. For more on Grant and his racial theories, see Jonathan Peter Spiro, *Defending the Master Race: Conservation, Eugenics, and the Legacy of Madison Grant* (Burlington: Vermont University Press, 2009).
29. Frye Jacobson, *Whiteness of a Different Color,* 69.
30. Charles H. Anderson, *White Protestant Americans: From National Origins to Religious Group* (Englewood Cliffs, N.J.: Prentice Hall, 1970), 58. On Italian-American and Swedish-American relations in Chicago, see Thomas Guglielmo, *White on Arrival: Italians, Race, Color, and Power in Chicago, 1890–1945* (New York: Oxford University Press, 2004), 25, 56. On the idea of a Germanic-Norse past of Anglo-Saxonism, see Reginald Horsman, *Race and Manifest Destiny: The Origins of American Racial Anglo-Saxonism* (Cambridge: Harvard University Press, 1981), chap. 2.
31. John G. Rice, "The Swedes," in *They Chose Minnesota: A Survey of the State's Ethnic Groups,* ed. June Drenning Holmquist (Saint Paul: Minnesota Historical Society Press, 1981), 263.
32. Adopting a concept from the memory studies scholars Jan Assmann and Aleida Assmann, this constitutes a transition from "communicative memory," which is "based exclusively on everyday communication" and has a temporal proximity to the remembered event, to "cultural memory," which is characterized by "its distance from the everyday" (Jan Assmann, "Collective Memory and Cultural Identity," *New German Critique* 65 [Spring–Summer 1995]: 126–29).
33. Christopher Endy, "Travel and World Power: Americans in Europe, 1890–1917," *Diplomatic History* 22, no. 4 (1998): 565–94; Lorraine Coons and Alexander Varias, *Tourist Third Cabin: Steamship Travel in the Interwar Years* (Basingstoke, U.K.: Palgrave Macmillan, 2003); and Wyman, *Roundtrip America,* 192–93.
34. Daniel T. Rodgers, *Atlantic Crossings: Social Politics in a Progressive Age* (Cambridge: Belknap Press of Harvard University Press, 1998), 3.
35. Ibid., 427–28. On the transnational history of the New Deal, see Kiran Klaus Patel, *The New Deal: A Global History* (Princeton: Princeton University Press, 2016). See also David W. Ellwood, *The Shock of America: Europe and the Challenge of the Century* (Oxford: Oxford University Press, 2012), 177–211. For a study of Depression-era commonalities among the United States, Italy, and Germany, see Wolfgang Schivelbusch, *Three New Deals: Reflections on Roosevelt's America, Mussolini's Italy, and Hitler's Germany, 1933–1939* (New York: Holt, 2006).

36. Kiran Klaus Patel, "How America Discovered Sweden: Reinventing Democracy during the 1930s," in *Transatlantic Democracy in the Twentieth Century: Transfer and Transformation,* ed. Paul Nolte (Berlin: Walter de Gruyter, 2016), 75.
37. Stig Hadenius, Björn Molin, and Hans Wieslander, *Sverige efter 1900: En modern politisk historia* (Stockholm: Bonnier Alba, 1993), 112–20; Per Thullberg and Kjell Östberg, *Den svenska modellen* (Lund: Studentlitteratur, 1994), 5–6; Francis Sejersted, *The Age of Social Democracy: Norway and Sweden in the Twentieth Century,* trans. Richard Daly, ed. Madeleine B. Adams (Princeton: Princeton University Press, 2011), 159–62.
38. Marquis W. Childs, *Sweden: The Middle Way* (New Haven: Yale University Press, 1936). On the impact and significance of Childs's book, see Carl Marklund, "The Social Laboratory, the Middle Way and the Swedish Model: Three Frames for the Image of Sweden," *Scandinavian Journal of History* 34, no. 3 (2009): 268–77; and Carl Marklund, "A Swedish *Norden* or a Nordic Sweden? Image Politics in the West during the Cold War," in *Communicating the North: Media Structures and Images in the Making of the Nordic Region,* ed. Jonas Harvard and Peter Stadius (Farnham, U.K.: Ashgate, 2013), 265–70. On the broader U.S. discussion about Swedish politics in the 1930s, see Merle Curti, "Sweden in the American Social Mind of the 1930s," in *The Immigration of Ideas: Studies in the North Atlantic Community,* ed. J. Iverne Dowie and J. Thomas Tredway (Rock Island, I.L.: Augustana Historical Society, 1968), 159–84.
39. Franklin D. Roosevelt, press conference no. 303, June 23, 1936, p. 293, FDR Presidential Library and Museum, http://www.fdrlibrary.marist.edu.
40. Mary Hilson, "Consumer Cooperation and Economic Crisis: The 1936 Roosevelt Inquiry on Cooperative Enterprise and the Emergence of the Nordic 'Middle Way,'" *Contemporary European History* 22, no. 2 (2013): 181–98. Although the commission amassed a considerable amount of information and its work was reported on extensively in the American press, it did not have any tangible political impact. Its message was stymied for several reasons: because of its unfortunate timing before a presidential election, because of opposition to the cooperative idea from U.S. businesses, and because of criticism about being un-American (Patel, "How America Discovered Sweden," 77–80).
41. John Logue, "The Swedish Model: Visions of Sweden in American Politics and Political Science," *Swedish-American Historical Quarterly* 50, no. 3 (July 1999): 162–71.
42. Kazimierz Musiał, *Roots of the Scandinavian Model: Images of Progress in the Era of Modernisation* (Baden-Baden: Nomos Verlagsgesellschaft, 2000), 21.
43. Martin Alm, "The New Deal in Sweden," in *Notions of America: Swedish Perspectives,* ed. Kerstin W. Shands, Rolf Lundén, and Dag Blanck (Huddinge: Södertörn Academic Studies, 2004), 75–93. The postwar reform of the Swedish school system was highly influenced by the work of Alva Myrdal who, with her husband, the prominent social scientist Gunnar Myrdal, had spent considerable time in the United States. See Jan Olof Nilsson, *Alva Myrdal: en virvel i den moderna strömmen* (Stockholm: Brutus Östlings Bokförlag Symposion, 1994), 138–58; and Dag Blanck, "We Have a Lot to Learn from America: The Myrdals and the Question of American Influences in Sweden," in *Angles on the English Speaking World: Trading Cultures,* vol. 2, *Nationalism and Globalization in American Studies,* ed. Clara Juncker and Russell Duncan (Copenhagen: Museum Tusculanum Press, 2002), 129–45.
44. Paul A. Levine, "Swedish Neutrality during the Second World War: Tactical Success or Moral Compromise?," in *European Neutrals and Non-Belligerents during the Second World War,* ed. Neville Wylie (Cambridge: Cambridge University Press, 2002), 304–30.

45. Martin Fritz and Birgit Karlsson, "Dependence and National Supply: Sweden's Economic Relations to Nazi Germany," in *Sweden's Relations with Nazism, Nazi Germany, and the Holocaust*, ed. Stig Ekman and Klas Åmark (Stockholm: Almqvist och Wiksell International, 2003), 114–19; John Gilmour, *Sweden, the Swastika, and Stalin: The Swedish Experience in the Second World War* (Edinburgh: Edinburgh University Press, 2010), 45–54; and Klas Åmark, *Att bo granne med ondskan: Sveriges förhållande till nazismen, Nazityskland och Förintelsen* (Stockholm: Albert Bonniers, 2016), 666–73.
46. Nikolas Glover, "Imaging Community: Sweden in 'Cultural Propaganda' Then and Now," *Scandinavian Journal of History* 34, no. 3 (2009): 248.
47. *Betänkande med utredning och förslag angående Sveriges kommersiella och kulturella förbindelser med transoceana länder: Del 1. . . . Avgivet den 14 april 1943 av Amerikautredningen* (Stockholm, 1943), 3, 8, 42.
48. Glover, "Imaging Community," 253–54; Nikolas Glover, *National Relations: Public Diplomacy, National Identity and the Swedish Institute, 1945–1970* (Lund: Nordic Academic Press, 2011), 57, 215; and Carl Marklund and Klaus Petersen, "Return to Sender: American Images of the Nordic Welfare States and Nordic Welfare State Branding," *European Journal of Scandinavian Studies* 43, no. 2 (2013): 245–57.
49. Wilhelm Agrell, "Den neutrala bundsförvanten: svensk-amerikanska säkerhetsrelationer i medgång och motgång," in *Det blågula stjärnbaneret: USA:s närvaro och inflytande i Sverige*, ed. Erik Åsard (Stockholm: Carlsson, 2016), 81–82.
50. Geir Lundestad, *America, Scandinavia, and the Cold War, 1945–1949* (New York: Columbia University Press, 1980), 47–63, 85–108, 200–202; and Agrell, "Den neutrala bundsförvanten," 193–94.
51. Eventually, plans for a Scandinavian alliance were dropped, and Denmark and Norway joined NATO in 1949, with Sweden opting to stay out (Lundestad, *America, Scandinavia, and the Cold War*, 208–12). On Sweden and NATO, see Mikael Holmström, *Den dolda alliansen: Sveriges hemliga NATO-förbindelser*, 4th ed. (Stockholm: Atlantis, 2015).
52. Mikael Nilsson, *Tools of Hegemony: Military Technology and Swedish-American Security Relations, 1945–1962* (Stockholm: Santérus Academic Press, 2007), chap. 3.
53. Charles Silva, *Keep Them Strong, Keep Them Friendly: Swedish-American Relations and the Pax Americana, 1948–1952* (Ph.D. diss., Stockholm University, 1999), 348–50; Nilsson, *Tools of Hegemomy*, 253; Lundestad, *America, Scandinavia, and the Cold War*, 214.

CHAPTER 2: CROSSING BORDERS

1. Hans Mattson, *250th Anniversary of the First Swedish Settlement in America: September 14th, 1888, Minneapolis, Minn.* (Minneapolis, 1889), 3–5, 15. On the 1888 commemoration, see Dag Blanck, "History at Work: The 1888 New Sweden Jubilee," *Swedish-American Historical Quarterly* 39, no. 2 (1988): 5–20; and Ulf Beijbom, "Olof Gottfrid Lange: Chicago's First Swede," in *Swedish-American Life in Chicago: Cultural and Urban Aspects of an Immigrant People, 1850–1930*, ed. Philip J. Anderson and Dag Blanck (Urbana: University of Illinois Press, 1992), 33–35.
2. Mattson, *250th Anniversary*, 2.
3. Byron Nordstrom, ed., *The Swedes in Minnesota* (Minneapolis: Denison, 1976); John G. Rice, "The Swedes," in *They Chose Minnesota: A Survey of the State's Ethnic Groups*, ed. June Drenning Holmquist (Saint Paul: Minnesota Historical Society Press, 1981), 248–76; Philip J. Anderson and Dag Blanck, eds., *Swedes in the Twin Cities: Immigrant Life and Minnesota's Urban Frontier* (Saint Paul: Minnesota Historical Society Press, 2001).

On the Scandinavian-American impact on Minnesota politics during the twentieth century, see Klas Bergman, *Scandinavians in the State House: How Nordic Immigrants Shaped Minnesota Politics* (Saint Paul: Minnesota Historical Society Press, 2017).

4. Mattson, *250th Anniversary*, 43. Sweden and Norway were in a personal union between 1814 and 1905. Although the two countries had separate parliaments, constitutions, administrations, legislations, and currencies, they had a common monarch, shared foreign policy, and thus also shared diplomatic representatives.

5. H. Arnold Barton, *A Folk Divided: Homeland Swedes and Swedish Americans, 1840–1940* (Carbondale: Southern Illinois University Press, 1994), 310–11; and Albin Widén, *Amandus Johnson: Svenskamerikan* (Stockholm: Norstedts, 1970), 133–48.

6. John Higham, "The Ethnic Historical Society in Changing Times," *Journal of American Ethnic History* 13, no. 2 (1994): 33–36.

7. April R. Schultz, *Ethnicity on Parade: Inventing the Norwegian American through Celebration* (Amherst: University of Massachusetts Press, 1994); and Steven Conn, "Melting Pots, Salad Bowls, Ethnic Museums, and American Identity," in *The Oxford Handbook of American Immigration and Ethnicity*, ed. Ronald Bayor (Oxford: Oxford University Press, 2016), 480–81.

8. On the Augustana Synod and Swedish-American ethnicity, see Dag Blanck, *The Creation of an Ethnic Identity: Being Swedish American in the Augustana Synod, 1860–1917* (Carbondale: Southern Illinois University Press, 2006); and Maria Erling and Mark Granquist, *The Augustana Story: Shaping Lutheran Identity in North America* (Minneapolis: Augsburg Fortress, 2008). The importance of other religious denominations in the Swedish-American community is, for example, discussed in George M. Stephenson, *The Religious Aspects of Swedish Immigration: A Study of Immigrant Churches* (Minneapolis: University of Minnesota Press, 1932); Sture Lindmark, *Swedish America 1914–1932: Studies in Ethnicity with Emphasis on Illinois and Minnesota* (Uppsala: Studia Historica Upsaliensia, 1971), 236–303; and Scott E. Erickson, *David Nyvall and the Shape of an Immigrant Church: Ethnic, Denominational, and Educational Priorities among Swedes in America* (Uppsala: Acta Universitatis Upsaliensis, 1996).

9. For descriptions of the early tercentenary planning, see Widén, *Amandus Johnson*, 133–37; and Julius Lincoln, "The Swedish-American Tercentenary," February 7, 1938, Delaware Tercentenary, Carl Gustaf Carlfelt Papers, box 1, Swenson Swedish Immigration Research Center, Rock Island, Illinois.

10. Minutes of the meeting to organize a general tercentenary committee, February 23, 1935, F1, vol. 843, UD 1920; and Francis J. Plym, "A Report to the Board of Directors of the Swedish American Tercentenary Association," October 8, 1938, TC. Having only elected a temporary chairman at the February meeting, Oscar Solbert was appointed chairman in June 1935.

11. Minutes, general tercentenary committee, February 23, 1935; *Worker's Bulletin* no. 2, January 1, 1938, and *Workers' Bulletin* no. 1, September 18, 1937, Swedish American Tercentenary Association, in TC.

12. Minutes, general tercentenary committee, February 23, 1935.

13. Act No. 31, "Celebration of 300th Anniversary of Earliest Settlement in Pennsylvania," July 28, 1936, Laws of the General Assembly of the Commonwealth of Pennsylvania, passed at the session of 1936, 79–80.

14. Act No. 542, "Celebration of Tercentenary Anniversary," July 2, 1937, Laws of the General Assembly of the Commonwealth of Pennsylvania, passed at the session of 1937, 2697–2700.

15. Michael Kammen, *Mystic Chords of Memory: The Transformation of Tradition in American Culture* (New York: Knopf, 1991), 395. On the Pennsylvania Works Progress Administration funding, see my discussion of Governor Printz Park (chap. 3).
16. "Official Biography," attachment in Frank W. Melvin, letter to Naboth Hedin, October 23, 1937, Folder Hallberg et al., box 2, #25.84, PAC.
17. François Weil, *Family Trees: A History of Genealogy in America* (Cambridge: Harvard University Press, 2013), chap. 4.
18. George H. Ryden, letter to C. Douglass Buck, February 9, 1935, F1, box 8, George Herbert Ryden Papers, MSS 31, Augustana College Special Collections, Rock Island, Illinois.
19. S. J. Res., Delaware Swedish Tercentenary, March 20, 1935, chap. 254, Laws of the State of Delaware, 105th Session of the General Assembly, vol. 40 (Wilmington: Taylor, 1935), 864–65.
20. S. J. Res., Appointment of the Delaware Tercentenary Commission, February 10, 1937, chap. 269, Laws of the State of Delaware, 106th Session of the General Assembly, vol. 41 (Wilmington: Taylor, 1937), 799–800; and Minutes, executive committee, Delaware Commission, March 19, 1937, Minute Book, 1330:10, box 1, DEC.
21. "George Herbert Ryden: Correspondence, 1927–1941," Special Collections Department, University of Delaware Library, http://www.lib.udel.edu; and "The Rev. Ernest E. Ryden Papers (1907–1962)," Evangelical Lutheran Church in America Library, Archivegrid, https://beta.worldcat.org.
22. H. Arnold Barton, "After the Great Migration: Swedish America and Sweden Since 1940," *Swedish-American Historical Quarterly* 46, no. 4 (1995): 335.
23. Harald Runblom, "Chicago Compared: Swedes and Other Ethnic Groups in American Cities," in Anderson and Blanck, *Swedish-American Life in Chicago*, 71.
24. John Higham, "From Process to Structure: Formulations of American Immigration History," Thomas J. Archdeacon, "Hansen's Hypothesis as a Model of Immigrant Assimilation," and H. Arnold Barton, "Marcus Lee Hansen and the Swedish Americans," in *American Immigrants and Their Generations: Studies and Commentaries on the Hansen Thesis after Fifty Years,* ed. Peter Kivisto and Dag Blanck (Urbana: University of Illinois Press, 1990), 11–63, 113–25. Examples of the second-generation interest also include the formation of Swedish-American fraternal societies, such as the Vasa Order of America (1896). See Barton, *A Folk Divided*, 85; and Lindmark, *Swedish America*, 304–20.
25. Gary Gerstle, *American Crucible: Race and Nation in the Twentieth Century* (Princeton: Princeton University Press, 2001), 114; and Matthew Frye Jacobson, *Whiteness of a Different Color: European Immigrants and the Alchemy of Race* (Cambridge: Harvard University Press, 1998), 91–96.
26. John Bodnar, *The Transplanted: A History of Immigration in Urban America* (Bloomington: Indiana University Press, 1985), 117–43.
27. Christopher L. Ward, "Autobiography of Christopher L. Ward, (1868–1943)," ed. Charles Lee Reese, Jr., *Delaware History* 15 (April 1972): 157–86, 219–55.
28. "Delaware Tercentenary Visitors' Guide, 1638–1938," TC.
29. Minutes of the Organization Meeting, New Jersey, June 28, 1937, F2, Swedish Tercentenary Records, 1937–38, MG 272, New Jersey Historical Society, Newark, New Jersey.
30. Joint Resolution No. 2, Commission to Arrange Celebration of the Settlement of Swedes in the Delaware Valley, May 29, 1937, Acts of the One Hundred and Sixty-Second Legislature of the State of New Jersey (1938), 656–57.

31. "Wollmar Boström," in *Vem är det: svensk biografisk handbok, 1953*, ed. Stina Svensson (Stockholm: Norstedts, 1953), 147.
32. See, for example, correspondence in folder "300th Correlation Meeting," September 24, 1937, box 6, #25.84, PAC.
33. Frank W. Melvin, letter to the members of the Swedish Colonial Society, November 1, 1937, part 2, vol. 67, F1f, P66, Utrikesdepartementet, Konsulatarkivet, New York, Riksarkivet Arninge, Stockholm, Sweden.
34. Frank W. Melvin, radio address, WPEN, n.d., Speeches Radio, box 7, #25.92, PAC.
35. *Observance of the Three Hundredth Anniversary of the First Permanent Settlement in the Delaware River Valley, 1938* (Washington, D.C.: U.S. Government Printing Office, 1940), 8.
36. Kammen, *Mystic Chords*, 375.
37. Frank W. Melvin, letter to Tercentenary Commission, Connecticut, November 6, 1936, and Frank W. Melvin, letter to Frank Devine, December 21, 1936, in Commissions (Other States), box 1, #25.84, PAC.
38. Kammen, *Mystic Chords*, 375–90.
39. John Seelye, *Memory's Nation: The Place of Plymouth Rock* (Chapel Hill: University of North Carolina Press, 1998), 3–4.
40. Peter Trubowitz, *Defining the National Interest: Conflict and Change in American Foreign Policy* (Chicago: University of Chicago Press, 1998), 3–4, 100–13.
41. Joseph A. Fry, "Place Matters: Domestic Regionalism and the Formation of American Foreign Policy," *Diplomatic History* 36, no. 3 (2012): 457–59, 482.
42. For Pennsylvania, see Richard Keller, *Pennsylvania's Little New Deal* (New York: Garland, 1982), 101–55; and Philip S. Klein and Ari Hoogenboom, *A History of Pennsylvania*, 2nd ed. (University Park: Pennsylvania State University Press, 1980), 455–58. For Delaware, see Roger A. Martin, *A History of Delaware Through Its Governors, 1776–1984* (Wilmington: McClafferty, 1984), 415; and John A. Munroe, *History of Delaware*, 5th ed. (Newark: University of Delaware Press, 2006), 209–12.
43. "Earle Was Amazed at Swedish Housing," *Berwick Enterprise*, December 17, 1937, Folder Dec 14–15, Box 9, PAC.
44. On Moore's governorship, see Richard J. Connors, "Moore, A. Harry," in *Encyclopedia of New Jersey*, ed. Maxine N. Lurie and Marc Mappen (New Brunswick, N.J.: Rutgers University Press, 2004), 534. During his time in the U.S. Senate, Moore was the only Democrat to vote against the 1935 Social Security Act.
45. J. Sigfrid Edström, letter to Rickard Sandler, January 22, 1935, F1, vol. 843, UD 1920.
46. Therese Nordlund, *Att leda storföretag: En studie av social kompetens och entreprenörskap i näringslivet med fokus på Axel Ax:son Johnson och J. Sigfrid Edström, 1900–1950* (Stockholm: Almqvist och Wiksell International, 2005), 54–55.
47. Minutes, ". . . det andra preliminära sammanträdet," May 20, 1936, F1, vol. 843, UD 1920.
48. Gustav Sundbärg, *Betänkande i utvandringsfrågan och därmed sammanhängande spörsmål jämlikt Kungl. brefvet den 30 januari 1907 afgifvet af Gustav Sundbärg* (Stockholm: Norstedts, 1913), 19–21, 661. On the work of the commission and Swedish reactions to the emigration, see Ann-Sofie Kälvemark, *Reaktionen mot utvandringen: Emigrationsfrågan i svensk debatt och politik 1901–1904* (Uppsala: Studia Historica Upsaliensia, 1972), 142–213; and Martin Alm, *Americanitis: Amerika som sjukdom eller läkemedel; Svenska berättelser om USA åren 1900–1939* (Lund: Studia Historica Lundensia, 2002), 64–85.

49. Fritz Henriksson, "V.P.M.," September 17, 1935, F1, vol. 843, UD 1920.
50. Wollmar Boström, letter to Fritz Henriksson, October 25, 1935, and Wollmar Boström to Ministern för Utrikes Ärenden, March 8, 1936, in F1, vol. 843, UD 1920.
51. H. J. Res. 499 (Pub. Res. 102), Delaware River Valley Tercentenary, June 5, 1936, United States Statutes at Large, 74th Congress, 2nd sess., vol. 49, chap. 533 (1936) 1486–87. For the House and Senate proceedings, see *Congressional Record*, 74th Congress, 2nd sess., vol. 80:6, 6136–37; and *Congressional Record*, 74th Congress, 2nd sess., vol. 80:8, 8434. On the U.S. invitation to Sweden, see James E. Brown, Jr., letter to Karl Gustaf Westman, July 27, 1936, 841.5, General Records 1936, box 6, DoS Sthlm.
52. *Observance of the Three Hundredth Anniversary*, 9–10.
53. Kammen, *Mystic Chords*, chap. 14; John Bodnar, *Remaking America: Public Memory, Commemoration, and Patriotism in the Twentieth Century* (Princeton: Princeton University Press, 1992), 175–79; Denise D. Meringolo, *Museums, Monuments, and National Parks: Toward a New Genealogy of Public History* (Amherst: University of Massachusetts Press, 2012); and Seth C. Bruggeman, "A Century of Teaching with Pennsylvania's Historic Places," *Pennsylvania History* 82, no. 1 (2015): 7–8.
54. Minutes, Bestyrelsen, September 16, 1936, vol. 1, BNS.
55. Fritz Henriksson, *Sweden's Participation in the U.S. Celebration of the New Sweden Tercentenary: Report Compiled by Fritz Henriksson* (Stockholm: Bonnier, 1939), 13.
56. J. Sigfrid Edström, letter to Per Albin Hansson, November 18, 1937, vol. 5, BNS.
57. Act No. 31, "To Provide for the Commemoration . . . of the Three Hundredth Anniversary," July 28, 1936, Laws of the General Assembly of the Commonwealth of Pennsylvania, passed at the session of 1936, 79–80; and Max Engman, "The Tug of War Over 'Nya Sverige' 1938," *Swedish-American Historical Quarterly* 45, no. 2 (1994): 81–82.
58. J. Parnell Thomas, August 21, 1937, *Congressional Record*, 75th Congress, 1st sess., vol. 81:8, 9622.
59. Engman, "The Tug of War," 84–85.
60. S. J. Res. 135 (Pub. Res. 71), Delaware River Valley Tercentenary, Invitation to Finland, chap. 781, *Congressional Record*, 75th Congress, 1st sess., 813.
61. Cordell Hull, letter to Franklin D. Roosevelt, September 2, 1937, 811.415, Chicago Jubilee–Delaware River Valley, box 5037, DoS. The commemoration has been described as "a watershed" because it for the first time united different political factions of the Finnish-American community. See Peter Kivisto, "Finnish Americans and the Homeland, 1918–1958," *Journal of American Ethnic History* 7 (Fall 1987): 13.
62. Engman, "Tug of War," 82–83, 86–87.
63. Oscar Solbert, letter to Christopher Ward, August 26, 1937, and "Paragraphs used as arguments against the Finnish participation . . . ," attached to Solbert, letter to Ward, September 22, 1937, in Subject File: Finland, 1330:0, box 7, DEC.
64. Joint Resolution No. 2, "For the Appointment of a Commission," February 28, 1938, Acts of the One Hundred and Sixty-Second Legislature of the State of New Jersey (1938), 998–1000.
65. Christopher Ward, to Richard McMullen, June 28, 1937, Subject File: Finland, and Christopher Ward, letter to Pierre S. du Pont, October 18, 1937, Subject File: Pierre S. du Pont, 1330:0, in box 7, DEC.
66. George H. Ryden, letter to Christopher Ward, November 18, 1936, Ward's Files: Swedish Tercentenary Commission, 1330:15, box 1, DEC.
67. Naboth Hedin, letter to the Board of Directors, Svensk-Amerikanska Nyhetsbyrån, October 26, 1945, F1, Vol. 243, UD Wash.

68. "Naboth Hedin," in *Vem är det: Svensk biografisk handbok 1963*, ed. Ingeborg Burling (Stockholm: Norstedts, 1962), 430–31; Dag Blanck, *Sverige-Amerika Stiftelsen: De första sjuttio åren 1919–1989* (Stockholm: Sverige-Amerika Stiftelsen, 1989), 49–50; and Allan Kastrup, *Med Sverige i Amerika: Opinioner, stämningar och upplysningsarbete; en rapport av Allan Kastrup* (Malmö: Corona, 1985), 30–37.
69. Hedin, letter to the Board of Directors, Svensk-Amerikanska Nyhetsbyrån, October 26, 1945.
70. P. O. Bersell, Oscar Benson, Emil Swenson, Herman Nelson, and Conrad Bergendoff, letter to undisclosed recipient, November 19, 1945, F1, box 3, SPCA.
71. Thomas Tredway, *Conrad Bergendoff's Faith and Work: A Swedish-American Lutheran, 1895–1997* (Rock Island, I.L.: Augustana Historical Society, 2014).
72. P. O. Bersell referenced in [Gösta Oldenburg], letter to Olof Lamm, February 6, 1946, doss. 1, vol. 81, UD Chi.
73. P. O. Bersell, "Det lutherska trehundraårsminnet," *Augustana*, July 26, 1938; and P. O. Bersell, "The Lutheran Tercentenary," *Lutheran Companion*, July 28, 1938, in Augustana Synoden, vol. 239, UD Wash. The accusations sparked a heated correspondence among Bersell, Oscar Solbert, and Wollmar Boström. Bersell eventually apologized to Boström and the Swedish-American commission while retaining his criticism of the Pennsylvania commission.
74. Conrad Bergendoff, letter to Mike Holm, August 19, 1947, F18, box 39, CBP.
75. Tredway, *Conrad Bergendoff's Faith and Work*, 273.
76. Barton, "After the Great Migration," 340. See also the declining interest in ethnic festivals in the Swedish-American town of Lindsborg, Kansas, in Lizette Gradén, *On Parade: Making Heritage in Lindsborg, Kansas* (Uppsala: Acta Universitatis Upsaliensis, 2003), 103–4.
77. Bodnar, *Remaking America*, 41–55.
78. Minutes, the Swedish Pioneer Centennial Association, January 26, 1946, F3, box 1, SPCA.
79. Gösta Oldenburg, letter to Herman Eriksson, July 13, 1946, F1, vol. 243, UD Wash; and Hellström, to Herman Eriksson, August 22, 1946, T, vol. 41, UD Mpls.
80. Herman Eriksson, letter to Carl F. Hellström, July 31, 1946, F1, vol. 243, UD Wash.
81. "A Trip To Holland" (poster), and Nils William Olsson to W. Wichers, August 19, 1947, in F16, box 1, SPCA.
82. Hedin, letter to the Board of Directors, Svensk-Amerikanska Nyhetsbyrån, October 26, 1945.
83. Gösta Oldenburg, letter to Naboth Hedin, November 10, 1945, doss. 1, vol. 81, UD Chi; and minutes, "Kommittén utsedd av styrelsen för Svensk-Amerikanska Nyhetsbyrån," November 28, 1945, T, vol. 41, UD Mpls.
84. Naboth Hedin, letter to Gösta Oldenburg, November 13, 1945, doss. 1, vol. 81, UD Chi.
85. [Gösta Oldenburg], letter to Olof Lamm, February 6, 1946, doss. 1, vol. 81, UD Chi.
86. Gösta Oldenburg, letter to Gunnar Granberg, March 25, 1947, T, vol. 41, UD Mpls.
87. Herman Eriksson, letter to Conrad Bergendoff, August 29, 1946, F1, vol. 243, UD Wash. See also invitations to Prime Minister Tage Erlander and King Gustaf V, November 25, 1946, attached to Alexis Aminoff, letter to Tage Erlander, December 5, 1946, in doss. 1, vol. 81, UD Chi.
88. Minutes, "Konstituerande sammanträde med svenska kommittén för pionjärjubileet i U.S.A.," March 31, 1947, T, vol. 41, UD Mpls.
89. Conrad Bergendoff, letter to Mike Holm, May 29, 1947, F1, box 3, SPCA.
90. Minutes, the Swedish Pioneer Centennial Association, June 5, 1947, F3, box 1, SPCA.

91. Newsletter, Pioneer Centennial, no. 3 (November 1947), and newsletter, Pioneer Centennial, no. 4 (March 1948), in F4, box 45, CBP.
92. Olof Rydbeck, letter to Per Sandberg, January 20, 1948, F10, box 5, SPCA; and Gunnar Granberg, letter to Allan Kastrup, May 4, 1948, X2b1, vol. 166, SI.
93. Nils William Olsson, letter to Henry Goddard Leach, July 2, 1947, F8, box 4, SPCA.
94. Veto of bill authorizing issuance of stamps commemorating the one hundredth anniversary of the coming of Swedish pioneers to the Midwest, March 30, 1948, *Public Papers of the Presidents of the United States, Harry S. Truman: Containing the Public Messages, Speeches, and Statements of the President, January 1 to December 31, 1948* (Washington, D.C.: U.S. Government Printing Office, 1964), 197.
95. *Congressional Record*, 80th Congress, 2nd sess., vol. 94:4, 4896, 5320.

CHAPTER 3: SETTLER COLONIAL HISTORIES

1. John Bodnar, *Remaking America: Public Memory, Commemoration, and Patriotism in the Twentieth Century* (Princeton: Princeton University Press, 1992), 33.
2. Lorenzo Veracini, *Settler Colonialism: A Theoretical Overview* (Basingstoke, U.K.: Palgrave Macmillan, 2010), 2–5. See also Daiva Stasiulis and Nira Yuval-Davis, introduction to *Unsettling Settler Societies: Articulations of Gender, Race, Ethnicity and Class* (London: Sage Publications, 1995), 3; Patrick Wolfe, *Settler Colonialism and the Transformation of Anthropology: The Politics and Poetics of an Ethnographic Event* (London: Cassell, 1999), 163. On settler colonialism and notions of righteous violence in U.S. history and foreign policy, see Walter L. Hixson, *American Settler Colonialism: A History* (Basingstoke, U.K.: Palgrave Macmillan, 2013).
3. Amandus Johnson, letter to Axel Wallenberg, n.d., F4, box 32, series 3, Amandus Johnson Papers, MSS 41, Historical Society of Pennsylvania, Philadelphia.
4. Minutes, Delaware Commission, December 10, 1936, Minutes, 1330:6, box 1, DEC.
5. Minutes, Delaware Commission, July 24, 1935, Minutes, 1330:6, box 1, DEC.
6. Report of Delaware Swedish Tercentenary Commission, Minutes, 1330:6, box 1, DEC.
7. W. J. T. Mitchell, *Image Science: Iconology, Visual Culture, and Media Aesthetics* (Chicago: University of Chicago Press, 2015), 153.
8. Minutes, Arbetsutskottet, September 22, 1936, Vol. 1, BNS.
9. Minutes, Delaware Commission, December 10, 1936, Minutes, 1330:6, box 1, DEC.
10. Wollmar Boström, telegram to Bestyrelsen, November 10, 1936, F2, vol. 843, UD 1920.
11. Minutes, Arbetsutskottet, November 25, 1936, vol. 1, BNS.
12. Frank Melvin, letter to George H. Earle, December 10, 1936, E, #25.84, box 2, PAC.
13. Frank Melvin, letter to Wollmar Boström, February 10, 1937, F4, vol. 844, UD 1920.
14. John G. Townsend, Jr., letter to Richard C. McMullen, February 11, 1937, Delaware Tercentenary Commission, Governor's Office, Governor's Papers, Richard McMullen, 1937 D-Elections, M03, series 7, RG 1302, Delaware Public Archives, Dover.
15. Christopher Ward, letter to C. Douglass Buck, March 29, 1937, Subject Files: "Rocks" Committee, 1330:0, box 14, DEC.
16. Christopher Ward, letter to Richard C. McMullen, April 12, 1937, Subject Files: "Rocks" Committee, 1330:0, box 14, DEC.
17. See, for example, George Ryden, letter to Oscar Solbert, April 30, 1937, Ryden's Files: O. N. Solbert, 1330:14, box 3, DEC.
18. *First Finnish Settlement in America, 300th Anniversary Celebration, Chester, Pennsylvania, June 29, 1938* (Chester, P.A., 1938); Max Engman, "The Tug of War Over 'Nya Sverige' 1938," *Swedish-American Historical Quarterly* 45, no. 2 (1994): 98. The mon-

ument, a rectangular block of red granite located at 1179 Concord Avenue in Chester, was made by Finnish sculptor Wäinö Aaltonen and, according to the inscription, stands in remembrance of "the Finnish pioneers of the first permanent settlement in the Delaware River Valley in 1638."

19. "Presentation of Governor Printz Park by the Swedish Colonial Society to the Commonwealth of Pennsylvania," June 29, 1938, Invitations and Programs, F1, #25.84, box 3, PAC.

20. *Proceedings of the Swedish Colonial Society at the Annual Meeting in the Assembly Rooms of the Historical Society of Pennsylvania, April 11, 1929* (Philadelphia: Swedish Colonial Society, 1931). On the Swedish Colonial Society's reverence for Tinicum Island, see Henry D. Paxson, *Sketch and Map of a Trip from Philadelphia to Tinicum Island, Delaware County, Pennsylvania* . . . (Philadelphia: Buchanan, 1926).

21. Report, "The 300th Anniversary," 83, Historical Data, #25.90, box 8, PAC.

22. Frank Melvin, letter to J. Sigfrid Edström, April 25, 1938, and J. Sigfrid Edström, letter to Frank Melvin, May 2, 1938, in Edstrom, #25.84, box 2, PAC.

23. "Resolution, addressed to the President of the United States by the Commonwealth of Pennsylvania and the United States Delaware Valley Tercentenary Commission," n.d., Legislation, #25.86, box 6, PAC.

24. Adam Hjorthén, "'Here is the Beginning of Pennsylvania': A Settler Commemoration and the Entangled Histories of Foundational Sites," *Journal of Transnational American Studies* 7, no. 1 (2016): 1–19. See also *The Brief History of the Colonization of New Sweden Thereby Establishing the Foundation of Pennsylvania* (Philadelphia: Pennsylvania 300th Anniversary Commission, 1938).

25. Mitchell, *Image Science*, 155.

26. Jean M. O'Brien, *Firsting and Lasting: Writing Indians out of Existence in New England* (Minneapolis: University of Minnesota Press, 2010), 7–20. On the American preoccupation with origins, as demonstrated by the proliferation of birthplace commemorations and monuments in the United States, see Seth C. Bruggeman, introduction, in *Born in the USA: Birth, Commemoration, and American Public Memory* (Amherst: University of Massachusetts Press, 2012), 1–25.

27. John Sutton Lutz, ed., *Myth and Memory: Stories of Indigenous-European Contact* (Vancouver: University of British Columbia Press, 2007).

28. Andrew Denson, *Monuments to Absence: Cherokee Removal and the Contest over Southern Memory* (Chapel Hill: University of North Carolina Press, 2017), 193, chap. 3.

29. Laura L. Peers, *Playing Ourselves: Interpreting Native Histories at Historic Reconstructions* (Lanham, M.D.: AltaMira, 2007); Amy Lonetree, *Decolonizing Museums: Representing Native America in National and Tribal Museums* (Chapel Hill: University of North Carolina Press, 2012). On notions of American innocence in settler memories, see Boyd Cothran, *Remembering the Modoc War: Redemptive Violence and the Making of American Innocence* (Chapel Hill: University of North Carolina Press, 2014). On the emergence of Native counter-memories of U.S.-Indian relations, including the Battle of the Little Bighorn and the Wounded Knee massacre, see Charles E. Rankin, ed., *Legacy: New Perspectives on the Battle of Little Bighorn* (Helena: Montana Historical Society Press, 1996); Larry J. Zimmerman, "Plains Indians and Resistance to 'Public' Heritage Commemoration of Their Pasts," in *Cultural Heritage and Human Rights*, ed. Helaine Silverman and D. Fairchild Ruggles (New York: Springer, 2007), 144–58; Michael A. Elliott, *Custerology: The Enduring Legacy of the Indian Wars and George Armstrong Custer* (Chicago: University of Chicago Press, 2007), chap. 6; Erika Doss,

Memorial Mania: Public Feeling in America (Chicago: University of Chicago Press, 2010), 328–56; and David W. Grua, *Surviving Wounded Knee: The Lakotas and the Politics of Memory* (Oxford: Oxford University Press, 2016).

30. S. J. Res., Delaware Swedish Tercentenary, March 20, 1935, Chapter 254, Laws of the State of Delaware, 105th Session of the General Assembly, vol. 40 (Wilmington: Taylor, 1935), 864; and Act No. 542, July 2, 1937, Laws of the General Assembly of the Commonwealth of Pennsylvania, passed at the session of 1937, 2697.

31. Joint Resolution No. 2, May 29, 1937, Laws of New Jersey, 1937, 656.

32. Gunlög Fur, *Colonialism in the Margins: Cultural Encounters in New Sweden and Lapland* (Leiden: Brill, 2007), 171.

33. Speech, Crown Prince Gustaf Adolf, June 27, 1938, in Fritz Henriksson, *Sweden's Participation in the U.S. Celebration of the New Sweden Tercentenary: Report Compiled by Fritz Henriksson* (Stockholm: Bonnier, 1939), 172.

34. Speech, Cordell Hull, June 27, 1938, in *Observance of the Three Hundredth Anniversary of the First Permanent Settlement in the Delaware River Valley, 1938* (Washington, D.C.: U.S. Government Printing Office, 1940), 24.

35. George H. Earle, "Over NBC Blue Network," April 8, 1938, Speeches, Radio, and [Richard C. McMullen], "Mr. Chairman, Your Excellency, Governor Earle," [April 8, 1938], Speeches, Forefathers' Day, in #25.92, box 7, PAC.

36. Gunlög Fur, "Romantic Relations: Swedish Attitudes towards Indians during the Twentieth Century," *Swedish-American Historical Quarterly* 55, no. 3 (2004): 145–64; and Gunlög Fur, "Fabrications of Friendship? The Historiography of European-Indian Friendship in the Delaware Valley," in *Notions of America: Swedish Perspectives*, ed. Kerstin W. Shands, Rolf Lundén, and Dag Blanck (Huddinge: Södertörn Academic Studies, 2004), 105–7.

37. Rachel Rubinstein, *Members of the Tribe: Native America in the Jewish Imagination* (Detroit: Wayne State University Press, 2010); and Christian F. Feest, "Germany's Indians in European Perspective," in *Germans and Indians: Fantasies, Encounters, Projections*, ed. Colin G. Calloway, Gerd Gemünden, and Susanne Zantop (Lincoln: University of Nebraska Press, 2002), 33–37.

38. Gunlög Fur, "Colonialism and Swedish History: Unthinkable Connections?," in *Scandinavian Colonialism and the Rise of Modernity: Small Time Agents in a Global Arena*, ed. Magdalena Naum and Jonas M. Nordin (New York: Springer, 2013), 18–21, 24; and Fur, "Romantic Relations," 147–8.

39. On Carl Milles's work in the United States, see Elisabeth Lidén, *Between Water and Heaven: Carl Milles Search for American Commissions* (Stockholm: Almqvist och Wiksell, 1986); and Erik Näslund, *Carl Milles: en biografi* (Höganäs: Wiken, 1991), 237–301.

40. Minutes, Bestyrelsen, November 11, 1936, vol. 1, BNS. A contributing reason for why the commission abandoned the idea of a statue was that the original design portrayed Gustavus Adolphus kneeling. Because Philadelphia had a large Catholic population, the commission feared that a kneeling figure of a Lutheran king, who had fought against Catholics in the Thirty Year War, might "invite manifestations" from some of the city's residents (minutes, Arbetsutskottet, September 29, 1936, vol. 1, BNS).

41. Carl Milles, letter to J. Sigfrid Edström, November 10, 1936, vol. 15, BNS.

42. Folke Bernadotte, letter to J. Sigfrid Edström, December 29, 1936, vol. 15, BNS.

43. Martin Kastengren, letter to J. Sigfrid Edström, February 5, 1937, vol. 15, BNS.

44. Carl Milles, letter to J. Sigfrid Edström, January 24, 1937, vol. 6, BNS.

45. Carl Milles, letter to J. Sigfrid Edström, December 21, 1936, vol. 15, BNS; and Aman-

dus Johnson, letter to Christopher Ward, March 31, 1937, Subject Files: Amandus Johnson, 1330:0, box 9, DEC.
46. Minutes, Arbetsutskottet, September 22, 1937, vol. 1, BNS.
47. See, for example, minutes, Arbetsutskottet, October 21, 1936, vol. 1, BNS.
48. Lidén, *Between Water and Heaven*, 43–54; and Näslund, *Carl Milles*, 263–66.
49. "Delaware to acquire Fort Christina Site as State Park," April 1937, Subject Files: Publicity Committee, 1330:0, box 14, DEC.
50. "An Act to Change the Name of the Christiana River in New Castle County to the Christina River," May 3, 1937, chap. 4, Laws of the State of Delaware, 106th Session of the General Assembly, vol. 41 (Wilmington: Taylor, 1937), 21.
51. This notion of progress and civilization can be understood through Bruno Latour's discussion about the concept of modernity. According to him, the "adjective modern designates a new regime, an acceleration, a rupture, a revolution in time" that always, through contrast, defines "an archaic and stable past." The word *modern* thus "designates a break in the regular passage of time, and it designates a combat in which there are victors and vanquished" (*We Have Never Been Modern* [Cambridge: Harvard University Press, 1993], 10).
52. "Inbjudan till nationalinsamling för Delaware-monumentet," December 1936, F3, vol. 844, UD 1920; and Henriksson, *Sweden's Participation*, 30–38.
53. Minutes, "vid konferens å Statsrådsberedningen . . . om en nationalinsamling . . . ," November 10, 1936, vol. 1, BNS.
54. Prince Bertil, speech no. 1, Wilmington, June 27, 1938, vol. 145, HRR.
55. Franklin D. Roosevelt, speech, June 27, 1938, *Observance of the Three Hundredth Anniversary*, 19.
56. Final Report of Delaware Tercentenary Commission, January 17, 1939, 13–14, Ryden's Files: Printed Materials, 1330:11, box 21, DEC.
57. Orm Øverland, *Immigrant Minds, American Identities: Making the United States Home, 1870–1930* (Urbana: University of Illinois Press, 2000), 54–86.
58. Bénédicte Deschamps, "Italian Americans and Columbus Day: A Quest for Consensus between National and Group Identities, 1840–1910," in *Celebrating Ethnicity and Nation: American Festive Culture from the Revolution to the Early 20th Century*, ed. Jürgen Heideking, Geneviève Fabre, and Kai Dreisbach (New York: Berghahn, 2001), 135.
59. John Bodnar's claim that the 1948 commemoration specifically celebrated the Swedish settlement in Bishop Hill, Illinois, is not supported by contemporary sources. See Bodnar, *Remaking America*, 43–48.
60. Pioneer Centennial Association newsletter 1 (November 1946), F4, box 45, CBP.
61. "Svensk-amerikanernas 100-årsjubileum," *Svenska Morgonbladet*, May 14, 1946, F1, vol. 243, UD Wash.
62. Conrad Bergendoff, "A Centennial of Swedish Pioneers," *American Scandinavian Review* (Summer 1946), F18, box 39, CBP.
63. Nils William Olsson, "Pioneer Centennial to Be Observed Throughout Middle West in 1948," *American Swedish Monthly* 42, no. 6 (November 1947), 6–7.
64. Naboth Hedin, letter to the Board of Directors, Svensk-Amerikanska Nyhetsbyrån, October 26, 1945, F1, vol. 243, UD Wash.
65. Bergendoff, "A Centennial of Swedish Pioneers."
66. William Cronon, "Revisiting the Vanishing Frontier: The Legacy of Frederick Jackson Turner," *Western Historical Quarterly* 18 (April 1987): 157–76.
67. Frederick Jackson Turner, *The Frontier in American History* (New York: Holt, 1921), 1, 21–37.

68. Kerwin Lee Klein, *Frontiers of Historical Imagination: Narrating the European Conquest of Native America, 1890–1990* (Berkeley: University of California Press, 1997), 19–20.
69. O'Brien, *Firsting and Lasting*, xii.
70. Edwin Carl Johnson, "The Swedish Invasion," June 13, 1948, F47, box 5, AKC.
71. Prince Bertil, speech [Chicago Stadium], n.d., F7, vol. 842, UD 1920.
72. On the adoption of the frontier myth in politics and popular culture, see, for example, Gerald D. Nash, *Creating the West: Historical Interpretations, 1890–1990* (Albuquerque: University of New Mexico Press, 1991), 41–42; and Richard Slotkin, *Gunfighter Nation: The Myth of the Frontier in Twentieth-Century America* (New York: Harper Perennial, 1992), 278–350.
73. Plaques at the Jenny Lind Chapel in Andover, Illinois, and at the intersection of Kellogg Boulevard East and Robert Street North in Saint Paul, Minnesota. A third plaque was unveiled during the centennial, at Pine Lake, Wisconsin, in memory of the settlement established in 1841 by clergyman Gustaf Unonius.
74. Prince Bertil, speech, June 30, 1948, Report, State of New York, 19–21, F11, box 1, SPCA.
75. Annette Kolodny, *The Lay of the Land: Metaphor as Experience and History in American Life and Letters* (Chapel Hill: University of North Carolina Press, 1975). This is essentially a discourse of Jeffersonian agrarianism. See Richard Slotkin *The Fatal Environment: The Myth of the Frontier in the Age of Industrialization, 1800–1890* (Norman: University of Oklahoma Press, 1994), 51–52.
76. David M. Wrobel, *Promised Lands: Promotion, Memory, and the Creation of the American West* (Lawrence: University of Kansas Press, 2002), 121–22.
77. Pioneer Centennial Association newsletter 1 (November 1946), F4, box 45, CBP.
78. Pioneer Centennial Association newsletter 4 (March 1948), F4, box 45, CBP.
79. Johan Enander, *Förenta Staternas historia*, 4 vols. (Chicago: Enander och Bohmans förlag, 1874–80); and Johan Enander, *Nordmännen i Amerika eller Amerikas upptäckt: Historisk afhandling med anledning af Columbiafesterna i Chicago 1892–1893* (Rock Island, I.L.: Lutheran Augustana Book Concern, 1893).
80. Donna R. Gabaccia, "The Minnesota School and Immigration History at Midwestern Land Grant Universities, 1890–2005," *Journal of Migration History* 1, no. 2 (2015): 171–99.
81. Ulf Beijbom, "The Historiography of Swedish America," *Swedish-American Historical Quarterly* 31 (October 1980): 282; and H. Arnold Barton, *A Folk Divided: Homeland Swedes and Swedish Americans, 1840–1940* (Carbondale: Southern Illinois University Press, 1994), 311.
82. An example is an overview of Swedish contributions to American history, in Adolph Benson and Naboth Hedin, eds., *Swedes in America, 1638–1938* (New Haven: Yale University Press, 1938).
83. "Essay Contest, Free Trips to Scandinavia" (poster), and Earnest B. Bearnarth, letter to Dear Contestant, n.d., in "Essay Contest," vol. 81, UD Chi.
84. Swedish American Line, "Swedish Pioneer Essay Contest Winners Named," June 26, 1948, F6, box 45, CBP; Adolph Benson, ed., *The Will to Succeed: Stories of Swedish Pioneers* (Stockholm: Bonnier, 1948), 7–16.
85. Byron J. Nordstrom, "The Swedish Historical Society of America: The Minnesota Years," in *Swedes in the Twin Cities: Immigrant Life and Minnesota's Urban Frontier*, ed. Philip J. Anderson and Dag Blanck (Saint Paul: Minnesota Historical Society, 2001), 104–16.
86. Vilas Johnson, letter to undisclosed recipient, n.d., F13, box 2, SPCA.

87. John Higham, "The Ethnic Historical Society in Changing Times," *Journal of American Ethnic History* 13, no. 2 (1994): 30–44.
88. Another commonality was that both societies were established as a result of commemorations—in the Norwegian-American Historical Association case, the Norse-American Centennial Celebration of June 1925. See Mark Safstrom, "Writing History Together: Norwegian American and Swedish American Historians in Dialogue," in *Norwegians and Swedes in the United States: Friends and Neighbors*, ed. Philip J. Anderson and Dag Blanck (Saint Paul: Minnesota Historical Society Press, 2012), 108–10.
89. Per Sandberg, letter to Ledamöterna, May 6, 1947, F6, vol. 842, UD 1920.
90. Naboth Hedin, letter to Conrad Bergendoff, November 5, 1945, F18, box 39, CBP.
91. Bodnar, *Remaking America*, 33.
92. The Swedish definition include words such as *nyodlare, föregångsman, banbrytare*, and *vägbyggare*. See *Svenska akademiens ordlista*, 13th ed. (Stockholm: Svenska Akademien, 2006), s.v. *pionjär*.
93. Erik Gustaf Geijer, "Odalbonden," in *Iduna: En Skrift för den Nordiska Fornålderns Älskare; Första häftet* (Stockholm, 1811), 24–27.
94. Patrik Hall, *Den svenskaste historien: Nationalism i Sverige under sex sekler* (Stockholm: Carlsson, 2000), 107–8, 118–25.
95. Henrik Berggren and Lars Trägårdh, *Är svensken människa? Gemenskap och oberoende i det moderna Sverige* (Stockholm: Norstedts, 2006), 41–44.
96. Ibid., 87–93.
97. Turner, *The Frontier in American History*, 21–37.
98. On Native Americans, national parks, and ideas about wilderness, see Robert H. Keller and Michael F. Turek, *American Indians and National Parks* (Tucson: University of Arizona Press, 1998); and Mark David Spence, *Dispossessing the Wilderness: Indian Removal and the Making of National Parks* (New York: Oxford University Press, 1999).

CHAPTER 4: MUTUAL MODERNITIES

1. "Prins Bertil reser samma väg som svenska pionjärerna i USA," *Västgöta-Demokraten*, February 5, 1948, vol. 1, NWOP.
2. Pierre Nora, general introduction, in *Realms of Memory: Rethinking the French Past: Conflicts and Divisions* (New York: Columbia University Press, 1996), 1:15.
3. Julia Creet, introduction, in *Memory and Migration: Multidisciplinary Approaches to Memory Studies*, ed. Julia Creet and Andreas Kitzmann (Toronto: University Press, 2011), 9.
4. Astrid Erll, "Travelling Memory," *Parallax* 17, no. 4 (2011): 12–13. See also Susannah Radstone, "What Place Is This? Transcultural Memory and the Locations of Memory Studies," *Parallax* 17, no. 4 (2011): 117–18.
5. Christopher Endy, *Cold War Holidays: American Tourism in France* (Chapel Hill: University of North Carolina Press, 2004), 15; Christopher Endy, "Travel and World Power: Americans in Europe, 1890–1917," *Diplomatic History* 22 (Fall 1998): 573. On how eighteenth- and nineteenth-century Americans defined themselves through travel, see Daniel Kilbride, *Being American in Europe, 1750–1860* (Baltimore: Johns Hopkins University Press, 2013).
6. John Bodnar, *Remaking America: Public Memory, Commemoration, and Patriotism in the Twentieth Century* (Princeton: Princeton University Press, 1992), 128–35. For other examples of commemorative travels and reenactments in national, not cross-border, contexts, see Ann Uhry Abrams, *The Pilgrims and Pocahontas: Rival Myths of Ameri-*

can Origin (Boulder, C.O.: Westview, 1999), 276; David M. Wrobel, *Promised Lands: Promotion, Memory, and the Creation of the American West* (Lawrence: University of Kansas Press, 2002), 95–119; Stephen Gapps, "Performing the Past: A Cultural History of Reenactments" (Ph.D. diss., University of Technology, Sydney, 2002), 156–58; Leslie Witz, *Apartheid's Festival: Contesting South Africa's National Pasts* (Bloomington: Indiana University Press, 2003), 216–41; and Stephen Gapps, "'Blacking Up' for the Explorers of 1951," in *Settler and Creole Reenactment*, ed. Vanessa Agnew and Jonathan Lamb (Basingstoke, U.K.: Palgrave Macmillan, 2009).

7. A delegation representing Finland also traveled with the 1938 Swedish delegation on the *Kungsholm*. This considerably smaller group consisted of nine people and had a political character. It was led by the minister for foreign affairs, Rudolf Holsti, and included the speaker of parliament, several members of parliament, as well as representatives of the Finnish press and church. See Max Engman, "The Tug of War Over 'Nya Sverige' 1938," *Swedish-American Historical Quarterly* 45, no. 2 (1994): 93–94.

8. J. Sigfrid Edström, letter to Frank Melvin, April 19, 1938, Edstrom, #25.84, box 2, PAC.

9. Fritz Henriksson, *Sweden's Participation in the U.S. Celebration of the New Sweden Tercentenary: Report Compiled by Fritz Henriksson* (Stockholm: Bonnier, 1939), 20–22, 147.

10. J. Sigfrid Edström, letter to Frank Melvin, June 12, 1938, Edstrom, #25.84, box 2, PAC.

11. Stig Hadenius, Björn Molin, and Hans Wieslander, *Sverige efter 1900: En modern politisk historia* (Stockholm: Bonnier Alba, 1993), 354–55.

12. "Ministern för utrikes ärenden anför efter gemensam beredning med statsrådets övriga ledamöter . . . ," n.d., F6, vol. 842, UD 1920.

13. "PM rörande konferensen den 15/9 1947," September 17, 1948, doss. 1, vol. 81, UD Chi.

14. Sven Dahlman, letter to Beskickningen, May 8, 1948, F7, vol. 842, UD 1920.

15. Gjöres was replaced by Karin Kock, a minister without portfolio, and, at the time, the only woman in the Swedish government.

16. On the difference between representing something by "standing for" and "acting for" it, see Hanna F. Pitkin, *The Concept of Representation* (Berkeley: University of California Press, 1972), 60–90.

17. For example, the entire issue of the *Annals of the American Academy of Political and Social Science* 197 (May 1938) was devoted to Sweden.

18. Marquis W. Childs, *Sweden: The Middle Way* (New Haven: Yale University Press, 1936).

19. George H. Earle, letter to Wollmar Boström, October 22, 1937, and George Messersmith, letter to Fred Morris Dearing, November 9, 1937, in 811.415, box 5038, DoS; and report, "The 300th Anniversary," Historical Data, #25.90, box 8, PAC.

20. [Franklin D. Roosevelt], letter to George H. Earle, October 8, 1937, 841.5, box 13, DoS Sthlm.

21. Richard Keller, *Pennsylvania's Little New Deal* (New York: Garland Publishing, 1982).

22. Report, "The 300th Anniversary," 83–84; and Kim-Eric Williams, "Ninety Years of Growth and Challenge: The Swedish Colonial Society, 1919–2009" (Philadelphia: Swedish Colonial Society, 2009), http://colonialswedes.net.

23. "Earle Was Amazed at Swedish Housing," *Berwick Enterprise*, December 17, 1937, Folder Dec. 14–15, #25.91, box 9, PAC. In the same folder, see also "Sweden Has Inspired Earle to Banish Slums, He Says," *Scranton Tribune*, December 17, 1937.

24. The most recent example was the participation of King Carl XVI Gustaf, Queen Silvia, and Princess Madeleine in the 2013 commemoration of New Sweden. See the Con-

clusions for more on the 2013 celebration. On the significance of royals to Swedish Americans, see Lizette Gradén, "Royal Symbolism and Swedish-American Heritage Making," *Swedish-American Historical Quarterly* 54 (July 2003): 185–201.

25. Ian Radforth, *Royal Spectacle: The 1860 Visit of the Prince of Wales to Canada and the United States* (Toronto: University of Toronto Press, 2004); and Heike Bungert, "Demonstrating the Values of 'Gemüthlichkeit' and 'Cultur,'" in *Celebrating Ethnicity and Nation: American Festive Culture from the Revolution to the Early 20th Century*, ed. Jürgen Heideking, Geneviève Fabre, and Kai Dreisbach (New York: Berghahn, 2001), 181–84.
26. J. Sigfrid Edström, letter to Wollmar Boström, April 30, 1937, vol. 5, BNS; and Nils Rudebeck, letter to Wollmar Boström, December 23, 1937, vol. 141, HRR.
27. See, for example, "Here's What Twin Cities' Girls Think of Prince Bertil," n.d., ASI 1938.
28. Report, "The 300th Anniversary," 87–88.
29. "PM rörande konferensen den 15/9 1947," September 17, 1948.
30. Fabian af Petersens, *Prins Bertil: Ett liv* (Stockholm: Fischer, 1992), 99–116, 135–41.
31. "Polisuppbåd mötte Prins Bertil: Televisionsdebut på flygfältet," *Stockholms-Tidningen*, June 2, 1948, Clippings, vol. 81, UD Chi.
32. Gösta Oldenburg, "Kring Pionjärjubileet," June 28, 1948, attachment to Gösta Oldenburg, letter to Nils William Olsson, December 29, 1948, F6, box 4, SPCA.
33. Franklin D. Roosevelt, press conference no. 303, June 23, 1936, p. 293, FDR Presidential Library and Museum, http://www.fdrlibrary.marist.edu.
34. Henriksson, *Sweden's Participation*, 148.
35. Prince Bertil, speech no. 1, Wilmington, June 27, 1938, vol. 148, HRR.
36. For discussions about reenacted colonial landings, see John Seelye, *Memory's Nation: The Place of Plymouth Rock* (Chapel Hill: University of North Carolina Press, 1998), 637–39; Richard M. Fried, *The Russians are Coming! The Russians are Coming! Pageantry and Patriotism in Cold-War America* (New York: Oxford University Press, 1998), 112; and Maria Nugent, "'An Echo of That Other Cry': Re-Enacting Captain Cook's First Landing as Conciliation Event," in *Conciliation on Colonial Frontiers: Conflict, Performance, and Commemoration in Australia and the Pacific Rim*, ed. Kate Darian-Smith and Penelope Edmonds (New York: Routledge, 2015), 193–209.
37. See, for example, Michael Kammen, *Mystic Chords of Memory: The Transformation of Tradition in American Culture* (New York: Knopf, 1991), 305; Wrobel, *Promised Lands*, 113; Gregory Clark, *Rhetorical Landscapes in America: Variations on a Theme from Kenneth Burke* (Columbia: University of South Carolina Press, 2004), 100; and Gapps, "'Blacking Up' for the Explorers," 211.
38. Crown Prince Gustaf Adolf, speech no. 1, "H.K.H. Kronprinsens anförande i radio," June 17, 1938, vol. 148, HRR.
39. Oscar Solbert, letter to Christopher Ward, March 30, 1937, Subject Files: Solbert, 1330:0, box 15, DEC.
40. Amandus Johnson, letter to Wollmar Boström, December 14, 1936, F3, vol. 231, UD Wash.
41. Image no. 37, "Members of party disembarking at the Rocks," F11, box 4, 1325:36, Department of State, General Photographic Collection, Delaware Public Archives, Dover; and "Wilmington, Del., Swedish Prince Dedicates Shaft to Early Settlers," presented by Graham McNamee, Universal Newsreel (1938), DVD, 76 min.
42. Fred Morris Dearing, letter to Cordell Hull, December 7, 1937, 811.415, box 5038, DoS; and George H. Earle, letter to Franklin D. Roosevelt, October 1937, 841.5, box 13, DoS Sthlm.

43. Report, "The 300th Anniversary," 87–88.
44. Engman, "Tug of War," 97.
45. Fred Morris Dearing, letter to Cordell Hull, December 7, 1937.
46. Nils William Olsson, "Swedish Delegation Follows the Path of the Pioneers," *American Swedish Monthly* 42 no. 6 (June 1948), 12, 27.
47. Nils William Olsson, letter to Per Sandberg, March 17, 1948, F2, box 5, SPCA.
48. J. Sigfrid Edström, "PM för den officiella svenska delegationen," April 28, 1938, vol. 14, BNS; Henriksson, *Sweden's Participation*, 91–113; and *Observance of the Three Hundredth Anniversary of the First Permanent Settlement in the Delaware River Valley, 1938* (Washington, D.C.: U.S. Government Printing Office, 1940), 37–51. Although some delegates followed the royals during the whole journey, the delegation officially dissolved in New York on July 6. Because of the importance of its figureheads, however, the royals' continued travels symbolized the seamless extension of the journey westward.
49. J. Sigfrid Edström, letter to Oscar Solbert, December 2, 1936, vol. 5, BNS.
50. J. Sigfrid Edström, letter to Oscar Solbert, October 31, 1936, F3, vol. 231, UD Wash.
51. J. Sigfrid Edström, letter to Wollmar Boström, April 30, 1937, vol. 5, BNS.
52. Oscar Solbert, letter to J. Sigfrid Edström, November 13, 1936, F3, vol. 231, UD Wash.
53. Carl F. Hellström, letter to Rickard Sandler, August 12, 1937, Minnesota, vol. 239, UD Wash.
54. Wollmar Boström, letter to Carl F. Hellström, September 22, 1937, EI, vol. 39, UD Mpls.
55. Wollmar Boström, letter to George T. Summerlin, March 17, 1938, 811.415, box 5038, DoS.
56. Wollmar Boström, letter to Birger Tinglöf, May 10, 1938, Kalifornien, vol. 239, UD Wash.
57. "Northwest Plans Special Train to Celebration," *New Sweden Tercentenary News* [1], TC.
58. *Observance of the Three Hundredth Anniversary*, 8.
59. Nils William Olsson, letter to A. Theodore Sohlberg, September 4, 1947, F4, box 5, SPCA.
60. Official itinerary of Swedish delegation, F3, vol. 243, UD Wash; Nils William Olsson, "Swedish Delegation Follows the Path of the Pioneers"; and Pioneer Centennial Association newsletter 5 (May 1948), X2b1, vol. 166, SI.
61. Pioneer Centennial Association newsletter 1 (November 1946), F4, box 45, CBP.
62. Prince Bertil, speech, City Hall, New York City, F7, vol. 842, UD 1920.
63. "The Swedish in America's Blood," *Newsweek*, n.d., attached to Niles W. von Wettberg, letter to Conrad Bergendoff, June 17, 1948, F6, box 45, CBP.
64. Oscar Solbert, letter to Christopher Ward, October 12, 1937, Subject Files: Solbert, 1330.0, box 15, DEC.
65. George H. Earle, speech, Gothenburg, Sweden, November 28, 1937, attached to Frank Melvin, letter to Cordell Hull, November 11, 1937, 811.415, box 5038, DoS.
66. Aviatar Zerubavel, *Ancestors and Relatives: Genealogy, Identity, and Community* (New York: Oxford University Press, 2012), 53–75. On the idea of a nation as family, see Etienne Balibar, "The Nation Form: History and Ideology," in *Race, Nation, Class: Ambiguous Identities*, ed. Etienne Balibar and Immanuel Wallerstein (London: Verso, 1991), 86–106.
67. François Weil, *Family Trees: A History of Genealogy in America* (Cambridge: Harvard University Press, 2013), 178.
68. The reality, of course, was more problematic. Sweden has a history of colonialism and

slavery, including the Caribbean colony of St. Barthélemy (1784–1878). In the twentieth century it imposed racist policies against the indigenous Sámi population in the country's northern regions. See Holger Weiss, *Slavhandel och slaveri under svensk flagg: Koloniala drömmar och verklighet i Afrika och Karibien 1770–1847* (Stockholm: Atlantis, 2016); and Lennart Lundmark, *"Lappen är ombytlig, ostadig och obekväm": Svenska statens samepolitik i rasismens tidevarv* (Umeå: Norrlands universitetsförlag, 2002).

69. Gunnar Myrdal, *An American Dilemma: The Negro Problem and Modern Democracy* (New York: Harper, 1944). On Myrdal's study and the impact of his book, see Dag Blanck, "Svenska uppfattningar om USA under två århundraden," in *Det blågula stjärnbaneret: USA:s närvaro och inflytande i Sverige*, ed. Erik Åsard (Stockholm: Carlsson, 2016), 62–67.

70. Elazar Barkan, *The Retreat of Scientific Racism: Changing Concepts of Race in Britain and the United States between the World Wars* (Cambridge: Cambridge University Press, 1992); Thomas A. Guglielmo and Earle Lewis, "Changing Racial Meanings: Race and Ethnicity in the United States, 1930–1964," in *Race and Ethnicity in America: A Concise History*, ed. Ronald H. Bayor (New York: Columbia University Press, 2003), 169–71.

71. Nancy Ordover, *American Eugenics: Race, Queer Anatomy, and the Science of Nationalism* (Minneapolis: University of Minnesota Press, 2003), xv–xvi; and Marouf A. Hasian, Jr., *The Rhetoric of Eugenics in Anglo-American Thought* (Athens: University of Georgia Press, 2017).

72. Matthew Frye Jacobson, *Whiteness of a Different Color: European Immigrants and the Alchemy of Race* (Cambridge: Harvard University Press, 1998), 93. See also David R. Roediger, *Working toward Whiteness: How America's Immigrants Became White; The Strange Journey from Ellis Island to the Suburbs* (New York: Basic Books, 2005), 139–45.

73. Johanna Schoen, "Reassessing Eugenic Sterilization: The Case of North Carolina," in *A Century of Eugenics in America: From the Indiana Experiment to the Human Genome Era*, ed. Paul A. Lombardo (Bloomington: Indiana University Press, 2011), 142.

74. See, for example, Molly Ladd-Taylor, "Eugenics and Social Welfare in New Deal Minnesota," in Lombardo, *A Century of Eugenics in America*, 118.

75. Susan Curell, introduction, in *Popular Genetics: National Efficiency and American Mass Culture in the 1930s*, ed. Susan Curell and Christina Cogdell (Athens: Ohio University Press, 2006), 3.

76. Gunnar Broberg and Mattias Tydén, "Eugenics in Sweden: Efficient Care," in *Eugenics and the Welfare State: Norway, Sweden, Denmark, and Finland*, ed. Gunnar Broberg and Nils Roll-Hansen (East Lansing: Michigan State University Press, 2005), 135; and Mattias Tydén, *Från politik till praktik: De svenska steriliseringslagarna 1935–1975*, 2nd ed. (Stockholm: Acta Universitatis Stockholmiensis, 2002), 53–57, 522, 553–56.

77. Gunnar Broberg and Mattias Tydén, *Oönskade i folkhemmet: Rashygien och sterilisering i Sverige* (Stockholm: Gidlunds, 1991), 90–96; and Karin Johannisson, "Folkhälsa: Det svenska projektet från 1900 till 2:a världskriget," *Lychnos: Årsbok för idéhistoria och vetenskapshistoria* (Uppsala: Lärdomshistoriska samfundet, 1991), 139–95.

78. Wollmar Boström, "The Swedish Part in the Delaware Tercentenary," *American Swedish Monthly* 29, no 4. (April 1935), 6.

79. Amandus Johnson, letter to Wollmar Boström, December 14, 1936, F3, vol. 231, UD Wash.

80. Ove Olsson, report, "Som Delawaredelegat till Amerika," attached to Olof Lamm, letter to Fritz Henriksson, February 7, 1939, vol. 14, BNS.

81. Carol E. Hoeffecker, *Corporate Capital: Wilmington in the Twentieth Century* (Philadelphia: Temple University Press, 1983), 111.

82. U.S. Bureau of the Census, *Fifteenth Census of the United States: 1930, Population*, vol. 3, part 1, *Reports by States, Alabama–Missouri* (Washington, D.C.: U.S. Government Printing Office, 1932), 382; and U.S. Bureau of the Census, *Sixteenth Census of the United States: 1940, Population*, vol. 2, part 1, *Characteristics of the Population* (Washington, D.C.: U.S. Government Printing Office, 1943), 896, 934.
83. U.S. Bureau of the Census, *Fifteenth Census of the United States: 1930*, Delaware, New Castle County, Wilmington, Representative District 1, Ward 8, ED 2–42, sheets 22A and 22B, NARA digital publication, T626, FamilySearch, https://familysearch.org; U.S. Bureau of the Census, *Sixteenth Census of the United States: 1940*, Delaware, New Castle County, Wilmington Representative District 1, Ward 8, ED 4–68, sheets 3A and 3B, NARA digital publication, T627, FamilySearch, https://familysearch.org.
84. Brett Gadsden, *Between North and South: Delaware, Desegregation, and the Myth of American Sectionalism* (Philadelphia: University of Pennsylvania Press, 2013), 8; and William W. Boyer and Edward C. Ratledge, *Pivotal Policies in Delaware: From Desegregation to Deregulation* (Newark: University of Delaware Press, 2014), 1–11.
85. For a useful definition of the concept of modernization, see Nils Gilman, *Mandarins of the Future: Modernization Theory in Cold War America* (Baltimore: Johns Hopkins University Press, 2003), 7. Notions of a time gap between the past and the present and ideas about progress are central to understanding how commemorations can manifest contemporary interests on the foundations of the past. See Reinhart Koselleck, *Futures Past: On the Semantics of Historical Time*, trans. Keith Tribe (New York: Columbia University Press, 2004), 11–25, 263–70; and Jürgen Habermas, *The Philosophical Discourse of Modernity* (Cambridge: Polity, 1987), 5–7.
86. Algot Mattsson, *Vägen mot väster: En bok om emigrationen och Svenska Amerika Linien* (Stockholm: Askild och Kärnekull, 1982), 123–29, 145–60.
87. Olsson, report, "Som Delawaredelegat till Amerika."
88. Johan Rådberg, *Drömmen om atlantångaren: Utopier och myter i 1900-talets stadsbyggande* (Stockholm: Atlantis, 1997), 7–16.
89. Crown Prince Gustaf Adolf, speech no. 1, "H.K.H. Kronprinsens anförande i radio."
90. Radio news, Swedish American Line, no. 2 [1937], TC.
91. Pamphlet, "Three White Viking Ships," Publications, #25.90, box 8, PAC.
92. Sven Dahlman, letter to Beskickningen, May 8, 1948, F7, vol. 842, UD 1920.
93. Pioneer Centennial Association newsletter 4 (March 1948), 1948, F18, box 39, CBP.
94. Prince Bertil, speech "New York City Hall 1st or 2nd June," F7, vol. 842, UD 1920.
95. George T. Summerlin, letter to Frank Melvin, March 19, 1938, Women's Executive, F2, #25.84, box 6, PAC.
96. George H. Earle, letter to Harry Moore, n.d., Women's Executive, F2, #25.84, box 6, PAC.
97. Carl A. Sorling, letter to Conrad Bergendoff, July 12, 1948, F5, box 45, CBP.
98. G. Hilmer Lundbeck, Jr., "A Tribute to the Pioneers," and Tore H. Nilert, "Now They Come by Air," in *American Swedish Monthly* 42, no. 6 (June 1948), 91–92, 95–96.
99. Endy, *Cold War Holidays*, 25.
100. Wrobel, *Promised Lands*, 104–5.
101. Amanda Lagerkvist, *Amerikafantasier: Kön, medier och visualitet i svenska reseskildringar från USA 1945–63* (Ph.D. diss., Stockholm University, 2005), 75 and chap. 3; Martin Alm, *Americanitis: Amerika som sjukdom eller läkemedel: Svenska berättelser om USA åren 1900–1939* (Lund: Studia Historica Lundensia, 2002), 36; and Anders Houltz, *Teknikens tempel: Modernitet och industriarv på Göteborgsutställningen 1923* (Hedemora: Gidlund, 2003), 125–34.

102. Alm, *Americanitis*, 167–68, 249–58.
103. David W. Ellwood, *The Shock of America: Europe and the Challenge of the Century* (Oxford: Oxford University Press, 2012).
104. Tom O'Dell, *Culture Unbound: Americanization and Everyday Life in Sweden* (Lund: Nordic Academic Press, 1997), 123–26, 136.
105. Kammen, *Mystic Chords*, 300.

CHAPTER 5: BONDS OF SWEDISHNESS

1. *New Sweden Tercentenary News*, no. 2, and *New Sweden Tercentenary News*, no. 4, in TC.
2. Len Travers, *Celebrating the Fourth: Independence Day and the Rites of Nationalism in the Early Republic* (Amherst: University of Massachusetts Press, 1997); Simon P. Newman, *Parades and the Politics of the Street: Festive Culture in the Early American Republic* (Philadelphia: University of Pennsylvania Press, 1997); Jürgen Heideking, "Celebrating the Constitution: The Federal Processions of 1788 and the Emergence of a Republican Festive Culture in the United States," in *Celebrating Ethnicity and Nation: American Festive Culture from the Revolution to the Early 20th Century*, ed. Jürgen Heideking, Geneviève Fabre, and Kai Dreisbach (New York: Berghahn, 2001), 25–43. On nineteenth- and twentieth-century histories of festivals in the United States, see Susan G. Davis, *Parades and Power: Street Theater in Nineteenth-Century Philadelphia* (Philadelphia: Temple University Press, 1985); David Glassberg, *American Historical Pageantry: The Uses of Tradition in the Early Twentieth Century* (Chapel Hill: University of North Carolina Press, 1990); and Beverly J. Stoeltje, "Festival," in *Folklore, Cultural Performances, and Popular Entertainments: A Communications-Centered Handbook*, ed. Richard Bauman (New York: Oxford University Press, 1992), 261–67.
3. See, for example, Geneviève Fabre and Jürgen Heideking, introduction, in Heideking et al., *Celebrating Ethnicity and Nation*, 1–24.
4. Orm Øverland, *Immigrant Minds, American Identities: Making the United States Home, 1870–1930* (Urbana: University of Illinois Press, 2000), 2. On ethnic festivals as interpreted in U.S. contexts, see April R. Schultz, *Ethnicity on Parade: Inventing the Norwegian American through Celebration* (Amherst: University of Massachusetts Press, 1994); Lizette Gradén, *On Parade: Making Heritage in Lindsborg, Kansas* (Uppsala: Acta Universitatis Upsaliensis, 2003); Heideking et al., *Celebrating Ethnicity and Nation*; Kathleen Neils Conzen, "Ethnicity as Festive Culture: Nineteenth-Century German America on Parade," in *Invention of Ethnicity*, ed. Werner Sollors (Oxford: Oxford University Press, 1989), 44–76; Olivia Cadaval, *Creating a Latino Identity in the Nation's Capital: The Latino Festival* (New York: Garland, 1998); Lon Kurashige, *Japanese American Celebration and Conflict: A History of Ethnic Identity and Festival, 1934–1990* (Berkeley: University of California Press, 2002); and Robert A. Orsi, *The Madonna of 115th Street: Faith and Community in Italian Harlem, 1880–1915*, 3rd ed. (New Haven: Yale University Press, 2010). Compare the transnational approach in Daron W. Olson, "On Both Sides of the Atlantic: Transnational Celebrations of Norwegian National Identity, 1925–1939," in *Norwegian-American Essays 2014: Migrant Journeys: The Norwegian-American Experience in a Multicultural Context*, ed. Terje Mikael Hasle Joranger (Oslo: Novus Forlag, 2014), 99–122.
5. On transnationalism, immigration, and ethnicity, see Elliot R. Barkan, introduction,

in *Immigration, Incorporation, and Transnationalism*, ed. Elliot R. Barkan (New Brunswick, N.J.: Transaction, 2007), 1–23; and Peter Kivisto, "Theorizing Transnational Immigration: A Critical Review of Current Efforts," *Ethnic and Racial Studies* 24 (July 2001): 549–77. On memory studies, see Michael Rothberg, "Multidirectional Memory in Migratory Settings: The Case of Post-Holocaust Germany," in *Transnational Memory: Circulation, Articulation, Scales*, ed. Chiara De Cesari and Ann Rigney (Berlin: Walter de Gruyter, 2014); Julia Creet and Andreas Kitzmann, eds., *Memory and Migration: Multidisciplinary Approaches to Memory Studies* (Toronto: University of Toronto Press, 2011). On migrant connections across borders, see Matthew Frye Jacobson, *Special Sorrows: The Diasporic Imagination of Irish, Polish, and Jewish Immigrants in the United States*, 2nd ed. (Berkeley: University of California Press, 2002); and Roger Waldinger, *The Cross-Border Connection: Immigrants, Emigrants, and Their Homelands* (Cambridge: Harvard University Press, 2015).
6. Daron W. Olson, *Vikings across the Atlantic: Emigration and the Building of a Greater Norway, 1860–1945* (Minneapolis: University of Minnesota Press, 2013), 215.
7. Donna R. Gabaccia, Dirk Hoerder, and Adam Walaszek, "Emigration and Nation Building during the Mass Migration from Europe," in *Citizenship and Those Who Leave: The Politics of Emigration and Expatriation*, ed. Nancy L. Green and François Weil (Urbana: University of Illinois Press, 2007), 65.
8. The vast majority of festivals were organized by local Swedish-American committees, but the largest celebrations, in Chicago and Minneapolis–Saint Paul, were planned in cooperation with Swedish consuls and diplomats stationed in the Midwest.
9. Report, "The 300th Anniversary," 90–92, historical data, #25.90, box 8, PAC.
10. "'I Have to Pinch Myself,' Crown Prince Confesses," *Minneapolis Star*, n.d., ASI 1938.
11. "Chicago Today May View Its Royal Guests," *Chicago Daily Tribune*, July 16, 1938, Illinois, vol. 240, UD Wash.
12. Poster, tercentenary celebration at Soldier Field, Chicago, July 16, 1938, Delaware, vol. 78, UD Chi; and souvenir program, Swedish Pioneer Centennial celebration, Minnesota State Fairgrounds, June 27, 1948, ASI 1948.
13. "Regal Grace Outlasts Busy Day," n.d., ASI 1938.
14. Martin Kastengren, letter to Oscar Solbert, May 14, 1938, F4, vol. 235, UD Wash.
15. Martin Kastengren, letter to Wollmar Boström, May 11, 1938, F3, vol. 235, UD Wash.
16. Oscar Solbert, letter to Martin Kastengren, May 12, 1938, F3, vol. 235, UD Wash.
17. Conrad Bergendoff, "The Centennial and After," *Augustana Bulletin* 43 (September 1948), F49, box 5, AKC.
18. Olof Rydbeck, memo, July 27, 1948, attached to Sten Aminoff, letter to Statsministern, July 26, 1948, Tb, vol. 41, UD Mpls.
19. "En 'Svenskarnas Dag' som helt säkert i långa tider skall minnas i dessa svenskbygder [sic]," *Svenska Amerikanska Posten*, July 20, 1938, and "Efterskörd från Svenskarnas Dag," *Svenska Amerikanska Posten*, July 27, 1938.
20. Richard Hofstadter, quoted in Seymour Martin Lipset, *American Exceptionalism: A Double-Edged Sword* (New York: Norton, 1996), 18.
21. Michael Ignatieff, *Blood and Belonging: Journeys into the New Nationalism* (London: BBC, 1993), 3–4.
22. Lawrence H. Fuchs, *The American Kaleidoscope, Race, Ethnicity, and the Civic Culture* (Hanover, N.H.: Wesleyan University Press, 1990), 7–34.
23. Gary Gerstle, *American Crucible: Race and Nation in the Twentieth Century* (Princeton: Princeton University Press, 2001); Paul Spickard, *Almost All Aliens: Immigration, Race,*

and Colonialism in American History and Identity (New York: Routledge, 2007); Matthew Frye Jacobson, *Whiteness of a Different Color: European Immigrants and the Alchemy of Race* (Cambridge: Harvard University Press, 1998), chaps. 1, 2, 7; and David R. Roediger, *Working toward Whiteness: How America's Immigrants Became White; The Strange Journey from Ellis Island to the Suburbs* (New York: Basic Books, 2005), chaps. 2, 3.

24. Michael Kammen, *Mystic Chords of Memory: The Transformation of Tradition in American Culture* (New York: Knopf, 1991), 438. On ethnic politics and U.S. foreign relations in the 1920s to the 1940s, see Alexander DeConde, *Ethnicity, Race, and American Foreign Policy: A History* (Boston: Northeastern University Press, 1992), 99–136.

25. See material in Assembly of Captive European Nations, Celebrations and Commemorations, box 140–42, Immigration History Research Center Archives, Archives and Special Collections, University of Minnesota, Minneapolis. See also Arthur L. Waldo, *First Poles in America, 1608–1958: In Commemoration of the 350th Anniversary of Their Landing at Jamestown, Virginia, October 1, 1608* (Pittsburgh, P.A.: Polish Falcons of America, 1957).

26. Olson, *Vikings across the Atlantic*, 188.

27. On the choice of songs during the festivals, see, for example, official souvenir program, Middle West Tercentenary, Soldier Field, July 16, 1938, vol. 80, UD Chi; and program, Swedish Festival, Central Park, New York July 6, 1938, F8, box 14, series 2, Amandus Johnson Papers, MSS 41, Historical Society of Pennsylvania, Philadelphia. "Svea" or "Mother Svea" is a patriotic symbol of Sweden.

28. Report, "Berättelse avgiven av Svenska kommittén," October 1949, X2b1, vol. 166, SI.

29. Panorama picture, Svenskarnas Dag tercentenary celebration, Minnesota State Fairgrounds, July 17, 1938, state fair celebration 1938, MSS/P: VC-20, photo box 1, American Swedish Institute, Minneapolis.

30. There were 580,000 second-generation Swedish Americans in the Midwest by 1930, compared to 314,000 who were Swedish-born. See Sture Lindmark, *Swedish America, 1914–1932: Studies in Ethnicity with Emphasis on Illinois and Minnesota* (Uppsala: Studia Historica Upsaliensia, 1971), 28–29.

31. H. Arnold Barton, *A Folk Divided: Homeland Swedes and Swedish Americans, 1840–1940* (Carbondale: Southern Illinois University Press, 1994), 264, 283.

32. Larry W. Danielson, "The Ethnic Festival and Cultural Revivalism in a Small Midwestern Town" (Ph.D. diss., Indiana University, 1972), 82–88, 147–93.

33. H. Arnold Barton, "Norwegians and Swedes in America: Some Comparisons," in *Norwegians and Swedes in the United States: Friends and Neighbors*, ed. Philip J. Anderson and Dag Blanck (Saint Paul: Minnesota Historical Society Press, 2012), 21–34; Olson, *Vikings across the Atlantic*, 30–40. See also Rebecca S. Miller, "Irish Traditional Music in the United States," in *Making the Irish American: History and Heritage of the Irish in the United States*, ed. J. J. Lee and Marion R. Casey (New York: New York University Press, 2006), 413–15.

34. Barbro Klein, "More Swedish Than in Sweden, More Iranian Than Iran: Folk Culture and World Migrations," in *Upholders of Culture: Past and Present; Lectures from an International Seminar Arranged by the Committee on Man, Technology, and Society at the Royal Swedish Academy of Engineering Sciences (IVA) in 2000*, ed. Bo Sundin (Stockholm: Royal Swedish Academy of Engineering Sciences, 2001), 67–73.

35. Orvar Löfgren, "Nationella Arenor," in *Försvenskningen av Sverige: Det nationellas förvandlingar*, ed. Billy Ehn, Jonas Frykman, and Orvar Löfgren (Stockholm: Natur och kultur, 1993), 45–58. On Swedish cultural traditionalism as a countermovement to the more

modernistic nationalism, see Jonas Hansson, *Humanismens kris: Bildningsideal och kulturkritik i Sverige 1848–1933* (Eslöv: Brutus Östlings Bokförlag Symposion, 1999), 159–205.
36. Patrik Hall, *Den svenskaste historien: Nationalism i Sverige under sex sekler* (Stockholm: Carlsson, 2000), 257–69.
37. "Parade Units Display Old Country Lore for Visitors from Sweden," n.d., vol. 3, NWOP.
38. "Dråplig Rockfordparad, Oscar II i skyltfönster," *Stockholms-Tidningen*, n.d., vol. 3, NWOP.
39. "Five Church Leaders Take Part," n.d., ASI 1938.
40. Minutes, executive committee of the Chicago committee, September 30, 1947, F4, box 45, CBP.
41. Audio recording, Conrad Bergendoff, June 28, 1938, record 8, All Lutheran Swedish Tercentenary, vol. 25, BNS.
42. "10.000 entusiastiska besökare på pioniärfest i Minneapolis," *Svenska Dagbladet*, n.d., F48, box 5, AKC.
43. Pioneer Centennial Association newsletter 5 (May 1948), and report, "Berättelse avgiven av Svenska kommittén," October 1949, in X2b1, vol. 166, SI.
44. "Väldigaste Sverigefesten i USA:s historia," March 3, 1948, Clippings, vol. 81, UD Chi. The first stanza of the Swedish version of "A Mighty Fortress Is Our God" is quoted in "Hear Us, Svea."
45. Richard F. Tomasson, "How Sweden Became So Secular," *Scandinavian Studies* 74 (Spring 2002): 66; and Thorleif Pettersson, "Sekularisering," in *Religion i Sverige*, ed. Ingvar Svanberg and David Westerlund (Stockholm: Dialogos, 2011), 32–38. On modernization and secularization, see Pippa Norris and Ronald Inglehart, *Sacred and Secular: Religion and Politics Worldwide* (Cambridge: Cambridge University Press, 2004), 24–25. Religion continued to be important among certain proponents of a conservative Swedish nationalism; see Charlotte Tornbjer, *Den nationella modern: Moderskap i konstruktioner av svensk nationell gemenskap under 1900-talets första hälft* (Lund: Nordic Academic Press, 2002), 249–50.
46. Dag Blanck, *The Creation of an Ethnic Identity: Being Swedish American in the Augustana Synod, 1860–1917* (Carbondale: Southern Illinois University Press, 2006), 43.
47. Thomas Tredway, *Conrad Bergendoff's Faith and Work: A Swedish-American Lutheran, 1895–1997* (Rock Island, I.L.: Augustana Historical Society, 2014), 241–49; Maria Erling and Mark Granquist, *The Augustana Story: Shaping Lutheran Identity in North America* (Minneapolis, M.N.: Augsburg Fortress, 2008), 95–111; Mark A. Granquist, "As Others Saw Them: Swedes and American Religion in the Twin Cities," in *Swedes in the Twin Cities: Immigrant Life and Minnesota's Urban Frontier*, ed. Philip J. Anderson and Dag Blanck (Saint Paul: Minnesota Historical Society Press, 2001), 270–71.
48. "Bertil fick pressberöm för Chicagotal," n.d., Vol. 3, NWOP.
49. Ibid.
50. Report, "Berättelse avgiven av Svenska kommittén."
51. Jonas Frykman, "Nationella ord och handlingar," in Ehn et al., *Försvenskningen av Sverige*, 166–80.
52. Øverland, *Immigrant Minds*, 19, chap. 2.
53. Crown Prince Gustaf Adolf, speech no. 25, fairgrounds, Minneapolis, July 17, 1938, vol. 148, HRR.
54. Program, folk festival, Rockford Stadium, June 8, 1948, vol. 3, NWOP.
55. Report, "Berättelse avgiven av Svenska kommittén."

56. "Iowasuccé för Bo Bergman och 'Svarta Höken,'" *Dagens Nyheter*, June 26, 1948, F48, box 5, AKC.
57. Glassberg, *American Historical Pageantry*, 114, 139–47.
58. Gunlög Fur, "Indians and Immigrants: Entangled Histories," *Journal of American Ethnic History* 33, no. 3 (2014): 63–65. As a parallel to midwestern homesteading, the relation on the Overland Trail was also distinguished by cooperation more than conflict. See Michael L. Tate, *Indians and Emigrants: Encounters on the Overland Trail* (Norman: University of Oklahoma Press, 2006).
59. Karen V. Hansen, *Encounter on the Great Plains: Scandinavian Settlers and the Dispossession of Dakota Indians, 1890–1930* (New York: Oxford University Press, 2013).
60. Prince Bertil, speech, Avon, July 10, 1938, vol. 148, HRR.
61. Crown Prince Gustaf Adolf, speech no. 25, Minneapolis, July 17, 1938.
62. The transition to the English language was gradual and displayed many local variations. The process was generally slower on the East Coast, which had more recent Swedish immigrants, than in the Midwest. Barton, *A Folk Divided*, 254–57; Lindmark, *Swedish America*, 191–218.
63. The number of Swedish speakers in the United States totaled about 830,000 in 1940 and 415,000 in 1960; see Joshua E. Fishman and John E. Hoffman, "Mother Tongue and Nativity in the American Population," in *Language Loyalty in the United States: The Maintenance and Perpetuation of Non-English Mother Tongues by American Ethnic and Religious Groups*, ed. Joshua A. Fishman (London: Mouton, 1966), 44–45. For recent research on Swedish as a "heritage language" in America, see Angela Falk, "Long after the Immigrant Language Shift: Swedish and Norwegian in Heritage Communities," in Anderson and Blanck, *Norwegians and Swedes*, 85–106.
64. Lennart Limberg, "Svenska lektoraten, åren 1913 till 1945," in *Internationell nationalism: Riksföreningen 100 år*, ed. Lennart Limberg (Gothenburg: Riksföreningen Sverigekontakt, 2008), 109–11, 128–31.
65. Crown Prince Gustaf Adolf, speech, Soldier Field, Chicago, July 16, 1938, vol. 148, HRR.
66. Martin Alm, *Americanitis: Amerika som sjukdom eller läkemedel; Svenska berättelser om USA åren 1900–1939* (Lund: Studia Historica Lundensia, 2002), 138.
67. Åsa Linderborg, *Socialdemokraterna skriver historia: Historieskrivning som ideologisk maktresurs 1892–2000* (Stockholm: Atlas, 2001), 329–31, 353–56.
68. Prince Bertil, speech, [Chicago Stadium], n.d., attached to Sven Dahlman, letter to Naboth Hedin, May 19, 1948, F7, vol. 842, UD 1920.
69. Edwin Carl Johnson, speech, press release, "The Swedish Invasion," June 13, 1948, F47, box 5, AKC.
70. Franklin D. Roosevelt, speech, audio recording, June 27, 1938, record 13–14, box 1, vol. 26, BNS. William (Wilhelmus) Beekman was appointed vice-director of the Dutch West India Company with responsibility for its colony on the Delaware River; see Philip W. White, *The Beekmans of New York in Politics and Commerce, 1647–1877* (New York: New York Historical Society, 1956), 33–51.
71. Crown Prince Gustaf Adolf, speech, Soldier Field, July 16, 1938.
72. Crown Prince Gustaf Adolf, speech no. 25, Minneapolis, July 17, 1938.
73. Crown Prince Gustaf Adolf, speech, Soldier Field, July 16, 1938; and Johnson, speech, "The Swedish Invasion," June 13, 1948.
74. Prince Bertil, speech, stadium, Rockford, Illinois, June 8, 1948, F47, box 5, AKC.
75. Program, folk festival, Elmwood Park, Omaha, June 20, 1948, F50, box 5, AKC; and

Roy Larson, "Ryden Warns of Losing Our Spiritual Heritage at Swedish Pioneer Service," n.d., Sigurd L. Anderson Papers, MSS P:15, Swedish Pioneer Centennial Association, Tri-City Local Committee, Swenson Swedish Immigration Research Center, Rock Island, Illinois.
76. "Centennial Group Seeks Typical Swedish Pioneer," *Minneapolis Sunday Tribune*, May 9, 1948, Te, vol. 41, UD Mpls.
77. Franklin D. Roosevelt, quoted in Olson, *Vikings across the Atlantic*, 205.
78. Werner Sollors, *Beyond Ethnicity: Consent and Descent in American Culture* (New York: Oxford University Press, 1986), 5–6.
79. Catherine Nash, *Of Irish Descent: Origin Stories, Genealogy, and the Politics of Belonging* (Syracuse, N.Y.: Syracuse University Press, 2008), 40, 183.
80. Catherine Nash, *Genetic Geographies: The Trouble with Ancestry* (Minneapolis: University of Minnesota Press, 2015); Steve Jones, *In the Blood: God, Genes and Destiny* (London: HarperCollins, 1996); Aviatar Zerubavel, *Ancestors and Relatives: Genealogy, Identity, and Community* (New York: Oxford University Press, 2012).
81. Vilas Johnson, "Reminiscences of the Swedish Pioneer Centennial," *Swedish-American Historical Quarterly* 20, no. 4 (1969): 174.
82. "The Nation: Truman on Tour," *New York Times*, June 6, 1948.
83. On the political preferences of Swedish Americans, see Sten Carlsson, "Swedes in Politics," in *From Sweden to America: A History of the Migration; A Collective Work of the Uppsala Migration Research Project*, ed. Harald Runblom and Hans Norman (Minneapolis: University of Minnesota Press, 1976), 291–300; and Hans Norman and Harald Runblom, *Transatlantic Connections: Nordic Migration to the New World after 1800* (Oslo: Norwegian University Press, 1987), 215–27.
84. Harry S. Truman, address in Chicago before the Swedish Pioneer Centennial Association, June 4, 1948, *Public Papers of the Presidents of the United States, Harry S. Truman: Containing the Public Messages, Speeches, and Statements of the President, January 1 to December 31, 1948* (Washington, D.C.: U.S. Government Printing Office, 1964), 287–88.
85. "DP Bill For Entry of 200,000 Is Voted by Senate, 63 To 13," *New York Times*, June 3, 1948; and "President Urges Wider Social Help as Offset to Reds," *New York Times*, June 5, 1948.
86. Truman, address in Chicago, 288–90.
87. John Bodnar, *Remaking America: Public Memory, Commemoration, and Patriotism in the Twentieth Century* (Princeton: Princeton University Press, 1992), 50.
88. Geir Lundestad, *America, Scandinavia, and the Cold War, 1945–1949* (New York: Columbia University Press, 1980), 208.
89. "Statement by the President Upon Signing the Displaced Persons Act," June 25, 1948, *Public Papers of the Presidents, Harry S. Truman, 1948*, 382.
90. Speech, Prince Bertil, [Chicago Stadium, 1948].
91. "Prince, President Celebration Stars," *Chicago Daily Sun Times*, June 5, 1948, Te, vol. 41, UD Mpls.
92. Anthony Kwame Appiah, "Racisms," in *Anatomy of Racism*, ed. David Theo Goldberg (Minneapolis: University of Minnesota Press, 1990), 16.
93. U.S. Bureau of the Census, *Negroes in the United States, 1920–32* (Washington, D.C.: U.S. Government Printing Office, 1935), 55. On the Great Migration and African American life in Chicago, see James R. Grossman, *Land of Hope: Chicago, Black Southerners, and the Great Migration* (Chicago: University of Chicago Press, 1989); James N.

Gregory, *The Southern Diaspora: How the Great Migrations of Black and White Southerners Transformed America* (Chapel Hill: University of North Carolina Press, 2005), 113–52; James Ralph, "Chicago, Illinois," in *The Great Black Migration: A Historical Encyclopedia of the American Mosaic*, ed. Steven A. Reich (Santa Barbara, C.A.: Greenwood, 2014), 63–69; and Davarian L. Baldwin, *Chicago's New Negroes: Modernity, the Great Migration and Black Urban Life* (Chapel Hill: University of North Carolina Press, 2014).

94. Nicholas Lemann, *The Promised Land: The Great Black Migration and How It Changed America* (New York: Vintage, 1991), 70; and Christopher Manning, "African Americans," in *Encyclopedia of Chicago*, http://www.encyclopedia.chicagohistory.org.

95. Edward R. Kantowicz, "Polish Chicago: Survival through Solidarity," in *Ethnic Chicago: A Multicultural Portrait*, 4th ed., ed. Melvin G. Holli and Peter d'Alroy Jones (Grand Rapids, M.I.: Eerdmans, 1995), 174. See also Melvin G. Holli and Peter d'Alroy Jones, introduction, in ibid., 5.

96. U.S. Bureau of the Census, *Sixteenth Census of the United States: 1940, Population*, vol. 2, part 1, *Characteristics of the Population* (Washington, D.C.: U.S. Government Printing Office, 1943), 655.

97. Anita Olson Gustafson, "Swedes," in *Encyclopedia of Chicago*, http://www.encyclopedia.chicagohistory.org.

CHAPTER 6: PERPETUAL FRIENDSHIPS

1. Crown Prince Gustaf Adolf, speech, "Sweden broadcast," July 22, [1938], vol. 148, HRR.
2. Crown Prince Gustaf Adolf, telegram to Cordell Hull, July 7, 1938; Cordell Hull, telegram to Gustaf Adolf, July 8, 1938; Cordell Hull, letter to Rudolf Holsti, July 6, 1938; and Rudolf Holsti, letter to Cordell Hull, July 7, 1938: all in 811.415, box 5038, DoS.
3. On the relation between food and memory, see Marcia Reed, ed., *The Edible Monument: The Art of Food for Festivals* (Los Angeles: Getty Research Institute, 2015); and David E. Sutton, *Remembrance of Repasts: An Anthropology of Food and Memory* (Oxford: Berg, 2001).
4. Carlnita P. Greene and Janet M. Cramer, "Beyond Mere Sustenance: Food as Communication/Communication as Food," in *Food as Communication, Communication as Food*, ed. Janet M. Cramer, Carlnita P. Greene, and Lynn M. Walters (New York: Lang, 2011), x.
5. Paul J. Burton, *Friendship and Empire: Roman Diplomacy and Imperialism in the Middle Republic (353–146 BC)* (Cambridge: Cambridge University Press, 2011), 25, 33–34, 39.
6. "Moore Curbs Jersey Elite List to 300 for Swedish Celebration," June 7, [1938], F2, Swedish Tercentenary Records, 1937–38, MG 272, New Jersey Historical Society, Newark.
7. Joanne Finkelstein, *Dining Out: A Sociology of Modern Manners* (New York: New York University Press, 1989), 2–21; and Robert Appelbaum, *Dishing It Out: In Search of the Restaurant Experience* (London: Reaktion, 2011).
8. Helen Zoe Veit, *Modern Food, Moral Food: Self-Control, Science, and the Rise of Modern American Eating in the Early Twentieth Century* (Chapel Hill: University of North Caroline Press, 2013), 128, chap. 6; Harvey Levenstein, *Paradox of Plenty: A Social History of Eating in Modern America* (New York: Oxford University Press, 1993), 28. On American middle-class food culture, the aristocratic abandonment of French cuisine, and

early-twentieth-century changes in public dining, see Andrew P. Haley, *Turning the Tables: Restaurants and the Rise of the American Middle Class, 1880–1920* (Chapel Hill: University of North Carolina Press, 2011); and James C. O'Connell, *Dining Out in Boston: A Culinary History* (Hanover, N.H.: University of New England Press, 2016).

9. Fritz Henriksson, *Sweden's Participation in the U.S. Celebration of the New Sweden Tercentenary: Report Compiled by Fritz Henriksson* (Stockholm: Bonnier, 1939), 100–101; and program, centennial banquet, Palmer House, June 5, 1948, F5, box 45, CBP.
10. Frank Melvin, letter to J. Sigfrid Edström, June 1, 1938, Minutes, #25.84, box 1, PAC.
11. Minutes, executive committee, November 15, 1937, Minutes, #25.84, box 1, PAC.
12. Recordings, banquet W.C.A.U., Philadelphia, WPA, 2-4383, PAC.
13. Report, "The 300th Anniversary," 60, Historical Data, #25.90, box 8, PAC.
14. Daron W. Olson, *Vikings across the Atlantic: Emigration and the Building of a Greater Norway, 1860–1945* (Minneapolis: University of Minnesota Press, 2013), 169.
15. Program, "vid firandet av staten Pennsylvanias helgdag Forefathers' Day i Stockholm stadshus," April 8, 1938, Invitations and Programs, F1, #25.84, box 3, PAC; and press release, from Pennsylvania Three Hundredth Anniversary Commission, April 4, [1938], Press Releases, #25.89, box 7, PAC.
16. Report, Ove Olsson, "Som Delawaredelegat till Amerika," attached to Olof Lamm, letter to Fritz Henriksson, February 7, 1939, vol. 14, BNS.
17. See, for example, enclosed menus for Delaware dinners in John S. McCallister, letter to Christopher Ward, January 28, 1938, Subject Files: Luncheon, 1330:0, box 6, DEC; and program, banquet, New York, Waldorf-Astoria, June 30, 1948, F6, box 45, CBP.
18. Food historians have maintained that immigration and cross-cultural intermingling are keys to understanding how food has evolved over time. See, for example, Donna R. Gabaccia, *We Are What We Eat: Ethnic Food and the Making of Americans* (Cambridge: Harvard University Press, 1998); and Jennifer Jensen Wallach, *How America Eats: A Social History of U.S. Food and Culture* (Lanham, M.D.: Rowman and Littlefield, 2013).
19. Jan-Öjvind Swahn, *Fil, fläsk och falukorv* (Lund: Historisk media, 2000), 25–27; Håkan Jönsson, "The Road to the New Nordic Kitchen: Examples from Sweden," in *The Return of Traditional Food*, ed. Patricia Lysaght (Lund: Lund Studies in Arts and Cultural Sciences, 2013), 54–55.
20. Levenstein, *Paradoxes of Plenty*, 120.
21. O'Connell, *Dining Out in Boston*, 136–37; and Waverly Root and Richard De Rochemont, *Eating in America: A History* (Hopewell, N.J.: Ecco, 1995), 343. Compare the ostentatious menus at Delmonico's, in Barry Werth, *Banquet at Delmonico's: Great Minds, the Gilded Age, and the Triumph of Evolution in America* (Chicago: University of Chicago Press, 2009), 277–78; and Root and Rochemont, *Eating in America*, 329.
22. "City Honors Royalty at Banquet; Prince Lauds Chicago Civil Spirit," *Herald Examiner*, July 16, 1938, Illinois, vol. 240, UD Wash.
23. For a similar discussion on late-nineteenth-century Europe, see Rachel Rich, *Bourgeois Consumption: Food, Space and Identity in London and Paris, 1850–1914* (Manchester, U.K.: Manchester University Press, 2011), 193–94.
24. Program, luncheon, Hotel du Pont, June 27, 1938, Subject Files: Photographs, 1330:0, box 12, DEC; and menu, University Club, New York, July 22, 1938, Invitations and Programs, F1, #25.84, box 3, PAC.
25. Program, centennial banquet, Palmer House; and program, Hotel Faust, Rockford, Illinois, June 9, 1948, F49, box 5, AKC.
26. Draft of program to banquet, Forefathers' Day, April 8, 1938, n.d., Invitations and Programs, F2, #25.84 box 3, PAC.

27. Program, Banquet, Forefathers' Day, April 8, 1938, Invitations and Programs, F1, #25.84, box 3, PAC.
28. Will Jewett, letter to J. Bruce Kramer, June 10, 1938, Commissions (Other States), #25.84, box 1, PAC.
29. Prince Bertil, speech, June 28, [1938], attached to Gunnar Hägglöf, letter to Frank Melvin, August 19, 1938, Speeches, 1937–38, #25.92, box 7, PAC.
30. John W. Kephart, speech, Barclay Hotel, Philadelphia, June 29, 1938, attached to John W. Kephart, letter to Will Jewett, September 22, 1938, Speeches, 1937–38, #25.92, box 7, PAC.
31. "Smash Berlin Jews' Shops," *Chicago Daily Tribune*, June 18, 1938.
32. See the front page of *New York Times* on June 4, 5, 20, and 26, 1938.
33. *Observance of the Three Hundredth Anniversary of the First Permanent Settlement in the Delaware River Valley, 1938* (Washington, D.C.: U.S. Government Printing Office, 1940), 31–32.
34. "Roosevelt Warns Nations All Must Keep Peace," *New York Times*, July 1, 1938.
35. Crown Prince Gustaf Adolf [read by Prince Bertil], speech no. 13, dinner by U.S. Delaware Valley Tercentenary Committee, July 3, 1938, vol. 148, HRR.
36. Cordell Hull, speech, June 27, 1938, in *Observance of the Three Hundredth Anniversary*, 25.
37. Frank A. Ninkovich, *The Diplomacy of Ideas: U.S. Foreign Policy and Cultural Relations, 1938–1950* (Cambridge: Cambridge University Press, 1981), 30; and George C. Herring, *From Colony to Superpower: U.S. Foreign Relations Since 1776* (Oxford: Oxford University Press, 2008), 502–15. On the development of state-controlled U.S. public diplomacy through the 1940s, see Nicholas J. Cull, *The Cold War and the United States Information Agency: American Propaganda and Public Diplomacy, 1945–1989* (Cambridge: Cambridge University Press, 2008), 1–51; and Wilson P. Dizard, Jr., *Inventing Public Diplomacy: The Story of the U.S. Information Agency* (Boulder, C.O.: Rienner, 2004), 17–62.
38. Franklin D. Roosevelt, speech, June 27, 1938, in *Observance of the Three Hundredth Anniversary*, 18–19.
39. On memory, commemoration, and diplomacy, see Alexis Dudden, *Troubled Apologies among Japan, Korea, and the United States* (New York: Columbia University Press, 2008); and Ann Rigney, "Scott 1871: Celebration as Cultural Diplomacy," in *Commemorating Writers in Nineteenth-Century Europe*, ed. Joep Leerssen and Ann Rigney (Basingstoke, U.K.: Palgrave Macmillan, 2014), 65–87. On the Swedish-German connection in the early twentieth century, see, for example, Andreas Åkerlund, *Mellan akademi och kulturpolitik: Lektorat i svenska språket vid tyska universitet, 1906–1945* (Uppsala: Acta Universitatis Upsaliensis, 2010).
40. Will Swift, *The Roosevelts and the Royals: Franklin and Eleanor, the King and Queen of England, and the Friendship That Changed History* (Hoboken, N.J.: Wiley, 2004), 83. On the royal Norwegian visit, see also Olson, *Vikings across the Atlantic*, 179–88.
41. Swift, *Roosevelts and the Royals*, 128–51.
42. "Roosevelts Treat Guests to Hot Dogs," *New York Times*, July 3, 1938.
43. Walter LaFeber, "The United States and Europe in an Age of American Unilateralism," in *The American Century in Europe*, ed. R. Laurence Moore and Maurizio Vaudagna (Ithaca, N.Y.: Cornell University Press, 2003).
44. Truman, address in Chicago, June 4, 1948, in *Public Papers of the Presidents of the United States, Harry S. Truman: Containing the Public Messages, Speeches, and State-*

ments of the President, January 1 to December 31, 1948 (Washington, D.C.: U.S. Government Printing Office, 1964), 287–90.
45. Michael Scott Van Wagenen, *Remembering the Forgotten War: The Enduring Legacies of the U.S.-Mexican War* (Amherst: University of Massachusetts Press, 2012), 162–65; and Laura A. Belmonte, *Selling the American Way: U.S. Propaganda and the Cold War* (Philadelphia: University of Pennsylvania Press, 2008), 3–35.
46. "Swedish Prince Calls for Unity to Bring Peace," *Chicago Sunday Tribune*, June 6, 1948, Clippings, Vol. 81, UD Chi.
47. Prince Bertil, speech, Hotel Fontenelle, Omaha, Nebraska, June 19, 1948, F47, box 5, AKC.
48. Program, Noon Day Club of Omaha, Hotel Fontenelle, June 19, 1948, F49, box 5, AKC.
49. Prince Bertil, speech, Hotel Fontenelle, Omaha, June 19, 1948.
50. Jussi Kurunmäki and Johan Strang, introduction, in *Rhetorics of Nordic Democracy*, ed. Jussi Kurunmäki and Johan Strang (Helsinki: Studia Fennica Historica, 2010), 9–11.
51. Carl Marklund, "Sharing Values and Shaping Values: Sweden, 'Nordic Democracy,' and the American Crisis of Democracy," and Jan Hecker-Stampehl, "Keeping Up the Morale: Constructions of 'Nordic Democracy' during World War II," in ibid, 114–64.
52. Sten Carlsson, "From Four Estates to Two Chambers: The Riksdag in a Period of Transition, 1809–1921," in *The Riksdag: A History of the Swedish Parliament*, ed. Michael F. Metcalf (New York: St. Martin's, 1987); Josefin Rönnbäck, *Politikens genusgränser: Den kvinnliga rösträttsrörelsen och kampen för kvinnors politiska medborgarskap 1902–1921* (Stockholm: Atlas Akademi, 2004); and Ebba Berling Åselius, *Rösträtt med förhinder: Rösträttsstrecken i svensk politik 1900–1920* (Stockholm: Acta Universitatis Stockholmiensis, 2005).
53. See, for example, program, Noon Day Club of Omaha, June 19, 1948.
54. Carl F. Hellström, letter to Wollmar Boström, March 14, 1938, and Carl F. Hellström, letter to Oscar Solbert, June 9, 1938, in EII, vol. 39, UD Mpls.
55. Audio recording, July 6, 1938, record 6, "His Royal Highness Gustaf Adolf at Luncheon given in His Honor at the Union Club, N.Y.," vol. 25, BNS. For the 1783 Treaty of Amity and Commerce, see Charles Jenkinson, *A Collection of All the Treaties of Peace, Alliance, and Commerce, Between Great-Britain and Other Powers . . .* (London: Debrett, 1785), 3:316–30.
56. David W. Ellwood, *The Shock of America: Europe and the Challenge of the Century* (Oxford: Oxford University Press, 2012), 144.
57. Crown Prince Gustaf Adolf, speech, July 6, 1938, in *Observance of the Three Hundredth Anniversary*, 50.
58. Thomas Bender, *A Nation among Nations: America's Place in World History* (New York: Hill and Wang, 2006), 235.
59. Douglas A. Irwin, *Peddling Protectionism: Smoot-Hawley and the Great Depression* (Princeton: Princeton University Press, 2011), 163.
60. Douglas A. Irwin, "From Smoot-Hawley to Reciprocal Trade Agreements: Changing the Course of U.S. Trade Policy in the 1930s," in *The Defining Moment: The Great Depression and the American Economy in the Twentieth Century*, ed. Michael D. Bordo, Claudia Goldin, and Eugene N. White (Chicago: University of Chicago Press, 1998), 333–42; Irwin, *Peddling Protectionism*, 192–94; and Herring, *From Colony to Superpower*, 500.
61. Donna R. Gabaccia, *Foreign Relations: American Immigration in Global Perspective* (Princeton: Princeton University Press, 2012), 124.

62. Irwin, "From Smoot-Hawley," 343–44.
63. U.S. Department of Commerce, Bureau of Foreign and Domestic Commerce, *Foreign Trade of the United States Calendar Year 1938*, part 2, *Trade by Regions and Countries* (Washington, D.C.: U.S. Government Printing Office, 1940), 78–83; and Eric W. Fleisher and Jörgen Weibull, *Viking Times to Modern: The Story of Swedish Exploring and Settlement in America and the Development of Trade and Shipping from the Viking to Our Time* (Stockholm: Almqvist och Wiksell, 1953), 87. On American influence on the development of Swedish automobile culture, see Per Lundin, *Bilsamhället: Ideologi, expertis och regelskapande i efterkrigstidens Sverige* (Stockholm: Stockholmia, 2008).
64. Prince Bertil, speech, Hotel Faust, Rockford, Illinois, June 9, 1948, F47, box 5, AKC.
65. Address of Prince Bertil, June 30, 1948, Report, State of New York, 20, F11, box 1, SPCA.
66. John Fousek, *To Lead the Free World: American Nationalism and the Cultural Roots of the Cold War* (Chapel Hill: University of North Carolina Press, 2000), 128.
67. Fleisher and Weibull, *Viking Times to Modern*, 90.
68. "Anteckningar rörande H.K.H. Prins Bertils resa i U.S.A.," vol. 148, HRR; and "List, Luncheon at DAC," June 14, 1948, doss. 2, vol. 81, UD Chi.
69. Gösta Oldenburg, letter to Alexis Aminoff, May 25, 1948, F3, vol. 243, UD Wash.
70. Sven Dahlman, letter to Olof Rydbeck, May 19, 1948, F7, vol. 842, UD 1920.
71. A. Theodore Solhberg, letter to Nils William Olsson, April 4, 1948, F4, box 5, SPCA.
72. "Pamparna trängs kring prins Bertil men pionjären glöms bort i jubileumsyran," n.d., vol. 3, NWOP.
73. "Pionjären och Karin Kock glömdes bort vid emigrationsfestligheterna i Detroit," *Stockholms-Tidningen*, June 15, 1948, vol. 3, NWOP.
74. Irwin, "From Smoot-Hawley," 349.
75. Crown Prince Gustaf Adolf, speech no. 21, state banquet, Chicago, July 15, 1938, vol. 148, HRR. The statistic refers to 1900, when 144,000 Swedish-born immigrants lived in Chicago, which—if one still counts those immigrants as Swedish nationals—would have made the city second in size to Stockholm. See Philip J. Anderson and Dag Blanck, introduction, in *Swedish-American Life in Chicago: Cultural and Urban Aspects of an Immigrant People, 1850–1930*, ed. Philip J. Anderson and Dag Blanck (Urbana: University of Illinois Press, 1992), 1.
76. Dwight H. Green, speech, Palmer House, June 5, 1948, F47, box 5, AKC.
77. Crown Prince Gustaf Adolf [read by Prince Bertil], speech no. 13, July 3, 1938.
78. Malte Jacobsson, speech, Gothenburg, November 28, 1937, Speeches, 1937–38, #25.92, box 7, PAC.
79. [Johan-Olov Johansson], speech, "by the chairman of the city council of Stockholm at the Banquet for the Hon. George H. Earle," December 1, 1937, Speeches 1937–38, in #25.92, box 7, PAC.
80. For a copy of the speech, see Prince Bertil, Waldorf-Astoria Hotel, New York, June 30, 1948, F47, box 5, AKC; for the printed version, see address of Prince Bertil, June 30, 1948, Report, State of New York.
81. "Fight to Stay Free Pledged by Bertil: Swedish Prince Says Support of U.S. Gives Courage to His People in Resolve," *New York Times*, July 1, 1948; and Truman, address in Chicago, June 4, 1948, 287.

CONCLUSION: THE RESILIENCE OF HISTORY

1. John Brolund, "Beskrivning av Delaware-skrinet," April 11, 1938, vol. 7, BNS.
2. J. Sigfrid Edström, letter to Christopher Ward, April 29, 1938, Subject Files: Bostrom, 1330:0, box 3, DEC.
3. Wollmar Boström, letter to Christopher Ward, May 11, 1938, Subject Files: Bostrom, 1330:0, box 3, DEC.
4. Fritz Henriksson, *Sweden's Participation in the U.S. Celebration of the New Sweden Tercentenary: Report Compiled by Fritz Henriksson* (Stockholm: Bonnier, 1939), 38–40.
5. H. Arnold Barton, *A Folk Divided: Homeland Swedes and Swedish Americans, 1840–1940* (Carbondale: Southern Illinois University Press, 1994), 326.
6. For example, the Swedish government in 1957 asked the minister of commerce to appoint a commission to investigate the possibility of "a Swedish manifestation in the United States." The purpose was to promote commercial and cultural relations, stimulate Swedish exports to America, and increase American tourism to Sweden. The report emphasized the success of the New Sweden Tercentenary and the Swedish Pioneer Centennial as demonstrations of affinity between the countries and suggested that Sweden should participate in future celebrations in America. See *Sverige i USA: Ett förslag till vidgad upplysningsverksamhet; Betänkande avgivet den 31 oktober 1957 av USA-kommittén* (Stockholm, 1957), 1–2.
7. *New Sweden '88: 350-årsfirandet av Nya Sverige-kolonins grundande 1638; Generalsekreterarens rapport* (Stockholm: Svenska nationalkommittén för New Sweden '88, 1989), 29.
8. Lyndon B. Johnson, speech, March 29, 1963, 1330:1, DE 325th; and *New Sweden '88: 350 Years of Friendship* (Stockholm: Swedish National Committee for New Sweden '88, 1989).
9. "H. M. Konungens tal vid galamiddag i Wilmington," May 11, 2013, Sveriges Kungahus, http://www.kungahuset.se/.
10. Press release, remarks of Prince Bertil of Sweden at Delaware Swedish Colonial Society dinner, Longwood Gardens, March 29, [1963], 1330:1, DE 325th.
11. S. J. Res. 289, Year of New Sweden, May 15, 1986, 99th Congress, U.S. Statutes at Large, vol. 100, part 1, 439–40.
12. Exhibit proposal, "New Sweden 88': The Fabric of a Friendship," December 15, 1986, and documentation on the exhibit and the film, in the folder New Sweden 88: Notes from Swedish Tobacco Company, NS '88.
13. Zoriana E. Siokalo, Clarissa Solmssen, and Vito Trimarco, *Before Penn: Swedish Colonists in the Land of the Lenape* (Philadelphia: American Swedish Historical Museum, 1988), 9. The exhibition received positive reviews; see James F. Turk, review of *Before Penn: Swedish Colonists in the Land of the Lenape* at the American Swedish Historical Museum, *Journal of American History* 76, no. 3 (1989): 849–51.
14. Clarissa Solmssen, letter to Lennart Espmark, November 2, 1987, Swedish Tobacco 1st proposal, NS '88.
15. Exhibit proposal, "New Sweden 88': The Fabric of a Friendship."
16. Zoriana E. Siokalo, letter to James Revey, February 25, 1988, Swedish Tobacco 1st proposal, NS '88.
17. Zoriana E. Siokalo, letter to James Revey, May 2, 1988, and James Revey, letter to Zoriana E. Siokalo, May 2, 1988, in Plans for 1988: Correspondence, NS '88.
18. *New Sweden '88: 350 Years of Friendship*, 27.

19. Amy Hill Hearth, *"Strong Medicine" Speaks: A Native American Elder Has Her Say: An Oral History* (New York: Astria, 2008), 26. On Native sovereignty struggles and the difference between state and federal recognition, see Amy E. Den Ouden and Jean M. O'Brien, eds., *Recognition, Sovereignty Struggles, and Indigenous Rights in the United States: A Sourcebook* (Chapel Hill: University of North Carolina Press, 2013).
20. *New Sweden '88; Generalsekreterarens rapport*, 9.
21. Lars Florin, ed., *Migrationsåret '96: Utvandrare & Invandrare i Sverige Historia, 1846–1996; ett 150-årsjubileum i Sverige och USA* (Stockholm: Migrationsåret '96, 1996).
22. *Emigrants and Immigrants in Swedish History, 1846–1996 / Utvandrare och Invandrare i Sveriges Historia, 1846–1996*, August 1994, bilingual print, committee appointed by the Swedish Ministry of Culture, collections of the Swedish Council of America, Minneapolis.
23. Press release, remarks of Prince Bertil, Longwood Gardens, March 29, [1963].
24. *New Sweden '88; Generalsekreterarens rapport*, 9.
25. Tammy S. Gordon, *The Spirit of 1976: Commerce, Community, and the Politics of Commemoration* (Amherst: University of Massachusetts Press, 2013), 3–7, 131–48.
26. Another example was the 1983 commemoration of the 1783 Treaty of Commerce and Amity. See Robert Skole, *USA, Sweden* (Stockholm: Gullers, 1984).
27. "H. M. Konungens tal vid galamiddag i Wilmington," May 11, 2013.
28. Johnson, speech, March 29, 1963.
29. Prince Bertil, speech, Fort Christina Monument, March 29, [1963], Delaware 1963, box 18, AKC.
30. "H. M. Konungens tal vid Buena Vista Plantation," May 11, 2013, Sveriges Kungahus, http://www.kungahuset.se.
31. "H. M. Konungens tal vid galamiddag i Wilmington," May 11, 2013.
32. On Swedish-American relations and the image of Sweden in the United States, see Erik Åsard, ed., *Det blågula stjärnbaneret: USA:s närvaro och inflytande i Sverige* (Stockholm: Carlsson, 2016); and Jeff Werner, *Medelvägens estetik: Sverigebilder i USA*, 2 vols. (Hedemora: Gidlunds, 2008). See also Carl Marklund, "From 'False' Neutrality to 'True' Socialism: U.S. 'Sweden-Bashing' during the Later Palme Years, 1973–1986," *Journal of Transnational American Studies* 7, no. 1 (2016): 1–18. On the popular notion of "the Swedish Sin" in the 1950s and 1960s, see Nikolas Glover and Carl Marklund, "Arabian Nights in the Midnight Sun? Exploring the Temporal Structure of Sexual Geographies," *Historisk Tidskrift* 129, no. 3 (2009): 487–510. A more recent image of Sweden appears in the popular fiction genre known as "Nordic Noir"; see Kerstin Bergman, *Swedish Crime Fiction: The Making of Nordic Noir* (Milan: Mimesis International, 2014).
33. Matthew Frye Jacobson, *Roots Too: White Ethnic Revival in Post–Civil Rights America* (Cambridge: Harvard University Press, 2006), 7–10. On regional commemorations in the early twentieth century, see Michael Kammen, *Mystic Chords of Memory: The Transformation of Tradition in American Culture* (New York: Knopf, 1991), chap. 12. On the colonial revival as a longer twentieth-century phenomenon, see Richard Guy Wilson, Shaun Eyring, and Kenny Marotta, eds., *Re-Creating the American Past: Essays on the Colonial Revival* (Charlottesville: University of Virginia Press, 2006).
34. Kerwin Lee Klein, *Frontiers of Historical Imagination: Narrating the European Conquest of Native America, 1890–1990* (Berkeley: University of California Press, 1997); and Richard Slotkin, *Gunfighter Nation: The Myth of the Frontier in Twentieth-Century America* (New York: Harper Perennial, 1992), 278.

35. John Seelye, *Memory's Nation: The Place of Plymouth Rock* (Chapel Hill: University of North Carolina Press, 1998), 637.
36. "First State National Historic Park," National Park Service, https://www.nps.gov; and "Resolution Authorizing Governor to Proclaim Delaware Swedish Colonial Day," chap. 207, *Laws of the State of Delaware, 107th Session of the General Assembly* (1939), vol. 42, 446–47.
37. New Sweden Alliance, Inc., https://www.newswedenalliance.org.
38. Richard M. Fried, *The Russians Are Coming! The Russians Are Coming! Pageantry and Patriotism in Cold-War America* (New York: Oxford University Press, 1998), 112–14.
39. *America's 400th Anniversary*, http://www.jamestown2007.org.
40. Peter Carrier and Kobi Kabalek, "Cultural Memory and Transcultural Memory: A Conceptual Analysis," in *The Transcultural Turn: Interrogating Memory between and beyond Borders*, ed. Lucy Bond and Jessica Rapson (Berlin: Walter de Gruyter, 2014), 53.
41. During the past two decades, reconciliation rituals and commemorations have become common between indigenous and non-indigenous peoples. See Penelope Edmonds, *Settler Colonialism and (Re)conciliation: Frontier Violence, Affective Performances, and Imaginative Refoundings* (Basingstoke, U.K.: Palgrave Macmillan, 2016). The public history of slavery is a parallel to settler commemorations that also deals with difficult pasts; see Elizabeth Kowaleski Wallace, *The British Slave Trade and Public Memory* (New York: Columbia University Press, 2006); and James Oliver Horton and Lois E. Horton, eds., *Slavery and Public History: The Tough Stuff of American Memory* (New York: New Press, 2006).
42. Stephen J. Summerhill and John Alexander Williams, *Sinking Columbus: Contested History, Cultural Politics, and Mythmaking during the Quincentenary* (Gainesville: University of Florida Press, 2000), 116–17. See also Frye Jacobson, *Roots Too*, 336–46; and Timothy Kubal, *Cultural Movements and Collective Memory: Christopher Columbus and the Rewriting of the National Origin Myth* (New York: Palgrave Macmillan, 2008), 57–75.
43. "African American Events" and "Virginia Indian Heritage Events," http://www.jamestown2007.org; and F. Richard Sanchez, introduction, in *White Shell Water Place: An Anthology of Native American Reflections on the 400th Anniversary of the Founding of Santa Fe, New Mexico, with a Traditional Native Blessing by N. Scott Momaday*, ed. F. Richard Sanchez, Stephen Wall, and Ann Filemyr (Santa Fe, N.M.: Sunstone, 2010), 16. On local critique of the public memory of Juan de Oñate in New Mexico, see Erika Doss, *Memorial Mania: Public Feeling in America* (Chicago: University of Chicago Press, 2010), 311–16, 356–59.
44. Louis Bickford and Amy Sodaro, "Remembering Yesterday to Protect Tomorrow: The Internationalization of a New Commemorative Paradigm," in *Memory and the Future: Transnational Politics, Ethics, and Society*, ed. Yifat Gutman, Adam D. Brown, and Amy Sodaro (New York: Palgrave Macmillan, 2010), 67.
45. Magdalena Naum and Jonas M. Nordin, eds., *Scandinavian Colonialism and the Rise of Modernity: Small Time Agents in a Global Arena* (New York: Springer, 2013); Kristín Lofsdóttir and Lars Jensen, eds., *Whiteness and Postcolonialism in the Nordic Region: Exceptionalism, Migrant Others, and National Identities* (Farnham, U.K.: Ashgate, 2012); and Suvi Kesikinen, Salla Tuori, Sari Irni, and Diana Mulinari, eds., *Complying with Colonialism: Gender, Race, and Ethnicity in the Nordic Region* (Farnham, U.K.: Ashgate, 2009). Paul Bijl has also noted a silence about the Dutch colonial past based on a "broadly held conception that the Dutch had a different, better type of colonialism" than France and England did (*Emerging Memory: Photographs of Colonial Atroci-*

ties in Dutch Cultural Remembrance [Amsterdam: Amsterdam University Press, 2014], 225).

46. Ylva Habel, "Challenging Swedish Exceptionalism? Teaching While Black," in *Education in the Black Diaspora: Perspectives, Challenges, and Prospects*, ed. Kassie Freeman and Ethan Johnson (New York: Routledge, 2012), 100.

47. Gunlög Fur, "Colonialism and Swedish History: Unthinkable Connections?," in Naum and Nordin, *Scandinavian Colonialism and the Rise of Modernity*, 26.

INDEX

Aaltonen, Wäinö, 213–14n18
acceleration and rupture, 106–8, 115, 216n51. *See also* modernization
actor-centered methodology, 199n25
African Americans, 111, 113–15, 129, 150, 192
air travel, 116
Albert Edward, Prince of Wales, 101
Alfvén, Hugo, 131
Alm, Martin, 141
America Inquiry, 29–30, 59
American culinary culture, 157
An American Dilemma (Myrdal), 111
American dream, 186, 189
American Indians. *See* Native Americans
American Jewish Historical Society, 36
American Pilgrim Museum (the Netherlands), 197n4
American Revolution, 18, 90
American Sons and Daughters of Sweden, 35–37
American Swedish Historical Foundation, 181
American Swedish Historical Museum, 36–37, 79, 122, 181–82, 190
American-Swedish News Exchange (ASNE), 54, 58
America's 400th Anniversary, 190
amnesia, 18, 70. *See also* foundational sites; The Rocks in Wilmington, Delaware
ancestry and ethno-racial belonging: consent and descent, 146; festivals and, 151; genealogy, 39–40, 110–11, 120, 144–45, 173–74
Anderson, Charles H., 26
Andover, Illinois, 82, 86, 178, 217n73
Anglo-Americans, 137
Anglo-Saxon heritage, 25–26, 39–40, 111–12
anti-communism, 148, 163, 169, 171
Archdeacon, Thomas, 41
ASNE. *See* American Swedish News Exchange
Assembly of Captive European Nations, 130
Assmann, Aleida, 5, 197n10, 205n32
Assmann, Jan, 205n32
Augustana College, 37, 41, 54–55
Augustana Synod, 37, 41, 44, 54–57, 83, 133–34, 136
Aztlán, 137

Baltic States, 20, 52, 130
Barkan, Elazar, 111
Barton, H. Arnold, 41, 131–32
Beekman, William, 143, 228n70
Before Penn (exhibit), 181

239

Bender, Thomas, 167
Benjamin Franklin Hotel (Philadelphia), 156–57, 159
Benson, Adolph, 89–90
Bergendoff, Conrad, 55–57, 59–60, 82–84, 86, 128, 133–34, 147
Bersell, P. O., 55–56, 212n73
Bertil, Prince: as chair of Swedish Sports Confederation, 98; at Chicago Stadium festival, 86, 135, 142, 147, 149, 163; at commemorative dinners, 155, 159, 163–64, 169, 171–74; at festivals in United States, 125–26; honored by youth of Escanaba, Michigan, 100; as leader of Swedish delegation (1938), 6–7, 101–3; as leader of Swedish delegation (1948), 80, 94, 102, 109; on love of the land, 86–87; at New Sweden 325th anniversary, 180, 187; speech in Avon, Massachusetts, 139–40; speech in Rockford, Illinois, 144–45, 151, 169; on technological progress, 117; at tercentenary inauguration, 6–7, 80–81, 103
Bickford, Louis, 192
Biden, Joe, 180
Bijl, Paul, 237–38n45
Bishop Hill, Illinois, 82, 185, 216n59
Blegen, Theodore C., 88
Boas, Franz, 111
Bodnar, John, 18, 22, 64, 90, 148, 216n59
Boston, Massachusetts, 124, 170
Boston Tercentenary (1930), 45
Boström, Gertrude, 117
Boström, Wollmar: Amandus Johnson's letter to, 1; copper box received by, 176–77; design of monument and, 76; at Forefathers' Day banquet, 156; letter to Los Angeles committee, 108; Philadelphia meeting requested by, 37; on Swedish stock in United States, 113; tercentenary planning and, 43, 49, 51, 56, 66–67, 212n73
Boy Heroes at Chapultepec (memorial), 163
Bradenton, Florida, 103
Brewster, William, 2–3
British settlers and colonies, 21, 25, 72, 181, 193. *See also* Jamestown Colony

Broberg, Gunnar, 112
Bruggeman, Seth C., 19
Burton, Paul, 153
Bush, George W., 190
Bush, Lewis Potter, 42

California, 24
Canada, 44–45, 101, 144
capitalism, 19, 22, 28, 99, 167, 169–70
Capitol Building rotunda (Washington, D.C.), 2
Carl XVI Gustaf, King, 1–2, 178, 180–82, 184, 186–87, 219–20n24
Cather, Willa, 87
Catholics, 215n40
chambers of commerce, 166
Chase Center (Wilmington), 180
Chattanooga, Tennessee, 71
Cherokee people, 71
Chester, Pennsylvania, 68, 213–14n18
Chicago, Illinois: banquet in (1948), 157–58; centennial planning committees in, 60; crown prince's address in, 140–41, 144; festivals in, 133–35, 225n8; racial and ethnic demographics in, 150; revisited by Swedish delegations, 178; Swedish Americans in, 24, 171, 234n75; Swedish delegation visits to, 107–9, 118, 125–27, 142, 170–71. *See also* Chicago Stadium festival; Soldier Field in Chicago
Chicago Stadium festival, 86, 126, 134–37, 142, 146–50, 163
Chicago Symphony Orchestra, 135
Childs, Marquis, 28, 99
Chinese Exclusion Act (1882), 129
Chiton (Lenape sachem), 20
Christina, Queen, 78–79, 176
Christina River, 20, 65, 76, 104
Church of Sweden, 136
civilization, claims about bringing: concept of modernity and, 216n51; to Delaware at The Rocks, 65; in Delaware resolution, 40, 72; delegation tours and, 121; by Edström, 48; myths of origin and, 11; New Sweden monument and, 7, 79, 81; pioneers in the Midwest, 84–87, 93; replacement of Native Americans and, 13–14, 71–73;

resilience of settler histories and, 188; struggle for freedom and democracy in Sweden and, 86
Coker, Dennis, 2
Cold War: anti-communism and, 148, 169; centennial commemoration timing and, 4, 31; commemorative landscape and, 130; Jamestown Colony commemoration during (1957), 190; Lyndon Johnson's speech (1963), 186–87; traveling during, 95–96; United States–Sweden relations and, 162, 171, 173–74
collective memory, 4–5, 197n10
colonialism vs. immigration, 19, 74, 183–85, 193
colonial landings, reenactments of, 103–4, 178. *See also under* The Rocks in Wilmington, Delaware
Colonial Williamsburg, 190
colonist as archetypal figure, 63–64
Columbus, Christopher, 8, 82, 191–92
Columbus Day, 24, 124
commemoration(s): defined, 4; memory and, 18–19; mixed media, 10; new future-oriented paradigm of, 192; practice first developed, 18; reenacting past travels, 96, 103–4; settler commemorations, 10–14. *See also* cross-border commemorations
commemorative dinners and friendship, 152–75; commercial friendship, 166–71; cross-border settings, 154–59; friendship as kinship, 171–75; political friendship, 159–65, 170
commercial friendship, 166–71, 186–87
communicative memory, 205n32
Connecticut Tercentenary (1935), 45
consent and descent, 146
constitutional debates (1788), 124
consumerism, 186
contested terrain, 18, 202n4
Conway, Brian, 5
Coolidge, Calvin, 36
Cooper, James Fenimore, 71
cooperative movement, 28, 206n40
corporations and Swedish settlement celebration, 186
Creet, Julia, 95

cross-border commemorations: asymmetrical power relations in, 178–79; defined, ix–x; overview, 4–10; in vogue, 3. *See also* New Sweden commemoration (1888); New Sweden commemoration (2013); New Sweden Tercentenary commemoration; Swedish Pioneer Centennial commemoration
culinary culture, American, 157
cultural memory, 4–5, 197n10, 205n32
Cummings, Homer S., 160
Curell, Susan, 112
Czechoslovakia, 130

Dakota tribe, 139
Daughters of the American Revolution, 39
Dawes Act (1887), 14, 139
Dearing, Fred Morris, 105
Dehlgren, Sten, 17–19
Delaware: Fort Christina State Park and, 7; as Jim Crow state, 114; *Kalmar Nyckel*'s (ship) arrival in, 77–78; power struggle with Pennsylvania, 52–53, 67–68, 106; The Rocks as foundational site and, 65–68, 70, 72, 81, 109; tercentenary planning and, 38, 40–47, 49–50, 52–53
Delaware Bay, 19–20
Delaware Historic Markers Commission, 66
Delaware Memorial Commission, 37
Delaware River, 19–21, 44, 228n70
Delaware Swedish Colonial Day, 189
Delaware Swedish Colonial Society, 189
Delaware Tercentenary Commission, 40, 42–44, 65, 67
The Delaware Tercentenary Visitors' Guide, 43
Delaware Valley: civilization claims in, 7, 13–14, 71–72, 79; conflict between Delaware and Pennsylvania, 52–53; European settlement of, 19–22; *Kalmar Nyckel*'s (ship) arrival in, 137; Lenape people in, 19–21; New Sweden colony and foundational history of, 3, 193; prior to William Penn's arrival, 181; regionalism of, 189–90; relations

Delaware Valley (*continued*)
  between Swedish settlers and Native Americans, 13–14, 21; revisited by Swedish delegations, 178; tercentenary commemoration and, 12–14, 44–47, 107, 109
delegation travels, 94–121; embodying the modern state of Sweden, 96–103; following in the footsteps of the past, 103–7; ideas about race and, 107–15; technological modernity and, 115–20
Delmonico's (restaurant), 154–55
democracy, promotion of, 85–86, 91, 163–65, 167, 172, 174
Democratic Party, U.S., 17, 46–47, 168
Denmark, 28–29, 31, 207n51
Denson, Andrew, 71
Depression. *See* Great Depression
Des Moines, Iowa, 109, 138
Detroit, Michigan, 107, 109, 170–71
Detroit Athletic Club, 170
dinners, commemorative. *See* commemorative dinners and friendship
Displaced Persons Act (1948), 147–49
Drottningholm (ship), 115–16
Dutch-American Friendship Commemoration (1982), 8
The Dutch and Swedes on the Delaware (Ward), 42
Dutch settlers and colonies, 19–21, 72, 181, 193, 237–38n45. *See also* Netherlands

Earle, George H.: civilization claim by, 73; delivery of invitations by airplane, 117; at Forefathers' Day banquet, 156; at local commemorative events, 103; Melvin and, 67; New Deal and, 46; visit to Sweden, 69–70, 99–101, 105–6, 110, 172
East Coast of United States: commemorative dinners in, 156; national myth and, 84–85, 90, 188–89; settler commemorations in, 9, 11; Swedish delegation tour of, 107; Swedish Pioneer Centennial and, 106; tercentenary focus on, 56; transition to English language and, 228n62
Eastern Bloc countries, 130

Edström, J. Sigfrid, 47–48, 97–98, 107–8, 176
Eisenhower, Dwight D., 190
elite public dining, 154–55
Elizabeth, Queen (the Queen Mother), 3, 162, 190
Ellis Island, 188
Ellwood, David, 167
Elupacken (Lenape sachem), 20
Enander, Johan, 88
Endy, Christopher, 95
English settlers. *See* British settlers and colonies
Engman, Max, 53
entangled history approach, 5–7, 9, 198n17
Ericsson, John, 128, 186
Erikson, Leif, 137, 145
Erll, Astrid, 5, 95
Esbjörn, Lars Paul, 82
Escanaba, Michigan, 100, 170–71
ethnic commemorations, 18, 24, 124–25
ethnic interest, second-generation, 41–42, 209n24
ethnicity: ancestral origins and, 146; transnational dimensions of, 124, 151
ethno-racial belonging and ancestry, 146, 151
eugenics, 111–13
European Recovery Program (Marshall Plan). *See* Marshall Plan
European settlers and settlements: claims of belonging to the landscape, 87; departure points and settlement histories, 3–4, 71, 197n4; discovery, exploration, and settlement, 11; festivals and, 124; Native Americans and, 19–20, 70–79, 85–86

The Fabric of A Friendship (traveling exhibit), 181
Fågel Grip (ship), 20, 105, 110
Fahlstrom, Jacob, 86
Felipe VI, King, 3
festivals, 122–51; American nationalism and, 129–30; migration as a legacy and thing of the past, 137–43; qualities of blood lineage, 143–51; Swedish delegation visits and, 125–31; Swedishness and the frictions of modernity, 131–37

Finland: commemoration planning and, 4, 9; commemorative dinners and, 156, 158–60; delegations from, 6, 94, 159–60, 178, 219n7; New Sweden commemoration (2013) and, 1–2; as part of kingdom of Sweden, 20; Pennsylvania delegation and, 105–6; relations with United States, 161–62, 174; Sweden's power struggle with, 106; tercentenary participation and, 51–53, 67–70, 156
Finnish Americans: commemoration planning and, 4, 9, 52, 70; commemorative dinners and, 156; Finland's participation in tercentenary and, 211n61; success in United States, 186
Finnish monument, 68–69, 213–14n18
Finnish settlers in New Sweden/Delaware Valley, 21, 203n13, 213–14n18
Finns Point, New Jersey, 68
food history, 231n18
Ford Motor Company, 170
Forefathers' Day banquet, 156, 158
foreign policy, U.S.: cultural relations and, 161; free trade, 166–69; isolationism, 161–62; protectionist trade policies, 168; regional diversity and, 45–46; Swedish criticism of, 187–88; traveling and, 95–96; unilateralism, 163
foreign relations, national interests in, 47–53
Fort Casimir, 21
Fort Christina, 20–21, 53, 66
Fort Christina State Park: closing and reopening of, 176; construction of, 67–68, 70; inauguration of tercentenary at, 80; national recognition of, 189; neighborhood surrounding, 114; New Sweden monument at, 68, 75–76; Swedish and Finnish delegations landing at, 6–7
Fort Elfsborg, 78
foundational histories, appropriation of, 33–62; from ethnicity to regionalism, 37–47; national interests in foreign relations, 47–53; New Sweden commemoration (1888) and, 33–35; New Sweden Tercentenary and, 35–53; recent events and, 193; Swedish Pioneer Centennial and, 54–61

foundational sites, 65–70
foundational stories or histories, 24, 32, 63, 83–84, 92, 137, 150. *See also* foundational histories, appropriation of
foundational violence, disavowal of, 13, 72–73, 85–86, 188
Fourteenth Amendment to the Constitution, 129
Franklin, Benjamin, 25
freedom and independence, 64, 86, 91–92, 193
free trade, 166–69, 174
French cuisine, 154–55, 157
French Revolution, 18
French settlement in America, 3
friendship: commercial friendship, 166–71, 186–87; as kinship, 171–75; kinship vs., 153; political friendship, 159–65, 170, 186–87; between Sweden and United States, 152–53, 180, 186–87. *See also* commemorative dinners and friendship
frontier, settlement of, 84–85
Fry, Joseph, 46
Fur, Gunlög, 14, 21, 72, 192

Gabaccia, Donna, 124, 168
Geijer, Erik Gustaf, 91
genealogy, 39–40, 110–11, 120, 144–45, 173–74
General Allotment Act. *See* Dawes Act
General Motors, 170
genetics, 146
George VI, King, 162
German-American Friendship Garden, 8
German American Historical Society, 36
German Americans, 11, 40, 130
German-American Tricentennial, 8
German emigrants, 124, 150
Germany, 20, 29, 73, 130, 162
Giants in the Earth (Rolvaag), 87
Gillis, John, 5, 18
Gjöres, Axel, 59, 98, 219n15
Glassberg, David, 138
Good Neighbor policy, 168
Gothenburg, Sweden, 20, 77–78, 104–6, 110
Gould, Mark "Quiet Hawk," 2, 184
Governor Printz Park, 68–69, 101–2, 178
Grant, Madison, 25

Great Britain, 28, 162. *See also* British settlers and colonies
Great Depression, 27–28, 39, 47, 150, 167
great divide, 131–32
Great Migration, 150
Green, Dwight H., 171
Guffey, Joseph F., 49
Guglielmo, Thomas, 25
Gunillaberg, 69
Gustaf Adolf, Crown Prince: at commemorative dinners, 156, 166–67; cornerstone of American Swedish Historical Museum laid by, 36; free trade and, 166–67; illness of, 6–7, 101–2, 162; represented by Prince Bertil, 101–2; as star of commemorative events, 103; Swedish Americans' interaction with, 123, 125–26, 138, 140–41, 143–44, 152, 171; on Swedish settler relations with Native Americans, 72–73; tercentenary delegation and, 101
Gustaf V, King, 101–2
Gustavus Adolphus, King, 20, 74, 78, 176, 215n40

Habel, Ylva, 192
Handel's *Messiah*, 135
handshake, symbolism of, 2, 196–97n3
Hansen, Karen, 14
Hansen, Marcus Lee, 41, 88
Hansson, Per Albin, 27
"Hear Us, Svea" (Wennerberg), 131, 135
Hedin, Naboth, 29, 54–55, 58–59, 83, 90
Hellström, Carl F., 108, 166
Henry, Prince (of Prussia), 101
Higham, John, 41
Hirdman, Gunnar, 136–37
historical representations, 7, 198n19
Historic Sites Act (1935), 49–50
histories, foundational. *See* foundational histories, appropriation of; foundational stories or histories
histories, mythical, 137
histories, settler. *See* settler colonial histories; settler histories
history: celebrations of ethnic heritages and, 24; of colonialism and immigration, 19; commemorations and perspectives on, 18–19; mass migration as, 26; nationalism and, 18; race issues throughout, 24–25; Swedish-Native relations and, 21
history, resilience of, 176–93; leaving national paradigm, 188–93; malleable settler histories, 180–88
Hjortzberg, Olle, 12
Hoerder, Dirk, 124
Hoffman, Harold G., 47
Hoffman, Martinus, 143–44
Hofstadter, Richard, 129
Holland. *See* Netherlands
Holland Centennial (1947), 57
Holsti, Rudolf, 219n7
homemaking myths, 24, 82–83, 185
Homestead Act (1862), 14
Hot Dog Diplomacy, 162
Hotel du Pont (Wilmington), 155, 158
Huguenots, 40
Hull, Cordell, 51, 72–73, 105, 152, 155, 160–61
Hungarian emigrants, 130

ICC. *See* International Chamber of Commerce
identity construction and memory, 4–5
Illinois, 56, 107, 109, 117, 185. *See also* Andover, Illinois; Chicago, Illinois; Moline, Illinois; Rockford, Illinois; Rock Island, Illinois
immigrants, Swedish. *See* mass migration from Sweden
Immigration Act (1924), 23, 112, 115
immigration vs. colonialism, 19, 74, 183–85, 193
independence and freedom, 64, 86, 91–92, 193
Independence Day celebrations, 124
Indiana, 112
Indian Americans, 129–30
indigenous people, 191, 237n41. *See also* Native Americans
individualism, American, 85, 91–92
industrialization, 19, 22
International Chamber of Commerce (ICC), 166–67
internationalism, 46–47

international relations, 26–31, 174–75, 190. *See also* friendship; Roosevelt, Franklin D.; Truman, Harry S.
Irish Americans, 24, 146, 205n25
Italian Americans, 25–26, 82, 124
Italian emigrants, 23, 124, 130, 150
Italy, 130, 161

Jacobson, Matthew Frye, 25, 112, 188–89
Jacobsson, Malte, 172
Jamestown, New York, 204n22
Jamestown Colony, 2–3, 45, 103, 190, 192
Jansson, Erik, 82, 185
Japanese Americans, 129–30
Järnefelt, Eero, 51
Jefferson, Thomas, 91, 95
Jenny Lind Chapel, 86, 178, 217n73
Jewish Americans, 137
Jewish claims of affinity with Native Americans, 73
Jewish emigrants, 23, 148
Jews and Nazi regime, 160
John of Colno, 137
Johnson, Amandus, 1, 35–37, 65, 76, 88, 113–14
Johnson, Edwin Carl, 85–86, 142–43
Johnson, Lyndon B., 186–87
Johnson, Vilas, 135, 147
Johnson-Reed Act (1924). *See* Immigration Act
Jordan, Terry, 203n13

Kalmar Nyckel (airplane), 117
Kalmar Nyckel (ship): commemorative stamps and, 13; departure point of, 105; mock replica of, 1, 104; on New Sweden monument, 74–78; plaque commemorating departure of, 110; ship modeled on, 1–2, 178, 184; story of arrival of, 137; trip from Sweden to Delaware Valley, 20
Kalmar Nyckel Foundation, 178, 189
Kammen, Michael, 120
Kaups, Matti, 203n13
Keynesian economic theory, 27
kinship, 153–54, 171–75
Klein, Barbro, 132
Kock, Karin, 219n15

Kohl, Helmut, 8
Kosciuszko, Thaddeus, 24
Kungsholm (ship), 104, 115–16, 219n7

The Last of the Mohicans (Cooper), 71
Latour, Bruno, 216n51
Lawn Festival, 122, 124
Leif Erikson Day, 145
Lenapehoking, 19
Lenape Indian Tribe of Delaware, 2, 183. *See also* Lenape people
Lenape people, 2, 19–21, 72, 79, 181–83, 203n13
Lenapewihittuck, 19
Letizia, Queen, 3
Levenstein, Harvey, 155, 157
Lincoln, Nebraska, 109
Lind, John, 34
literacy rates, 24, 205n26
Lonetree, Amy, 71
Long Island Settlement Tercentenary (1936), 45
Louise, Princess (formerly Louise Mountbatten), 101–3, 125–26, 162
love of land, 86–87
Lundeen, Ernest, 156
Lutheran religion and Swedish heritage, 55–56, 82–83, 133–35, 215n40
Lutheran state church, 22

Madeleine, Princess, 219–20n24
Mahomen (Lenape sachem), 20
Mankato, Minnesota, 139
Margaret, Princess (of Connaught), 101
Markell, Jack, 180
Marshall, George, 148–49
Marshall Plan, 30–31, 61, 95–96, 98, 162, 170–71
Märtha, Crown Princess, 130, 162
mass migration and festivals, 122–24
mass migration from Sweden (1840–1930): appropriations of history and, 61–62; celebration of, 3–4; changes in attitude about, 48–49; conflation with Swedish colonization, 81–82; distinction from colonial settlement, 19; Migration Jubilee and, 185–86; as national problem in Sweden, 35, 48–

mass migration from Sweden (*continued*) 49; New Sweden connected to, 120, 138, 185; overview of, 22–26; Prince Bertil on, 169, 172–74; religion and, 135–36; separation between Sweden and Swedish America and, 131–32; Swedish Historical Society of America and, 89; Truman's speech and, 147, 163

Mattahorn (Lenape sachem), 20

Matthews, Freeman H., 30–31

Mattson, Hans, 33–34

May, Karl, 73

Mayflower (ship): commemoration of sailing of, 3; descendants of Pilgrims on, 39; mythical stories of, 137; reenactment of landing of, 103

Mayflower Hotel (Washington, D.C.), 160

Mayflower Museum (Plymouth, England), 197n4

McMullen, Richard C., 6–7, 46, 67, 73, 81, 155, 177

Melvin, Frank, 39–42, 44–45, 67, 69, 97–98

memory: commemorations and, 18–19; as contested terrain, 202n4; history and, 95; identity construction and, 4–5; location of, 95; migration and, 95; narratives of founding and, 70. *See also* collective memory; communicative memory; cultural memory; social memory; transcultural memory; transnational memory

memory sites (Nora), 95

Menéndez, Pedro, 103

menus for commemorative dinners, 158–59

Mexican Americans, 137

Mexico, 163

microhistorical approach, 199n25

Middle Way, 28, 46–47, 99, 206n40

Midwest United States: New Sweden commemoration (1888) and, 33–35; pioneers and westward expansion and, 64, 84, 86–87, 90; revisited by Swedish delegations, 178; Swedish Americans in, 31–32, 54–55, 58–59, 89, 107–8, 148, 226n30; Swedish delegations in, 125, 142, 171–72; Swedish Pioneer Centennial and, 54–61, 83, 106, 109; Swedish settlement in the, 3–4, 9, 13–14, 22, 24, 138, 144; tercentenary delegation tour of, 107–9; transition to English language and, 228n62

"A Mighty Fortress Is Our God" (song), 135

migrants vs. settlers, 64

migration, conflating colonial settlement and, 73–82, 187

Migration Jubilee (1996), 185

Milles, Carl, 6–7, 68, 74–76, 81, 176

Minneapolis Club, 166

Minneapolis–Saint Paul, Minnesota: celebrations at, 129, 225n8; centennial planning committees in, 60; commemorative dinners at, 166; memorial plaque unveiled in, 86, 217n73; New Sweden commemoration at (1888), 33–34, 81–82; revisited by Swedish delegations, 178; Swedish Americans in, 24, 26; Swedish Pioneer centennial delegation and, 109, 118, 125–26; tercentenary delegation and, 107–8, 123, 125–28, 131, 140

Minnesota, 107–8, 112, 131, 133, 139, 144. *See also* Minneapolis–Saint Paul, Minnesota

Minnesota River Valley, 138

Minnesota State Fair, 123, 125–26, 131, 133, 138, 140, 144–45

Minquas Kill, 20

Minuit, Peter, 20

Mississippi River, commemorations of settlements west of, 11

Mississippi Valley, 12, 14, 71, 82, 84, 86, 107

Mitatsimint (Lenape sachem), 20

Mitchell, W. J. T., 10, 65, 70

modernity: concept of, 85, 216n51; Swedish and American, link between, 143, 169; Swedishness and friction of, 131–37; transportation technologies and, 115, 119; traveling-as-reenactment and, 118–19; United States as model of, in Europe, 119

modernization: commemorations and, 223n85; old-fashioned notions of Swedishness and, 133; physical education in Sweden and, 137; of Sweden, 140–43; Swedish pioneering and immigration and, 151, 169, 172–73; transportation of delegates and, 115, 119–20
Moline, Illinois, 109, 145, 204n22
Monitor (warship), monument to, 128
Monument of Peace, 76
Moore, A. Harry, 47, 210n44
Muelle de las Carabelas (Wharf of the Caravels), 197n4
museums and historic sites at settlers' departure points, 197n4
Musiał, Kazimierz, 28
My Antónia (Cather), 87
Myrdal, Alva, 206n43
Myrdal, Gunnar, 111, 206n43
mythical stories and histories, 137
myths of origin, 11, 14–15, 63, 84–85, 188–89, 193. *See also* national mythology, American

Nanticoke Lenni-Lenape Tribal Nation, 2, 183–84. *See also* Lenape people
Nash, Catherine, 146
national collective identity formation, 5, 197–98n13
nationalism: American civic, 129–30; festivals and, 124, 129; methodological, 8; Norwegian, 132; practice of commemoration and, 18; racial, 129–30; regionalism commingled with, 53; Swedish, 132–33, 191, 227n45; transnationalism's relationship to, 201n43
national mythology, American: founding of civilization and, 81; handshake at The Rocks, 2, 196–97n3; settler histories, 12, 63, 188–89; settling of the frontier, 84–85, 90, 92. *See also* myths of origin
national mythology, Swedish, 91–92, 185
national paradigm, 4–5, 8; leaving, 188–93
National Society for the Preservation of Swedishness Abroad, 97
National Society of the Sons of the American Revolution, 39

nation building, 12, 124, 186
Native Americans: commemorative stamps and, 12–13; dispossession and replacement of, 71–72, 83, 92–93, 121, 183, 188, 191; European settlers and, 19–20, 70–73; handshake with U.S. soldier, 2, 196–97n3; Jamestown Colony commemoration and, 192; at New Sweden commemoration (2013), 2; Overland Trail and, 228n58; reconciliation rituals and, 237n41; at Santa Fe commemoration, 192; Swedish settler relations with, 13–14, 19–21, 38, 71–79, 85–86, 138–39, 181
NATO. *See* North Atlantic Treaty Organization
Naturalization Act (1790), 129
Nazi Germany, 29, 57, 111, 160
Nelles, H. V., 197–98n13
neoliberalism, 186
Netherlands: exploration and settlement in Delaware Valley, 19–20; *Mayflower* commemoration and, 3; New Sweden Company and, 20–21; New Sweden surrendered to, 21
New Deal and New Dealers, 17, 28, 32, 46–47, 49, 101–2
New England, 22, 45, 65, 107, 137
New England Historic Genealogical Society, 110
New Jersey, 38, 43, 47, 72, 153, 183
New Jersey Sand Hill Band of Lenape and Cherokee Indians, 182
New Netherlands, 19–21
New Sweden (1638–55): as Delaware and regional history, 42, 47, 193; first years of, 21; foundational site of, 65–70; Lenape people and, 19–21, 72–73, 79; love of land and, 86–87; Melvin's descent from, 39; peace and friendship connected to, 161–62, 180; Prince Bertil on, 172, 186; religious significance of, 134; Roosevelt's associations with, 143–44; settlement of, 3; surrendered to Dutch, 21–22; Swedish mass migration and, 31–32, 49, 120, 138, 185; trading and, 186. *See also* New Sweden commemoration (1888);

New Sweden (1638–55) (*continued*)
    New Sweden commemoration (2013);
    New Sweden Tercentenary commemoration; Swedish Pioneer Centennial commemoration
New Sweden Alliance, Inc., 189–90
New Sweden commemoration (1888), 33–35, 81–82
New Sweden commemoration (1938). *See* New Sweden Tercentenary commemoration
New Sweden commemoration (1948). *See* Swedish Pioneer Centennial commemoration
New Sweden commemoration (1988), 180–86
New Sweden commemoration (2013), 1–2, 178, 180, 183–84, 186–87, 189–90, 219–20n24
New Sweden Company, 20–21
New Sweden Memorial Commission, 37, 41, 44
New Sweden monument (1938), 65–68, 74–83, 89
New Sweden's 325th anniversary (1963), 180, 186–87
New Sweden Tercentenary commemoration (1938): Amandus Johnson on plans for, 1; American myth of origin and, 10–11; American Swedish Historical Museum and, 36; Augustana's participation in, 55–56; as celebration of settlement, 12–14; civilization claim as foundation for, 72–73; commemorative dinners during, 155–61; commemorative stamps for, 12–13; continuities emphasized in, 74; Dehlgren's observations of, 17–19; free trade promotion during, 169; future cross-border commemorations and, 177–78, 235n6; institutional epicenter for, 35; introduction to, 3–4; landing ceremony at The Rocks, 6–7; location chosen for, 56; material legacies of, 9–10; moments of opportunity for organizing, 19; monument for, 65–68, 74–82, 176–77; national involvement in, 26–27; in New Jersey, 153; Pennsylvania delegation to Sweden, 96,
99–101, 104–6; planning of, 43–53, 56, 178–79; racial tensions during, 113–15; religion and, 133–34; repertoires with Swedish national romantic theme, 131; resilience of, 176–78; Sweden and planning of, 47–48, 50, 56, 178–79; Swedish exceptionalism and, 193; Swedish Pioneer Centennial compared to, 57–58, 61, 83, 87–89, 92–93, 99, 177–78; timing of, 161; transatlantic relations and, 31–32. *See also* Swedish delegation to Tercentenary commemoration
New York City, 106–7, 109, 116, 128, 169–70, 172–74, 221n48
Ninkovich, Frank, 161
Nora, Pierre, 95
Nordic democracy, 165
Nordic Museum (Stockholm), 181
"Nordic race," 25, 112
Norse-American Centennial (1925), 36, 218n88
North Atlantic Treaty Organization (NATO), 31, 61, 190, 207n51
North Dakota, 14, 139
Northwest Territory Sesquicentennial (1938), 45, 96
Norway: immigrants from, 139; Nazi occupation of, 29, 145; royalty visits to United States, 130–31, 162; Scandinavian alliance and, 31, 207n51; union with Sweden, 35, 208n4
Norwegian-American Historical Association, 89, 218n88
Norwegian Americans, 11, 24, 36, 87, 124, 130–32, 156
nostalgic modernism, 120

Obama, Barack, 189
O'Brien, Jean, 85
Observations Concerning the Increase of Mankind (Franklin), 25
ocean liners, 115
Odalbonden (Geijer), 91
odalbonden, mythology of, 91–92
Olav, Crown Prince, 130, 162
Oldenburg, Gösta, 58–59, 147
old-settler societies, 11, 87
Old Swedes churches, 22, 189

Old Swedes Foundation, 189
Olson, Daron, 124
Olsson, Nils William, 60, 82–83, 106, 109, 170–71
Olsson, Ove, 114
Omaha, Nebraska, 140, 145, 163–64
opportunity, moments of, 17–32; international relations, 26–31; for organizing a commemoration, 19; transatlantic connections, 19–26
Ordover, Nancy, 112
Oscar II, King, 35
Overland Trail, 228n58
Ozawa v. the United States (1922), 129–30

Pacific Northwest, 23
Palme, Olof, 187–88
Palmer House (Chicago), 155
Park, Robert E., 111
The Passing of the Great Race (Grant), 25
peace as theme of commemorative dinners, 159–61, 167, 172–74
Peers, Laura, 71
Penn, William, 2–3, 78–79, 181
Pennsylvania: call for commemoration in, 38–39; choice of foundational site and, 67–70; commemorative dinners in, 156–60; delegation to Sweden, 96, 99–101, 104–6, 110, 116, 172; Finnish monument placed in, 67–68; Governor Printz Park created in, 68–69; power struggle with Delaware, 52–53, 67–68, 106; tercentenary planning and, 43–47, 49–53, 72. *See also* Philadelphia, Pennsylvania; Pittsburgh, Pennsylvania
"Pennsylvania" (song), 156
Pennsylvania 300th Anniversary Commission: on arrival of Prince Bertil, 102; creation of, 38; Governor Printz Park and, 68–69; monument placement and, 67–68; Pennsylvania celebration and, 44; Swedish delegation and, 98; tercentenary planning and, 56, 212n73; on visit to Sweden, 105, 110; on water pageant and fireworks display, 125
Pennsylvania Commonwealth banquet, 159–60

Pennsylvania Federation of Historical Societies, 38–40, 72
the people's body (*folkkroppen*), 113
the People's Home (*Folkhemmet*), 132–33
the people's stock (*folkstammen*), 113
Peterson, Val, 164
Philadelphia, Pennsylvania: All-Lutheran convention in, 133–34; Catholic population in, 215n40; festivals in, 122, 124; invitations to celebrations in, 117; museum built in, 35–38; revisited by Swedish delegations, 178; The Rocks as foundational site and, 65–67; Swedish American Tercentenary Association and, 38; Swedish delegation visits to, 107, 109, 170; tercentenary epicenter in, 35; water pageant and fireworks display in, 125
Pilgrim mythology, 137, 188–89
Pilgrim Tercentenary (1920–21), 45
pioneer as archetypal figure, 63–64
pioneers, Swedish, 82–92, 148–51, 163–65, 169, 171–73, 175, 185. *See also* Swedish Pioneer Centennial commemoration
pioneers and American national mythology, 189
pionjär, 90–91, 218n92
Pittsburgh, Pennsylvania, 107, 170
Plymouth colony, 11, 45, 84, 103
Plymouth Rock, 2, 14–15, 45, 65, 70, 188–89
Poland, 130
Polish Americans, 24, 137, 150
Polish emigrants, 124, 130, 150
political friendship, 159–65, 170, 186–87
politics: American feelings about Sweden and, 17; international, 19, 26–31; regional, 46–47; successful commemorations and, 17–19; travel and, 95; Truman's speech at Chicago Stadium festival and, 146–49
Ponce de León, Juan, 103
Pony Express (monument), 76
pre-Columbian histories, 137
Printz, Johan, 21, 68–70, 74–76, 78, 158, 181
Printzhof, 68, 158
Pulaski, Casimir, 24
Pullman Palace Car, 118–19

Quebec Tercentenary (1908), 197–98n13

race and racism: Chicago and, 150; dining preferences and, 154–55; ethno-racial belonging and ancestry, 24–26, 42, 120–21, 146, 151; friendship between nations and, 32, 153–54, 173–74; genealogy and, 39–40, 111, 120; Prince Bertil's speech and, 144–45; racial tensions during commemorations, 113–15; scientific racism and eugenics, 111–12; shared bloodlines and, 113, 120–21; Swedish exceptionalism and, 192–93; Truman's speech and, 149–50; United States compared to Sweden, 111
Randall, Ruth, 48
Reagan, Ronald, 8
Reciprocal Trade Agreement Act (1934), 168
reenactment: of colonial landings, 103–4, 178; of landing at The Rocks in Wilmington, Delaware, 1–2, 6–7, 104, 178, 184; performed by Swedish delegations, 1–2, 15, 96, 104, 117–19, 178, 184; traveling as, 118–19
regionalism, American, 45–47, 53, 70
religion and festivals, 133–35. *See also* Lutheran religion and Swedish heritage
religious freedom, 136, 160
Republican Party, U.S., 46–47
Restaurationen (immigrant sloop), 24
Revey, James "Lone Bear," 182–83
Rhode Island Tercentenary (1936), 45
Ribault, Jean, 3
Riksdag of the Estates (*ståndsriksdagen*), 165
Rockford, Illinois, 109, 133, 138, 144–45, 158, 169, 204n22
Rock Island, Illinois, 37, 54, 204n22
The Rocks in Wilmington, Delaware: current regional importance of, 189–90; Delaware resolution and, 40; as foundational site, 44, 65–70; monument at, 80–81, 83, 177; Prince Bertil's address at, 103; racial tension and surroundings of, 42, 113–15; reenactments of landing at, 1–2, 6–7, 104, 178, 184; revisited by Swedish delegations, 178; Roosevelt's address at, 162–63
Rodgers, Daniel, 27
Roediger, David, 130
Rolvaag, Ole Edvart, 87
Rome, founding of, comparisons to, 84
Roosevelt, Franklin D.: attention to tercentenary, 17, 49–51, 53; Good Neighbor policy, 168; Leif Erikson Day and, 145; Middle Way and, 28, 46–47; peace and, 160–61; Pennsylvania's delegation to Sweden and, 100; resolution on Printz's body sent to, 69; royal visits and, 162; Swedish modernity and, 103; at tercentenary inauguration, 6–7, 80–81, 143–44, 151, 161–62; trade policy and, 168
Rosenberg, Hilding, 135
Rothberg, Michael, 5
Royal Commission on Emigration, 48–49
Royal New Sweden Tercentenary Memorial Commission: delegation travels and, 107; on Finland's participation in tercentenary, 52; formation of, 50; government bureaucracy represented by, 59; Melvin's letter to, 69; monument plans of, 65–67, 74, 76; New York City celebration and, 128; Pennsylvania delegation to Sweden and, 104–5
Russian emigrants, 150
Ryden, Ernest, 41
Ryden, George H., 40–42, 44, 53

Sahlgaard, Hagbarth, 25
Saint Patrick's Day, 24, 124
Sámi people, 203n13, 221–22n68
Sandberg, Per, 90, 92
Sandburg, Carl, 135, 149
Sandler, Rickard, 47–48
Sankikas Kill, 20
Santa Fe, New Mexico, 3, 192
SAS. *See* Scandinavian Airlines System
Savage, Kirk, 197–98n13
Scandinavian Airlines System (SAS), 116, 118
Scandinavian Defense Union, 31, 207n51
Scandinavian progressiveness, 28

INDEX 251

Schlesinger, Arthur, Sr., 88
Scottish Americans, 40
Seelye, John, 45, 189
semiotics, 10
settler as archetypal figure, 63–64
settler colonial histories, 63–93; conflating colonial settlement and migration, 73–82; creating a foundational site, 65–70; founding of the modern age, 82–87; regional importance of, 189–90; settlers and Native Americans, 70–76; transatlantic pioneer, 87–92
settler colonialism, 11, 64
settler colonial legacy, 144, 164, 183
settler commemorations, 10–14
settler histories: cross-border significance of, 191; malleable, 180–88. *See also* settler colonial histories
settlers vs. migrants, 64
Shevchenko, Taras, 205n25
The Significance of the Frontier in American History (Turner), 84
Silvia, Queen, 1–2, 178, 181–83, 219–20n24
Siokalo, Zoriana, 182–83
Smith, John, 2–3, 103
Smoot-Hawley Act, 167–68
Social Democratic Party (Sweden), 27–29, 46, 97–98, 141
social engineering in Sweden, 112–13
social memory, 4, 197n10
Social Security Act (1935), 210n44
Sodaro, Amy, 192
Sofia Girls (*Sofiaflickorna*), 136–37
Solbert, Oscar, 37, 104, 107–8, 128, 208n10, 212n73
Soldier Field in Chicago, 126–27, 141, 144
Sollors, Werner, 146
Soto, Hernando de, 103
Spanish settlement in America, 3, 72
SPHS. *See* Swedish Pioneer Historical Society
Spirit Lake Dakota Indian Reservation, 14, 139
stamps, commemorative, 12–13
"The Star Spangled Banner," 156
Stasiulis, Davia, 12
St. Augustine, Florida, 3, 103
St. Barthélemy, 221–22n68

St. Catarina (ship), 137
Stephenson, George M., 88
sterilization laws, 112
Stockholm, Sweden, 48, 58, 76, 88, 105, 156, 172
Stuyvesant, Peter, 21
suffrage reforms, 165
Susan Constant (ship), 190
Susquehannocks, 20
Svenska Amerikanska Posten, 129
Sweden: Age of Greatness in, 176, 201–2n3; Chicago and Minneapolis–Saint Paul celebrations and, 225n8; colonialism and slavery, 73, 192–93, 221–22n68; commemorations in nineteenth and early twentieth centuries, 201–2n3; commemorative stamps of, 12–13; contemporary vs. nineteenth century, 139–40, 143; Earle's visit to, 46; eugenics in, 112–13; Finland's power struggle with, 106; Forefathers' Day banquet and, 156; friendship with United States, 152–53, 159–75, 186–87; housing program in, 101; kingdom of (1637), 20; mass migration and, 48–49; Migration Jubilee and, 185–86; as model of modern state, 27, 117; modernization of, 140–43, 151, 169; NATO and, 207n51; neutrality and Cold War, 148–49, 162; neutrality in WWII, 29–32, 57, 162; New Sweden commemoration (1888) and, 34–35; New Sweden monument and, 74–80; Pennsylvania delegation to, 96, 99–101, 104–6; racism and, 111, 221–22n68; returned emigrants in, 23; Scandinavian Defense Union and, 31, 207n51; secularization of, 135–37, 188, 227n45; Social Democratic Party in, 27–29; Swedish Americans' separation from, 131–33, 135–37; Swedish Pioneer Centennial and, 58–61, 86, 89–92, 94, 128, 162–63; tercentenary planning and, 47–48, 50, 56, 178–79; Truman's praise of, 163; union with Norway, 35, 208n4; United States as technological role model for, 119. *See also* Swedish-American relations; Swedish government

Sweden: The Middle Way (Childs), 28, 99. *See also* cooperative movement
Swedish-American Chamber of Commerce, 190
Swedish-American fraternal societies, 209n24
Swedish-American historical research, 88–89
Swedish-American Historical Society, 89
Swedish American Line, 88, 97, 104, 115–16, 118
Swedish-American relations: centennial planning and, 58–61; Cold War and, 162, 171, 173–74; commemorations and, 177; festival speakers and, 144; mass migration and, 22–23, 31–32; New Sweden monument and, 74–81, 177; during postwar period, 30–31; Sweden as model of modern state and, 27–29, 32; tercentenary delegation and, 97; tercentenary planning and, 47–49; World War II and, 29–30, 32
Swedish Americans: American civic nationalism and, 130; appropriation of history and, 33; biological relationship to Swedes, 113; in Chicago, 150; commemorative dinners and, 156, 159; conflation of colonization and immigration by, 81–82; Dakotas and, 139; Finland's inclusion in tercentenary plans and, 51–52; language maintenance and, 141; in the Midwest, 31–32, 54–55, 58–59, 226n30; modernity and, 143; New Sweden commemoration (1888) and, 33–35; numbers and impact of, 23–24, 32; pioneer celebrations and, 11; relative ease of assimilation for, 24–25; The Rocks as foundational site and, 65, 70; success in United States, 186; Sweden's involvement in tercentenary and, 47–49; Sweden's separation from, 131–33, 135–37; Swedish delegation interactions with, 122–26, 138, 140–41, 143–44, 152, 171; Swedish Pioneer Centennial and, 4, 31, 54–58, 83, 89, 128; at tercentenary inauguration, 7; tercentenary planning and, 1–2, 4, 35–44, 55–56, 107–9; Twin Cities celebration and, 129
Swedish American Tercentenary Association: Bersell's criticism of, 55–56, 212n73; festival at Soldier Field Stadium, 127; formation of, 37–38, 40; joint planning with regional commissions, 43–44; monument location and, 65–67; New York City celebration and, 128; pilgrimage to Delaware encouraged by, 109; Swedish lawn festival planned by, 122
Swedish Colonial Society, 35, 37, 39–40, 44, 68–69, 156, 180
Swedish Commission for the Pioneer Jubilee, 59–60, 89–90, 137
"Swedish Delegation Follows the Path of the Pioneers" (Olsson), 106
Swedish delegations: continued visits by, 178; reenactments performed by, 1–2, 15, 96, 104, 117–19, 178, 184. *See also* delegation travels; Swedish delegation to Centennial commemoration; Swedish delegation to Tercentenary commemoration
Swedish delegation to Centennial commemoration: at commemorative dinners, 163–64, 170, 172–74; at festivals, 125–26, 134, 136, 142–43; honored by children in Michigan, 100; journey to United States, 116–17; Prince Bertil as leader of, 80, 94, 102, 109; royals and attention to, 102–3; Swedish government appointment of, 98–99; travels throughout United States, 106–7, 109–10, 117–18
Swedish delegation to Tercentenary commemoration: at commemorative dinners, 157, 159–60, 162, 166–67; at festivals, 122–23, 125–28, 131, 143; journey to United States, 104; landing at The Rocks, 6–7, 178; Prince Bertil as leader of, 6–7, 101–3; royals and attention to, 101–3; Swedish government appointment of, 96–99; travels throughout United States, 107–9, 171
Swedish exceptionalism, 192–93

INDEX 253

Swedish folk and dance songs, 131–32
Swedish government: continuation of Swedish settlement celebrations and, 235n6; Finnish participation in tercentenary commemoration and, 52; involvement in centennial commemoration, 59, 94, 96–97; involvement in tercentenary commemoration, 48–50, 96–97, 104–5; social democratic model of, 27–29, 32; during and after WWII, 29–31
Swedish Historical Society of America, 89
Swedish immigrants of nineteenth and twentieth centuries. *See* mass migration from Sweden
Swedish Institute for Cultural Exchange with Foreign Countries, 30
"The Swedish Invasion," (speech), 85–86
Swedish language, 140–41, 228nn62–63
Swedish Ministry of Culture, 185
Swedish model, 27–28
Swedish modernity, 28–30, 103
Swedishness: beginning of, in America, 109, 189–90; biological dimension of, 145, 149–50; comparison of celebrations, 61; in festival context, 144; festivals as celebration of, 129; the frictions of modernity and, 131–37, 143; Milles's monument and, 81; role of royals during commemorations, 125–26; Swedish language and, 140; transatlantic sense of, 31; transcultural dimensions of, 151; Truman's speech and, 148–50; Ward's involvement in Delaware commission and, 42
Swedish Pioneer Centennial Association: at Chicago Stadium, 126, 134; Earle's trip to Sweden and, 110; formation of, 57–58; goals for commemoration, 87–89, 109; invitation to Swedish government, 96; religion and centennial planning by, 82–83; Sweden's involvement in commemoration and, 58–60; Swedish delegation and, 98, 102, 116–17
Swedish Pioneer Centennial commemoration (1948): ambiguous foundation of, 82, 216n59; American myth of origin and, 10–11; business interests and, 170–71; as celebration of settlement, 12–14; Chicago Stadium festival, 86, 126, 134–37; Cold War and timing of, 4, 31; commemorative dinners during, 157–58; commemorative stamps for, 12–13; founding of modern age and, 82–87; future cross-border commemorations and, 177–78, 235n6; historical society formation and, 89; history writing and, 87–89; introduction to, 3–4; material legacies of, 9–10; memorial plaques, 86–87, 217n73; moments of opportunity for organizing, 19; national involvement in, 26–27; Native American representations in, 138; parade in Rockford, Illinois, 133; planning of, 54–61; religion and, 134, 136; Sweden and, 58–61, 86, 89–92, 94, 128, 162–63; Swedish exceptionalism and, 193; Swedish pioneers at, 145; tercentenary commemoration compared to, 57–58, 61, 83, 87–89, 92–93, 99, 177–78; transatlantic relations and, 32; Truman and, 146, 163. *See also* Swedish delegation to Centennial commemoration
Swedish Pioneer Historical Society (SPHS), 89, 218n88
Swedish school system reform, 28–29, 206n43
The Swedish Settlement on the Delaware (Johnson), 35
Swedish Sports Confederation, 98
Swedish Tobacco Company, 181

Tariff Act (1930), 167–68
Texas Centennial (1936), 39
Tinicum Island, 53, 68–70
Tomasson, Richard, 135
Trail of Tears, 1938 centennial, 71
train travel, 117–19
transatlantic connections, 19–26; bloodlines, 113; commemoration festivals and, 128; commemorations as opportunities for, 59–60, 92–93; delegations and, 99; ethnicity, 125; genealogical bonds, 173–74; monument and,

transatlantic connections (*continued*)
  79–80; sense of modernity, 103; technological modernization, 120
transcultural memory, 5–6, 92, 95
transnationalism, 7, 124, 191, 198n18, 201n43
transnational memory, 5–6, 95
The Transplanted (Bodnar), 22
transportation, 115–20
traveling and power, 95–96
travelling memory, 95
Treaty of Amity and Commerce between Sweden and the United States (1783), 166–67, 187
Tredway, Thomas, 56
Trubowitz, Peter, 46
Truman, Harry S.: at Chicago Stadium festival, 86, 126, 134–35, 146–49, 163; on genealogical bonds with Sweden, 174; interest in centennial, 31, 60–61; Swedishness and, 151
Truman Doctrine (1947), 163, 169
Turner, Frederick Jackson, 45–46, 84–85
Tydén, Mattias, 112

Undén, Östen, 30–31
Union Club (NYC), 166
United Kingdom, 3, 190. *See also* British settlers and colonies
United States: British royal visit to (1860), 101; building of, 151; colonization mythologies in, xi; commemorative stamps of, 12–13, 61; consumerism, 186; delegation travels to, 94; ethnic commemorations in, 24; eugenics in, 112; European settlement of, beginning of, 2; festivals in, 123–24; friendship with Sweden, 152–53, 159–75, 186–87; immigration restrictions, 23, 112, 115, 168; *Mayflower* commemoration and, 3; myths of origin, 11, 14–15, 63, 84–85, 188–89, 193; patriotic commemorations in, 201–2n3; relations with Finland, 161–62; as role model for technological modernization, 119; royal visits to, 101–3; Sweden's neutrality and, 30–32, 57; Swedish bloodlines in, 109–10, 113, 120–21,

151, 172–74; Swedish delegations to, 96–103; Swedish immigration to, 3, 22–24, 27, 197n7; Swedish modernity in, notion of, 28–30. *See also* Swedish-American relations; U.S. government
United States v. Thind (1923), 129–30
University Club (NYC), 158
Unonius, Gustaf, 82, 217n73
Upland (New Sweden), 68
U.S.-Dakota War (1862), 138
U.S. Delaware Valley Tercentenary Commission, 49–50, 69, 160, 167
U.S. government, 28–31, 49–53, 60–61, 95–96
U.S.-Mexican War, 163

"Värmland" (Swedish folk song), 156
Veit, Helen Zoe, 154
Vesterheim Norwegian-American Museum, 36
Vietnam War, 187–88
Vikings, 91, 116, 133, 145
Vinland, 137
Virginia, 190
Von Steuben, Baron, 130
von Sydow, Max, 181
The Voyage to America (opera), 135

Walaszek, Adam, 124
Waldorf-Astoria (New York), 155, 173
Ward, Christopher, 40, 42, 52–53, 67, 176–77
Washington, D.C., 38, 107, 172
Washington State, 24
water pageant and fireworks display, 125
We Are What We Remember (Meriwether and Mattoon D'Amore), 5, 197–98n13
Weil, François, 111
welfare state, 28, 47, 141
Wennerberg, Gunnar, 131, 135
Westin, Gunnar, 136
westward expansion, 64, 84–85, 87
white privilege, 42
The Will to Succeed: Stories of Swedish Pioneers (Benson), 89–90
Wilmington, Delaware: African American population in, 114–15; Fort Christina State Park created at, 42, 67–68,

70; revisited by Swedish delegations, 178; Swedish American Tercentenary Association and, 38; Swedish Colonial Society and, 35; tercentenary delegation and, 1–2, 6–7, 107, 161. *See also* The Rocks in Wilmington, Delaware
Wilson, Woodrow, 167
Wilson Line shipyard, 65–67

Woodring, Harry Hines, 160
World War II, 4, 27, 29–30, 32, 58, 150
Wrobel, David, 118

Year of New Sweden, 180
Yorktown Victory Sesquicentennial (1931), 45
Yuval-Davis, Nira, 12

ADAM HJORTHÉN was born in Stockholm, Sweden. He holds an M.A. from Uppsala University and a Ph.D. from Stockholm University and has been a visiting scholar at both the University of Minnesota and George Washington University. He has taught courses in public history, historical theory and methodology, and the history of race and ethnicity in America. A recipient of the 2015 Orm Øverland Graduate Student Essay Prize and scholarships from the Sweden-America Foundation, the American-Scandinavian Foundation, and the Swedish Research Council, he serves as the president of the Swedish Association for American Studies (SAAS). He is currently a postdoctoral researcher with a dual affiliation at Stockholm University and the Free University of Berlin in Germany. Together with his wife, Nevra, and son, Emin, he divides his time between Stockholm and Berlin.

www.ingramcontent.com/pod-product-compliance
Lightning Source LLC
Chambersburg PA
CBHW020643230426
43665CB00008B/300